D1553259

The Ecological Life

DATE

Nature's Meaning

Series Editor:

Roger S. Gottlieb, Professor of Philosophy,
Worcester Polytechnic Institute

Each title in Nature's Meaning is created to have the personal stamp of a passionate and articulate spokesperson for environmental sanity. Intended to be engagingly written by experienced thinkers in their field, these books express the comprehensive and personal vision of the topic by an author who has devoted years to studying, teaching, writing about, and often being actively involved with the environmental movement. The books will be intended primarily as college texts, and as beautifully produced volumes, they will also appeal to a wide audience of environmentally concerned readers.

Integrating Ecofeminism, Globalization, and World Religions, by Rosemary Radford Ruether

Environmental Ethics for a Postcolonial World, by Deane Curtin

The Ecological Life: Discovering Citizenship and a Sense of Humanity, by Jeremy Bendik-Keymer

The Ecological Life

Discovering Citizenship and a Sense of Humanity

Jeremy Bendik-Keymer

ROWMAN & LITTLEFIELD PUBLISHERS, INC.
Lanham • Boulder • New York • Toronto • Oxford

ROWMAN & LITTLEFIELD PUBLISHERS, INC.

Published in the United States of America
by Rowman & Littlefield Publishers, Inc.
A wholly owned subsidiary of The Rowman & Littlefield Publishing Group, Inc.
4501 Forbes Boulevard, Suite 200, Lanham, Maryland 20706
www.rowmanlittlefield.com

PO Box 317
Oxford
OX2 9RU, UK

British Library Cataloguing in Publication Information Available

Library of Congress Cataloging-in-Publication Data

Bendik-Keymer, Jeremy, 1970–
   The ecological life : discovering citizenship and a sense of humanity /
Jeremy Bendik-Keymer.
      p. cm.
   Includes bibliographical references and index.
   ISBN 0-7425-3447-2 (cloth : alk. paper) — ISBN 0-7425-3448-0 (pbk. : alk. paper)
   1. Human ecology—Philosophy. 2. Environmental ethics. 3. Environmental justice.
I. Title.
GF21.B46 2006
179'.1—dc22   2005021900

Printed in the United States of America

♾™ The paper used in this publication meets the minimum requirements of
American National Standard for Information Sciences—Permanence of Paper for
Printed Library Materials, ANSI/NISO Z39.48-1992.

All the world's creatures are the truthful signs of our life.

—Alain de Lille, paraphrased

Life is beautiful, not because of colors or diversity, but just because it is life. And we should all respect it and not destroy it without proper justification.

—Razib Khan, a university student from Bangladesh

Respecting nature should come out of our sense of humanity.

—Nisreen Alzahlawi, a university student from Syria

For my New York family—Ruth, Esther, Dave

The Sky inside the City

Life among humans is more than you mentioned.

In the city, alone, live lives

A thousand times too deep within the ground,

I know. Silently, I watched them fall

Inside the space of my memories of other lives,

I dreamed. Timelessness makes sense only

Across the elements where species rise and descend.

As loved-ones, too, we walk

Out into the twilight as lavender as kisses—

The air intractable, an ether in change.

Contents

~

A Note to the Reader

1. Andrey Tarkovsky's film *Mirror* shows recurring scenes of a windstorm near the narrator's childhood home. These scenes are shot in black, white, and slow motion. In this respect, they echo the newsreel footage in the film: the bombing of Barcelona, a saltwater battle along a Russian plain in World War II, a bullfight, children fleeing Spain. The windstorm is the inversion of these shots, clearing away in the turbulence of the narrator's childhood home marked by the separation World War II brought to his parents. The wind rolls along the front of a wood and upsets objects on a wooden table outside. It precedes moments when the narrator, mute before the world's events, realizes that life can be beautiful, too.

2. When I was a child, I woke up by the rush of trees in the rain. Later, they swayed without noise in the night. That was high school. In France, again, the rain came down, but so fully that the windows of cafés steamed and beaded into rivers. Rest returned. College was a night in New York in mid-November, when the air was cold and clear in Brooklyn, and everything was as still as possibility. Many years later, humidity mixed with breezes off the lake, along Chicago's side streets as trees flickered yellow and green. Then Pikes Peak rose up in the morning, lit rose and cold with snow and altitude. And this morning a wind makes the feathers of an African bird ruffle up along its neck and crown. There is a whole phenomenology of life in just the weather.

3. In June 2003, I went to Arches National Park. This park is the scene of Edward Abbey's *Desert Solitaire*—a romantic meditation on what we have lost in losing our experience of wilderness. Abbey fills his book with mournful, angry experience of our civilization's discontinuity with the natural world. I was struck in Arches with something more continuous, though. To walk among the rocks can be to connect, and not across an insurmountable alienation. It can be a way of relating oneself to something slow and clarifying. Of course, becoming accustomed to nature takes time, and it takes know-how about how to live away from society. But we, too, are contours of wind patterns, waterlines: dryness reaches into our throats until we swallow; tunnels of lung expand; salt water is in our veins.

4. In Jerusalem, there is an avenue of trees, each tree representing a just person who helped the oppressed.[1] Why would a tree be a more apt symbol for justice than, say, a sign that reads "One Just Person"?

5. When people say of another that she is together as a person, with solid judgment and a moral core, they often say she is *rooted,* or, she is *grounded.* Why does nature express what is best in us?

6. As this year began, the world dealt with the aftermath of one of the largest humanitarian crises on record: a tsunami caused by an underwater earthquake so large it stuttered the Earth's rotation for a millisecond. Almost two hundred thousand people died; towns were washed away; people were stranded and left without a shelter or a place in an economy. For generations now, people along the Southeast Asian rim will hear the expression "it washed over us like a wave" with grief and unrest. Nature shows us some of the worst that can happen to our lives, and we remember it in our sense of life.[2]

7. There is a powerful connection between humanity and what we come out of and live in. Our fast-paced, anxious world can make it easy to ignore our connection. But it is there in our dreams, cultures, and sense of society at some of their most meaningful points. That is what this book is about.

*

None of these lectures were actually given. I chose to write this book *imagining* each part as a lecture, because my editors and I decided we wanted an accessible book and because it is important to our view of philosophy that philosophy feel like a natural conversation. In the words of colleagues, we're not here to win an argument but to start a conversation.[3] I hope these lectures allow me to speak naturally with you across distance and lack of acquaintance. Doing so is important, too, because in this book you will be introduced—or reintroduced—to some hard questions and abstract ideas, and I don't want you to lose the *trees* for the forest. I want you to be real keeping in mind the big questions.

I've placed the location of these lectures in an imagined American liberal arts university. This allows me to indirectly promote two ends. First, it allows me to work within the advantages of liberal arts education. This is broad, innovative education aimed at helping students think for themselves, develop a holistic picture of their role in life, and become lifelong learners. Liberal arts education is not preprofessional, because it judges—wisely—that the best vocational development for a human over long periods of time is to learn how to think creatively and critically about the ends of life. Thus I intend to make an indirect pitch for liberal arts education.

Second, the imagined location of these lectures allows me to criticize American culture and its economic excesses indirectly. I think this is important to do as a patriot, but my end is not polemical. The American way of life is hegemonic in today's global consumer culture and in the expectations swiftly being picked up by many parts of the developing world. This way of life has serious limitations from an ecological point of view. It is important to provide grounds to criticize this way of life from within, challenging the inhumane while protecting the humane. I hope this book will be instructive to those inside and outside the United States who are searching for reasons to refine a powerful culture.

This book is introductory and is meant to stir discussion. Nonetheless, it contains arguments that could be treated in technical philosophical journals, and I have tried to produce positions reflecting what I take to be several innovative areas of environmental work. The book presents some difficult matters through an accessible medium. Many times while writing, I was aware of voices that would want a more technical elaboration of arguments made herein. I would be happy if students or colleagues felt free to handle these matters more, criticizing or developing them. I would like to know, too, which matters, if any, deserve more treatment. Feel free to send me your comments.

Above all, thank you for your time.

Jeremy Bendik-Keymer
September 2005
Sharjah, United Arab Emirates

Notes

1. The place is Yad Vashem. See Martha Nussbaum, "Reply," in *For Love of Country: Debating the Limits of Patriotism*, Boston: Beacon Press, 1995.

2. As I finish the copyediting for this book, we are dealing with the aftermath of Hurricane Katrina. It is sad to think children for many years may have nightmares about flooding.

3. David Schmidtz, personal correspondence, and Elizabeth Willott, course material on arguing in philosophy. See their *Environmental Ethics: What Really Matters, What Really Works*, New York: Oxford University Press, 2002.

~

Becoming a Citizen of Earth

Hi you all! Good morning. Excuse me for being late today. The traffic from the airport was thick. We were stuck for an hour on the bridge. I'm glad you had to wait only ten minutes. If some of your classmates left, would you call them on your cell phones?

I was away in the Middle East doing work on the conditions of outsourced laborers there. The Sheikhs of Dubai, the Maktoums, have made a point over the last years of improving the working conditions of the hundreds of thousands of laborers working in that city. There was a conference around the theme of humanizing the city more. This is something the ruler of the city, Sheikh Maktoum, placed on the agenda during his Arab World 2020 conference in December 2004.

There is a lot to work on with your education: people who will use your services and insight, and people who will teach you on the job. So I hope you never stop taking your education seriously. And I hope especially that you don't succumb to cynicism or apathy. Too many people count on those fortunate enough to earn an education. This is something my coal miner grandpa Bendik taught me, he with only a sixth-grade education. In fact, I call the belief that with education comes responsibility "the Grandpa Bendik rule."

This lecture series' organizers tell me you're intelligent and hardworking people. I don't doubt it from the reputation of this school. Since leaving full-time academia to do organization-building projects, I've lived in upstate New York near where I grew up. I'm looking forward to coming back into the classroom this quarter. Thanks for having me. I will try to challenge you, and I will also try to meet you.

As students, *you have a right to clarity*. This is the first right of a self-educating mind. Without exercising this right, you cannot effectively learn, because you—insofar as you *do* have anything unclear in your minds—will not be clear about the lesson . . . Yes, what is your name?

Nashwa. What is a right to clarity?

The right to clarity is your right to have the teacher make the discussion as clear to you as she can, given the constraints of the format. It is your right to stop me to ask for clarification, or if the lecture does not favor interruption, to have me be available after class, during the midclass break, during office hours, or over e-mail to clear up your questions about the class material. *You should not feel you have to sit back in your chair as ideas or arguments fly over you and remain outside the conversation because it is vague or unclear to you.* You should be protected by a right that fends off intimidation at asking a question you fear peers or the teacher may think is stupid. No true question clarifying the material for your understanding is inappropriate. Perhaps you may have to ask it later or in a manner respectful of how others might hear it, but you have a right to ask it.

Thus a right to clarity is the pedagogical norm reinforcing what Immanuel Kant called *enlightenment*: the courage to use your own understanding.[1] Having courage is a personal virtue. Yet we can enable it through an environment that validates the virtue, gives it an open pathway, and provides an accessible means for its performance. Thanks, Nashwa.

*

These lectures are about something that matters. The question of the environment has been put on the agenda of almost every country in the world over the past ten years, and it is increasingly urgent as the twenty-first century proceeds. With a world population that is near seven billion and growing exponentially, and with a global economy that has consumed more resources in the past hundred years and altered more natural environments, made more species extinct and affected more large scale biotic processes than humans have ever done in history, there is cause for concern. Given how fast we are growing in numbers and how much we alter and use the Earth's life and living conditions, it is sensible to make sure that what we are doing is safe for our future and also moral. Are we ecologically sound and moral?

What I want to do in this quarter is to perform some philosophical background work to that safety and morality check. This is not a policy course. I will not pretend to perform the work of:

- population biologists
- statisticians
- climatologists
- urban planners
- economists
- healthcare analysts
- zoologists
- botanists
- agricultural scientists
- entomologists
- toxicologists
- and so forth

What I can do instead is perform general philosophical work that helps you assess how you think humanity should be in this world of life, the Earth. Big picture work is one use of philosophy. It does not supplant other uses of philosophy—for example, analysis of argument, conceptual clarification, and self-knowledge. Still, it can help us keep in mind the forest, when the bush-whacking is harsh and we need a cairn in sight.[2]

How should humanity relate to the Earth on which it lives? How should we view ourselves ecologically? En route to helping you find your answers to these questions, I'm going to speak with you today about two things: a claim and its justification. Let me write these on the blackboard.

Today's Class

1. I'm going to claim we should be *ecological citizens of this world*, and I'm going to explain what that means.
2. I'm going to justify the claim by saying *our sense of humanity demands it.*

This course will explain number two, the justification, and present some ideas of how we can live accordingly.

*

What is an "ecological citizen of this world"? It's a large expression in the mouth. It is also unclear how the adjective "ecological" modifies the noun "citizen." I will use "ecological" in a nonstandard way. By my usage, it means "logical with respect to living on Earth." "Eco" comes from the Greek *oikos*, the root of *economy*, too, by the way. The *oikos* is the home, dwelling, or realm of daily household transactions. It's where we live. For our purposes, that's *Earth*. When we are logical about living on Earth, we are ecological. If it helps, you can imagine a dash between "eco" and "logical" ("eco-logical"). My main point this quarter will be that *given* a number of realizations about our sense of humanity, being humane includes being ecological, and being ecological includes respecting life on Earth. Moreover, respecting life on Earth is part of being a true citizen in this world, what common humanity demands.

The Main Point of This Course

Given a number of realizations about our sense of humanity, being humane includes being ecological, and being ecological includes respecting life on Earth. *Respecting life on Earth is part of being a true citizen in this world, what common humanity demands.*

Let's start philosophizing toward this point.

*

We need to know how to proceed. Our method is philosophizing. So we should be aware of what that is. I've already noted there are a number of uses for philosophy: to visualize big issues, analyze arguments, clarify concepts, and achieve self-knowledge—among other uses. In all of these, philosophy is something people *do*. We learn philosophy by doing it. This is because "philosophy" means the love of wisdom. "Philia" is the Greek word for the kind of love friends have for each other, for a love that is not primarily erotic but grounded in care. "Sophia" is the Greek word for wisdom, which includes practical know-how. In considering this ancient definition of philosophy, we should remember above all that love is practiced—shown more than said. No matter how many times someone *says* she loves someone, almost the only thing that matters is whether she *acts* that way. Telling people we love them is part of the act of loving, but only in that act does it have its home. Otherwise, "I," "love," and "you" are just "words, words, words."

Wisdom is worth loving. It's one of the best things in life, ranking alongside love and the sacred. Love makes life meaningful at the end of the day. The sacred is innocence. Wisdom shows us how to live a life worthy of love and the sacred, how to get by, and how to be true in thought and deed. Its pointers are not trivial. Wisdom is good by itself, too, because an enlightened human should see life clearly.

Furthermore, we owe wisdom to others, to ourselves, and to our parents. An unwise life is likely to harm others, and we owe it to people to respect them. An unwise life is also likely to waste our potential. Yet we owe it to ourselves to develop. Furthermore, no matter that our parents are flawed, they gave us life—the most basic potential. It's an abuse of that gift to waste it. Also, because wisdom is extremely helpful for a life worth living, and because all humans deserve a life worth living, you and everyone your life touches deserve your love of wisdom.

So there are many reasons for wisdom being worth our love. I don't have a satellite link to what is wise. I am imperfect, as is any human. You are young: while imperfect, you have a fresh perspective, can shape your life in new ways, and can avoid some mistakes older people have made. I want to do my best to give you a head start into what you will discover for yourselves, but the wisdom is something you will have to work out yourselves, and only by loving it.

It may seem strange to think our primary method in this course will be a form of love. Yet that is the essential thing to say. The course will appear abstract, conceptual, analytic, argumentative, moralizing, and political at times. The most important thing, though, is that it express love for wisdom. I will do my best at that, and you do, too.

*

Here is a place for us (I count myself) to start growing up. Many schools in the United States do not teach becoming a citizen in the *world*. Even fewer teach becoming a citizen of *Earth*. Our world involves the environment. It's not just a human world, and it's not just a set of concrete streets, a car or a living room with a television set in it; it is not just a cell phone, a night out at dinner, a classroom, or a CD player. It's also the air we breathe, the water, the temperature we endure. It is the animals killed for our dinners, the beetles stepping persistently through forests, the disruption of a cloud above a range. I don't want us to forget these things and will argue from week three and following that it is a loss to forget them. What is it to be a citizen in that world, too?

Yet don't we need a government to be citizens? There isn't a world government. So how can we be citizens of the world, not just in a state or city? By speaking of a "citizen in the world," I want to suggest an old expression. "Citizen of the world" is the translation of "cosmopolitan." The Greek word "cosmos" means, roughly, "universe," and "polis" means, roughly, "city." A "cosmopolitan" is someone whose city is the universe—who is *social in a way that includes the whole world*, not just a particular city like Syracuse, Dubai, or New York. A cosmopolitan is guided by common humanity and is universally social, you might say. Hold that thought for a month.

People usually speak of a "cosmopolitan" in one of two senses. The first refers to people who are very worldly—people who travel a lot, have lived abroad and who feel comfortable mixing different cultures like the way New Yorkers go out one night to eat Indian food and the next night to eat French. This meaning of "cosmopolitan" carries an undercurrent of social class. People who are cosmopolitan in this way are wealthy (you need money to travel and eat out), and seem glamorous enough to be the subject of magazines like *Cosmo* (the fashion magazine).

The second sense of "cosmopolitan" is more scholarly and precise. It designates people who subscribe to a political ideal. This ideal has its roots in Greek thinkers who lived over two thousand years ago, and was first explored by a group of Roman politicians and philosophers called "Stoics." The Stoics thought that what unites people is our common capacity to reason and that anyone who can reason should be considered an equal citizen. Secondly, because reason according to them admits of very few cultural barriers (no nation owns it), someone with reason can be an equal citizen among reasoners anywhere in the world. The only community to which we must ultimately be responsible is the moral community of reason. Accordingly, cosmopolitans in this ancient sense are citizens of the moral community of reason anywhere in the world. They are worldwide citizens, not because they've traveled around or eat at different ethnic restaurants, but because they think themselves the moral equals of people everywhere. Moreover, they think this moral connection provides the rudimentary outlines of a community that is more important than any national. That's their radical thought.

Today, among other things, this second sense of being cosmopolitan suggests membership in the human rights movement. Modern human rights are global and try to structure the legal and political order. They do so through invoking the moral community of humans "endowed with reason and conscience," to quote the first article of the Universal Declaration of Human Rights.[3] Human rights try not to be religiously based, so as to avoid conflict, and claim their source in our convergent moral reason. Whether or not there is such a thing is another discussion, but the point is that if you support human rights, you support today's version of the cosmopolitan moral community the Roman Stoics had. With the aid of human rights, you can challenge any nation anywhere to right its injustice, and you are to be treated everywhere as a citizen with rights. Even in our world, it's not completely figurative to think yourself a citizen of the world. There's already some institutional reality to it.[4]

These are our two standard senses of "cosmopolitan," one from popular culture and the other from a political tradition. By speaking of being a citizen in our *ecological* world, therefore, am I introducing something new? Yes, I think so. To explore what appears new, I want to start with a distinction a twentieth century philosopher made, and I will omit his name for the moment, because it evokes strong antipathy for some good and some bad reasons. I want to avoid the connotations and focus on the useful distinction. This philosopher made a distinction between the "world" and the "earth." In our language, he would have spelled "earth" with a lower case "e." He was not speaking of the name of our planet. What was he speaking of then?

The answer may seem complicated at first. It will be simple by the end. It's helpful to think of the distinction between "world" and "earth" as a kind of mythology. Some mythological writers, like the ancient Greek Hesiod, use words like "world" and "earth" as names for dimensions of existence.[5] "Night," for instance, is not just the space between sunset and sunrise, but is a region of obscurity and fertile chaos. Similarly, for the philosopher who distinguished between the world and earth, the "world" is everything that means something. It's like *light* in some mythologies. By contrast, whatever is meaningless is not a part of our world. It's realm is the "earth." The earth is like *darkness* in some mythologies. Since we can't present what is outside meaning, we use an expression like "the earth" to invoke the fact we sometimes find our world blind and meaning at its limit. The "earth" is another name for what is unknown but pregnant with possible meaning.

We can't represent what is meaningless to us, but we can present the fact that there are meaningless things in life and that there could be things that matter outside what we currently find meaningful. Doing so reminds us that there is more to existence than what we take it to mean, although we have no idea what that "more" might be. For the philosopher we're considering, the earth limits and supports the world by being a place of fertile meaninglessness. It marks the experience of meaninglessness in our lives, but also the experience of having to find new meaning. Every night when we dream, for example, we let the earth act on our world. The earth is not a thing. It's not some image you have in your dream. Rather, it's the very need to *have* to dream, to *have* to sort through the meaning of your day by dreaming. The earth is like an empty space that cries out for organization.[6]

I think this philosopher called this region of fertile meaninglessness the "earth," because of the way the Earth—capital "E"—relates to our world (notice I am now switching from mythology to the daily language of our planet Earth and our world). The Earth—capital "E"—is where our world has been at home while the human species has been formed and has formed itself. In so being, the Earth—capital "E"—has long remained a source of trepidation, mystery, fascination and also love, shaping a pervasive sense of being part of something larger than ourselves, something that is both strange and familiar. We relate to the Earth, but it also slips our minds and grasp. The Earth is a source of relationship.

This philosopher's distinction got me thinking. Do we, in our current world, acknowledge what makes our world possible—namely, the Earth? When advertisements from the world's major corporations flood our televisions, stores and streets, do these advertisements present our world as involving an ecological dimension that can be destroyed, which is often fragile, which doesn't just work on our time and which deserves respect for its countless species of life? You answer this question for yourself. My answer was "No."

For the most part, our consumer world avoids the Earth. As a mass culture, we do not see how our consumption relies on ecological conditions and how our consumption exacts a heavy ecological price. Ironically, the Earth is mostly absent from the daily world of business. When it is there, the Earth has usually been reduced to a resource or an image for our pleasure. The environmental crisis is a sound bite on TV, easily displaced by the flood of advertisements selling junk food, beauty products, or cars. Yet if the Earth should be a source of a two-way *relationship* as this philosopher imagined, what then? It is one thing to realize the Earth is present in our world as something strange and familiar about which we should care, because it speaks to us in some sense. It is another thing to realize that concerns about the Earth are for the most part systematically absent from our major cultural expressions and from the way in which our world, especially our economy, operates. What then?

Thinking about this philosopher, Heidegger, I discovered a particular situation expressing his general picture.[7] I realized that in our world, the Earth *is* in some respects meaningless. It remains absent from our concerns. But it does *not* do so in an evocative, fertile way that makes the Earth a vital part of human meaning. Rather, it is meaningless as something that is systematically ignored. I found it bitterly ironic that in our dominant cultural world, the Earth is so meaningless it is not even mysterious. Knowing the ecological interests of Heidegger, this might be another reason he phrased his abstract concepts as he did, and if so, he was sending us a warning signal around 1950 as he tried to rationalize his own failure to see the error of fascist technology when he was involved with Nazism in the 1930s. (Heidegger's failure in the 1930s was that he didn't see his fellow humans; yet this doesn't mean his warning circa 1950 was wrong.)

*

When I thought more about the distinction between the Earth and the world, I realized that the Earth is absent from our world in ways that go beyond the present world. Cosmopolitanism as we have inherited it does not involve a substantial discourse of responsibility for the Earth. Its citizenship is not also ecological citizenship. This is not to say it couldn't be, or that there aren't moments in the cosmopolitan tradition that give room for some environmental considerations. It's just to say the main way we have inherited the ideal isn't solidly ecological. What would it be to be a citizen of the world that includes the Earth? What would it be to see our common humanity in relationship with the Earth?

For one thing, it would involve being a citizen in *this* world—not some other world, and not out of this world. It would be to understand who we are as situated in this planet with its ecology and other forms of life. It would be to see our humanity located here in relationship with life on Earth.

Moreover, seeing ourselves as ecological citizens in this world might have surprising and visionary implications. As we noted just a while ago, we are increasingly committed in our world to the discourse and institution of human rights. These are the major legacy of the cosmopolitan tradition today. They are grounded in our sense of common humanity. What would it be for our sense of humanity to ground ecological responsibilities also? What if being a citizen of the world out of common humanity also entailed being a citizen of the Earth out of an earthly sense of humanity?

When you think about it, our sense of humanity *does* include a relationship with the Earth. We cannot imagine our human world without the Earth being a large part of it. We *cannot*. So much of every widespread human culture involves the Earth. Materially, we all depend on such things as air and water, not to mention much else. Semantically, all widespread and historical cultures use representations of animals, of the weather, or of natural elements to express all manner of important things from love to religion to beauty to fear. We will discuss examples of these uses in a month.

Someone may object and say that we already *do* imagine humans living on some asteroid somewhere, no Earth in sight. So we *can* detach ourselves from the Earth. But even those humans living there would have to deal with their natural history: human beings come from the Earth and our having done so shapes who we are and have been. We will always be humans: beings who evolved on the Earth. The meaning of our world is made of the Earth, just not consistently and faithfully. So it seems absurd to speak of being a citizen of the world as if that meant only the human world.

Moreover, it is immoral to exclude the world's ecology from our citizenship, because we live on this Earth with other living beings, and life is not something that does not deserve any respect. People may have arguments for why *some* lives do not deserve any respect, but these are exceptions to the rule. The rule is that life deserves some respect. People then argue about which lives do and how much they do. Yet if life as a rule deserves some respect, it is immoral to exclude nonhuman life from what we think about when we think of being citizens in this world. As citizens, one of the things we have to think about is how to respect what deserves some respect, and that means we have to think about the Earth. How should we respect life on Earth?

Excluding this question from the meaning of being a citizen of the world makes cosmopolitanism immoral. Rather, we should build ecological citizenship into being a citizen in this world. When we hear the word "world," we should hear "the Earth" not far behind. To be a citizen in this world is then to be a citizen on this Earth.

I think we can now answer the question with which we began this train of thought easily. The new and yet potentially common sense idea here is that being a citizen of the world should involve ecological citizenship. To be a citizen in *this* world is to be a citizen of Earth, as well. The reasons why it is right to hold this idea are that, first, it is false that the human world does not already include the Earth, and that, second, it is immoral to forget that life is not something that does not deserve any respect.[8]

*

What I've said so far leaves open whether it is a good idea to be a citizen of the world at all. After all, most people throughout history and currently are citizens of specific cities, countries or regions. Why should we be citizens of the world as well? To start with the obvious, there is no world city. Yes, there are what people call "global cities."[9] I've lived near one of them, Dubai. It happens to have more nationalities living in it than you can count on several people's hands and feet. Still, it is a city in the United Arab Emirates, and when you drive out of this city for half an hour, you run into the desert, the "red sands" as locals call it. There is no city in the desert, let alone covering the entire world. But a *citi*-zen is a member of a city, technically speaking. The word "citizen" includes the Latin word for "city."

Of course, we now mean something more metaphorical by "citizen." Since we no longer live in small city-states, but usually under large nation-states, we think of our citizenship as our nationality. Still, there is no one-world nation. There are many of them, or else there wouldn't be a need for the *United*

Nations. Since there is no nation granting "world citizenship," but only nations granting American citizenship, Emirati citizenship, French citizenship, Indian citizenship . . . it seems implausible we should think of ourselves as world citizens. This is the *semantic argument* against cosmopolitanism: an argument proceeding from the way we use words.

There is also a *political argument* against cosmopolitanism. In fact, there are many, but I will give only one major kind of them. The one I will give comes from the Swiss philosopher Jean-Jacques Rousseau, perhaps the most influential writer of the eighteenth century. In his major work on the philosophy of education called *Émile*, Rousseau claimed that cosmopolitans do not serve their neighbors well.[10] Because they have to think about the entire world, they tend to lose sight of their home town. Because they try to stretch their sentiments to feel empathy for very distant people, they tend to have less sentiment for their neighbors. Cosmopolitanism, he claimed, makes them bad citizens. Hence, cosmopolitanism undermines citizenship and so shouldn't be an ideal for it. Many arguments against being a citizen of the world bear close resemblance to Rousseau's claims. Many assume that by setting our horizons too wide, we will lose sight of what is nearby.

The problem is, claims such as Rousseau's are psychological. They depend on whether people's psychologies really do work a certain way. But as a matter of fact, psychologies need not. Psychologies are adaptable and vary across humans. Often seeing the suffering of distant others *reminds* us of the suffering of our neighbors. We might live in a country with very poor and run-down cities and get used to that fact. However, one day we see a report on the poor of Calcutta, the war-torn citizens of Sarajevo or rebuilding and residual violence in Rwanda. Suddenly we remember that Chicago has areas that are very poor and filled with bullet-holes. Opening our horizons *can* remind us of where we live. If this were always so, it would be good to be a citizen of the world *so that* we could be a citizen in our hometown.

The argument Rousseau advanced can be stated more forcefully, however. Dividing our loyalties with our fellows around the world will inevitably take away some of our loyalties to our neighbors. This is not an emotional matter, but a conceptual one. When we should care for an Iraqi's rights just as much as we care for an American's rights, we will inevitably have to side with the Iraqi against the American if and only if the American has done something unjust to the Iraqi and the Iraqi hasn't done an injustice to the American. Or if both are victims of injustice, we will have to think they ideally *both* deserve our care, and equally so. Being a citizen of the world involves a form of moral equality across nations that may seem to take one away from loyalty to one's own.[11]

The reply to this kind of political argument is simple, though. It's *good* we oppose an injustice our own nation has committed. That is loyalty to the nation, and not the converse. After all, who is loyal: the person who lets her country do bad things or the person who keeps her country to what is good? Who is the loyal friend: she who lets her friend fall into bad ways or she who helps her friend out of the muck of the bad? Loyalty involves wanting the good for the one to whom you are loyal. Here, cosmopolitanism helps. By being a citizen of the world, you are on guard against national selfishness. You are on the lookout for human rights. Who wants to forget that no human should suffer injustice? Being a citizen of the world supports the cause of justice, and the cause of justice supports *true* loyalty to any nation or town.

Still, there is a last version of Rousseau's argument that goes like this. Yes, upholding universal moral norms is necessary for being a good citizen anywhere, and yes, finding common humanity abroad can help us be good neighbors domestically. But being a good citizen involves much more than basic moral responses. It requires, additionally, rich identifications with one's fellow citizens. Americans, for instance, understand a Brooklyn accent as coming from a place where people are gruff but known to be tolerant unless allied around specific ethnic tensions. Few Americans understand the ways of someone from Kalba, Sharjah, UAE. In a sense, we don't really share a life with folks we can't understand at the level of cultural accents and mannerisms. And this makes it hard to handle disagreements and political differences charitably, hard to forge a common purpose to civic life.

All that is true. Yet it isn't clear common citizenship depends on it. I don't share the accent of someone from Boise, but we can and easily do share a common political space all the same. That space is made up mostly of duties we have to each other and of our shared political process. In short, the norms, institutions, and official languages of our political order constitute an understanding sufficient for citizenship. People are so adaptable and creative that citizenship seems capable of going where the moral bonds and political institutions are.

Even in disagreement, moral responsibility and political process can take over and deal with the absence of a deeply felt common life. We shouldn't underestimate the cultural power of shared political structures. But even if we do, practices like listening to others in a methodical and fair way, giving people the benefit of the doubt, and trying to repeat back to the other side your most generous interpretation of what you took the other to mean can go a long way to forming a common purpose.

Moreover, there is much to learn from different viewpoints and breadth of experience gained in being worldly. Our cultural differences make citizenship interesting, *nyet*, no, *n'est-ce pas?* Regional differences within politically constituted common space can just as easily serve as points of learning. So even if cultural differences can sometimes strain citizenship, cultural diversity can also *strengthen* it. Moreover, since people tend to disagree about important matters even in the same culture, it is possible cultural difference could help *resolve* sticking points in a political order. We meet fresh viewpoints, and that stirs creativity. Thus in the absence of rigorous psychological and sociological studies, claims like Rousseau's are just too indecisive. I suspect they are conservative with human elasticity, too.

The semantic argument also does not make good sense. First of all, it is clear we do not have to stick to the literal meaning of the word "citizen." By speaking of "national citizenship," we have already let the literal meaning become figurative. Few if any nations are one big city. Why, then, should we let nationality stop us from using citizenship in yet another figurative sense, namely, in being a citizen of the world? What is more, the main things that have stayed the same between citizenship of a city and citizenship in a nation are the ideas of obligation and entitlement. Let me explain.

Political obligations are obligations we have to every member of our political community and to the community as a whole just because of our membership in that community. For instance, we have a political obligation to respect the property of our fellows. We can't just back our cars into theirs for fun without having to face the law. We also have a political obligation to help the government run. For example, in democracies we should vote, and in most forms of government we should pay taxes. Second, political entitlements are what we have a right to claim by virtue of being a member of the political community. For example, we have certain rights to due process or a minimum wage.

I do not see why, in principle, we cannot have obligations to our fellow world citizens and to some form of world governance. After all, we have a duty based on human rights not to torture anyone anywhere in the world. If we do torture someone, we should expect to be brought before a court of human rights (e.g., the International Criminal Court). Second, we have a duty to obey international law, a form of world governance. It is conceivable we could pay some form of tax to world organizations responsible for international services. After all, we would benefit from those services. Finally, we all have human rights, political entitlements of our common humanity. In principle, it does not seem impossible to think of citizenship in the context of the world. We already do.

Why, then, should we consider ourselves citizens in this world? We have already mentioned one reason. Doing so keeps us in touch with what every human being is due just for being human. We keep a sense of justice. There are other reasons as well.

One is that, like it or not, we are every day affected by the political order of the world and should have a say in how we are affected. Today, there is a massive global economy composed mostly of transnational corporations (TNCs) whose activities already affect, or will soon affect, everyone. This is nowhere more true than in ecological matters. Even people living in the most remote areas of the world with economies that are very local will have to deal with global pollution: the thinning of the ozone layer from industrial gasses, any global warming from the burning of fossil fuels, the poisoning of oceans and waterways from industrial toxins, and the waste generated by the more than six billion people currently living on this planet. These ecological issues affect or will soon affect everyone, at least indirectly. Shouldn't we all have a say in how those effects go? We should be citizens in this world, because we are affected by the world's economy and the way we regulate or do not regulate it.

Finally, another reason we should be citizens of the world is that we do have some responsibility to nonhuman life, and that life does not belong to any nation.

*

These are just some reasons why we should be citizens in this world, but I think that in and of themselves they are already sufficient for making it the case we should be cosmopolitan, in fact, ecologically cosmopolitan, citizens of Earth. Our being so is a matter of *justice*, a matter of *economy* and a matter of *respect for life*. These are no small matters. They become heightened when we think of the following (I'll write it out on the board):

> At this point in world history, humans should become ecological citizens, because without being so we erode our sense of humanity

This claim involves both an historical argument and an anthropological one. Let me explain.

Our sense of humanity is our sense of what is good for a human, and it is our sense of fellowship among all human beings as sharing a similar condition and fate. In lecture four, we will explain what a sense of humanity is in some detail. For now, let me point out that our sense of humanity is both moral and pragmatic. Morally, it is opposed to thoughtless destruction of life, and it is for relationships that deepen our understanding of our place in the universe. It is also for relationships that help us understand how to live a meaningful life. Pragmatically, our sense of humanity is opposed to self-destructiveness and is for what makes us live good lives. The problem is, a great deal of our current world culture goes violently against both what is pragmatic and what is moral from this humanistic perspective.

That hints at the anthropological claim, a claim about our sense of humanity. The "anthropo" in "anthropology" comes from the Greek word for human being. To start understanding the claim's historical dimension, take one example: our current global economy includes the fishing industry and the unregulated pollution of oceans. And the fishing industry goes against what our sense of humanity should support. One of its most respected critics shows this. Her name is Dr. Sylvia Earle.[12] Dr. Earle is one of the National Geographic Society's explorers in residence. Her specialty is deep-sea exploration, and she has had an impressive life between the ocean and Washington, DC, where she has worked on policy. Her major life focus is discovering truths about oceans. As she has grown older, Earle has developed a passion for preserving the oceans. In her presentations, she shows digital footage of strange, ocean life, such as that of jellies coursing with a colored electrical current like a marquis, or the vampire squid with its eyes the color of water.

Earle is increasingly worried about the oceans and the ways our fishing and pollution have begun to devastate them. For example, there is an increasing number of areas around the world called "dead zones" where, at the mouths of rivers, whole coastal waters go dead. The reason is that a form of algae takes over, feeding on nitrates coming from the rivers as they pour into the sea. The nitrates come from our fertilizers. And the algae they nourish pushes out almost all other life.

Or think about commercial fishing. In the North Atlantic, giant nets will trawl the ocean bottom to capture fish. These nets are so big that six transcontinental airplanes could fit inside them. The nets are heavy and scrape the ocean bottom. As they do, they devastate the habitat for thousands of miles. Fishing nets also capture more than their intended target. In the Gulf of Mexico, shrimp fishing captures many other species of plants and fish besides the shrimp. To get one cupful of shrimp, many cupfuls of life are taken. These other species are seen as waste and are thrown away. The combined worldwide effect of practices like these is so great, especially in industries like the tuna industry, that the Earth's ocean populations have been dramatically reduced, often by 90–99 percent.

Moreover, because all Earth life depends on complex food chains, when one species is fished toward extinction, other species dwindle away as well. A chain reaction can occur when we devastate smaller fish inadvertently caught in nets. Larger fish feed on smaller fish. Ripple effects occur along food chains where cycles of feeding balanced out in marine ecosystems over thousands of years are disrupted. It is like taking out a card from the middle of a house of cards. More crash down.

Dr. Earle looks at dead zones, devastated habitats across thousands of miles of ocean floor, almost extinct fish species, and she hopes we realize how our consumption devastates the Earth. Is this who we are, beings who devastate the oceans and turn them into dead zones, trenches of rubble, and ghost canyons where many fish no longer live? Are we beings who, out of the desire to make a profit now and to have more food than we need on our tables, eliminate species of life that took millions of years to evolve? Even if it were moral, which it is not, is this destruction good for us and our descendents?

Along with Earle, we might claim that the practices of the fishing industry and of unregulated ocean pollution are inhumane, because they thoughtlessly destroy life *and* because they engage in self-destructive behavior that limits our ability to have a fully good life. In these ways, they violently undermine what our sense of humanity should tell us to do. They dehumanize us. What is best in us does not thoughtlessly destroy life, and it does not extinguish possibilities for meaningful connections that allow us to understand who we are and have been. It does not let us act oblivious and insensitive to the beauty of life either. Finally, what is best in us does not send our future generations—our children's children—hurtling into a situation rife with potential danger. How safe can it be to kill off the Earth's first zones of life, the oceans?

Because the practices of the current industrial fishing industry and ocean waste-siting are inhumane, we should oppose them. One good way to do so is to be a citizen of Earth. After all, the political obligation to take care of the oceans has its proper reference point in the world not in any one nation, for the oceans circulate throughout nations. And that reference point is an ecological one. We should dive in and get involved.

The larger point, too, is that our global economy and population explosion cannot continue to destroy life and modify the Earth's environment at the pace they are going without seriously risking harm to a great many humans and without being thoughtless of other living beings to a degree that is massively immoral.[13] Especially at this point in history, we are morally obliged to respect life on Earth, and it would be prudent to do so as well. As I will speak throughout these lectures, we are looking at a matter of our *ecological humanity*. What is faithful to our human core is supposed to be respectful and thoughtful. But our current global economy is violently undermining that core. And the growing urbanization of human life insulating people in artificial environments with little to no contact with wild nature is not helping matters either.[14]

This is the sum of what I've been calling a historical and anthropological argument. At this point in world history, being true to the logic of our humanity is at stake. We should be more *ecological*.

*

Now that I have said a little more about what I think our sense of humanity involves, I want to come back to what I said about the word "ecological" near the beginning of today's lecture. Given the view of our sense of humanity I'll develop here, what will we mean by something being "ecological"? As I will use the term throughout the course, the word "ecological" will designate *being in a moral and healthy relationship with the natural world*. It is being "logical" about living on Earth, given what the Earth is to us and given our moral sense of humanity. We are ecological when we relate morally and healthily with the Earth's sphere of life—its biosphere—so that we allow it to maintain the environmental conditions in which we express what is best in us and have a healthy human life, including of course a moral one. People who take care to respect the Earth's life are ecological in this sense, and as we will examine later, being ecological in this way includes a moral dimension that respects life.

Being ecological

- is being in a healthy relationship with the natural world;
- includes a moral dimension: humans are considered inhumane when habitually immoral;
- may therefore include moral relations with nonhuman life; and
- is not therefore defined completely by the science of ecology.

Alongside the ecological, I will also speak a few times, and only when necessary for precision, of matters being "environmental." Here I refer to some matter bearing on the world of life, but not necessarily in a healthy relationship with it. Something can thus be environmental but not ecological, while all ecological things in my use of the word are also environmental. A car factory that produces cars contributing to global warming has an environmental impact. It is not in a healthy relationship with the natural world, but does affect the Earth's biosphere significantly. . . . Yes, what is your name?

I'm Joel. Could you write out on the board what you mean by "environmental" too? It sounds different from how I use it.

Yeah, sure. Thanks for exercising your right to clarity!
An environmental matter

- bears on the world of life, but does not assume a healthy or moral relationship to it;
- is not necessarily ecological, although all ecological things are environmental; and
- should *not* be confused with the everyday use of the word in activist circles. They assume being an "environmental" person is what I would call instead being an "eco-logical" one.

Thanks, Joel. These lectures, of course, invoke being ecological. The lectures could just as well be called "ecological humanity."[15] There is a link between being environmental and being ecological. *Because* human life is shaped by, draws on and profoundly affects the environment, and because it is part of being human to have some respect for life, we should be ecological. We should have the right relation to the sphere of life that sustains and has formed us. We will need these lectures to explain why this reasoning is sound.

*

To conclude for the day, I hope you now have a sense of what we will be discussing and why it is important. We're after citizenship on Earth, and we're after it because much of our world destroys an immense amount of life for no good enough reason, and because much of our world erodes our sense of humanity. We have to search for arguments supporting the assertions I have made about what is moral, prudent and true about today's world. Please do not accept what I have said just because it resonates with you. Also, please do not dismiss what I have asserted, if it's unwelcome. Rather, let good argument convince us of the soundness of a position so that we end up believing what is reasonable.

In this lecture so far, I have made brief arguments and ended with bold assertions. I have not yet argued thoroughly for why being an ecological citizen is the truly human thing to do. That argument will follow in time. Instead, today I have made two points. First, I've claimed that we should become ecological citizens of the world, and second I've justified that claim by saying we should be ecological out of our sense of humanity. This course will explain that justification and point toward what ecological citizenship involves.

Put your pens down for a moment and think about one more thing. Why does the title of this lecture suppose we should *become* citizens of Earth? Why does it assume we are not already citizens of Earth?

A citizen is a member of a political order who has political obligations to that order and to the lives in it. The contention in this chapter has been, first, that citizenship grounded in common humanity is global and, second, that our citizenship should be ecological, too. We should be ecological citizens of this world, the Earth.

I assume we are not yet fully ecological citizens, first, because our world governance has not yet found a way to be adequately ecological, and because very little civics training around the world includes a significant ecological focus.[16] How much of American public schooling, for example, involves a prudent and critical look at consumption, global warming or the treatment of meat animals?

I have made my assumption we should become citizens, second, because the very idea of being a citizen of the world—in either the popular or the precise, scholarly sense— has not historically included the Earth in the world. I claimed this when I summarized the idea of cosmopolitanism. It's not, historically, focused much at all on respect for nonhuman life.

Finally, I have made my assumption, because fulfilling one's obligations to justice and what is good for human life in a community is not something one simply does once and for all. It is something on which one should continually and consistently *work*. One becomes a citizen, because citizenship endures throughout our mature life, with duties repeatedly arising. As with most important human roles, one continues to mature in citizenship if and only if one attends to it. So as you go away for the week and read about justice for next week, I want you to remember that citizenship is an obligation, and it is also a deepening art.

Notes

1. Immanuel Kant, "What Is Enlightenment?" in *What Is Enlightenment? Eighteenth Century Answers and Twentieth Century Questions*, ed. James Schmidt, Stanford: University of California Press, 1996, 58–64.

2. Bushwhacking is hiking through a terrain without a path. A cairn is a small pile of rocks or other natural debris arranged so that it becomes a clear marker of the way to proceed. When there are no paths, there are often cairns on a hiking route people use.

3. "Humans are endowed with reason and conscience and should act toward one another in a spirit of brotherhood." *Universal Declaration of Human Rights*, 1948, article 1.

4. On the cosmopolitan tradition, see Martha Nussbaum, *The Cosmopolitan Tradition*, New Haven: Yale University Press, forthcoming.

5. See Hesiod's *Theogony*, trans. Richard Caldwell, Focus Publishing, 1987.

6. This reading of the anonymous philosopher is largely due to Irad Kimhi's reading of the French psychoanalyst Jacques Lacan.

7. See the essays collected in the volume, Martin Heidegger, *Poetry, Language and Thought*, New York: Harper & Row, 1974.

8. In developing an argument for ecological citizenship of *Earth*—the name we've given this planet—and not an argument for traditional cosmopolitanism, I could be taken to develop an approach to what Andrew Dobson calls "the post-cosmopolitan." However, I am not moving beyond the notion of the cosmopolitan, but *greening* it. To be a citizen of the world properly is to be a citizen of Earth, and this because the sense of humanity important for cosmopolitanism is substantially ecological. Moreover, our sense of humanity should become more ecological. If you are interested in the question of ecological critiques of cosmopolitanism, see Dobson's book *Citizenship and the Environment*, Oxford: Oxford University Press, 2003. Due to when I became aware of it and moving to Sharjah, I have not yet read Dobson's book, but only a summary. From what I can tell, my inquiry might be thought of as differing from Dobson's by exploring the *moral*, rather than the political, basis of ecological citizenship. If so, the two approaches can support a growing discussion of ecological citizenship from different angles.

9. See Saskia Sassen, *The Global City: New York, London, Tokyo*, 2nd edition, Princeton: Princeton University Press, 2002.

10. Jean-Jacques Rousseau, *Emile*, trans. Alan Bloom, New York: Basic Books, 1978, book 1.

11. This is a theme in Martha Nussbaum's *For Love of Country*.

12. I am grateful for the Lindeman Memorial Lecture on Colorado College's Earth Day 2004 for bringing Dr. Earle to speak.

13. The theme of that massive immorality—or "eco-cide"—is found in Roger Gottlieb's *A Spirituality of Resistance: Finding a Peaceful Heart and Protecting the Earth*, New York: Crossroad Publishing Company, 1999 and also in Frederic Bender's *The Culture of Extinction: Toward a Philosophy of Deep Ecology*, Boulder: Humanity Press, 2003.

14. Nisreen Alzahlawi reminded me of this point.

15. Candace Vogler first suggested this expression in the summer of 2001.

16. See Dobson, *Citizenship and the Environment*, for applied reflection on citizenship curricula with an ecological focus. Also, see Cornell professor David Driskell's *Growing Up in Cities* project. This latter is a community-based mapping and ecological awareness project done by poor children in many cities of the world. See his *Creating Better Cities with Children and Youth: a Manual for Participation*, Paris / London: UNESCO Publishing / Earthscan, 2002.

~

Moral Attention and Justice

For Andrew Bendik, coal miner

I hope you had a good weekend. It's fun being back in a liberal arts environment. I remember what it was like to see people again in the fall. There were all these "hellos" on the way to the Daily Caffé.[1] Everyone passed speaking to several people at once. "Hey." "What's up?" "Did you go home?" "See you later." "Oh, hi." You are lucky to have time to live in a small world of friends, ideas, and idealism. I hope that's what it is for you, and not too much partying and especially not cynicism. This may sound corny, but I think it's good, at least once in one's life, to devote oneself wholeheartedly to ideals. It's hard enough to do this in the professional world. It helps to start early. Politics on the job and economic pressures tend to make things complicated once one enters a profession.

Last week, I claimed we should be citizens of Earth. I claimed our humanity calls for it. In today's lecture, we will explore one kind of argument for these claims. That will be an *argument from justice*.

I will argue, first, that justice involves an ecological dimension. I believe there's a justice owed everyone with regard to what one needs from the environment. To make this point, I will point to facts about our life form that, when connected with assumptions about justice, commit us to being ecological. I will argue, second, that justice is global and long-term in reach, especially now. Then I will discuss some of the ways we can develop habits that are just. Let me write these objectives on the board.

Points for Today

1. Justice is ecological.
2. Especially today, it is global and long-term in reach.
3. There are a number of habits we can develop so as to be just.

I want to begin with an anecdote.

Not too long ago, I was in Vancouver and saw a documentary about Mark Rudd, a late '60s antiwar activist.[2] Rudd was once a questionable person, because he believed in the anarchic destruction of property and in terrorism that destroyed governmental institutions (happily, always with due warning to clear the area of people so that no one was ever hurt). Later, members of his terrorist group, the Weathermen Underground, became even more extreme and blew themselves up while making a bomb intended to kill off-duty police officers in New York City. Rudd then left the group, to his credit. By chance, I heard him speak at Fort Lewis College in Colorado a year after seeing the film, and he expressed a good deal of self-criticism at his early anarchy and nonmortal terrorism.[3]

In the film, what interested me about Rudd was his motivation. He was Columbia University educated and gave up a promising future to become an activist. Why? It is possible vanity or the love of power was part of the reason, since he became a leader in one of the hippest and most powerful student movements at the time, SDS (Students for a Democratic Society). But I felt that there was more to it than that. There is a powerful scene in the film where Rudd explains what it was like to wake up to Vietnam. What he explains is not unlike a conversion experience in religion.

Rudd said that when he finally saw *for a fact* how the American military was used to dominate many foreign countries, he realized his entire life had been missing an injustice so great he had to change completely. In other words, a fact that expanded his moral horizon changed his life and made him become an activist for justice. It was his point about the life-changing fact that interested me, not his immoral approach. I believe that we often screen out or push away truths that are uncomfortable or destabilizing. Yet they are truths.

Rudd's point was larger, too. People can live in a bubble of work, consumption, and entertainment, and as a result, people can miss much. One thing people can miss are things that are gravely wrong. This generalization is nowhere more true than with injustice against people far from the public eye. That is the kind of people ecological injustice frequently visits. Rudd's anecdote might then apply as well to justice concerning people's ecological

needs. Does justice call us to conceive of our lives in accordance with ecological facts we've not faced, facts that concern powerless or invisible people?

*

Here are two facts:

1. *Humans form relationships with lands.*

Think of us as those statues you go see at the Museum of Natural History
in New York City. Wax replicas of our ancestors, the statues stand in large
dioramas alongside remarks about the emergence of agriculture or iron
weapons. What they portray is this: over countless generations, we evolve
within lands, near waters, and under skies. We form relationships with lands,
and these relationships form not only our physical abilities, even features, but
also our cultures.[4] The ecologies in which we live give sense to our lives. For
instance, now is the time when leaves begin to change color—a mood our
culture reflects in poems, songs, autumn movies and clothes. When our culture harvested in early autumn, the meaning of this season was even stronger.
We would have harvest festivals and harvest times. We make the meaning of
life out of our natural place in the world.

2. *The effects of our actions extend greatly over space and time and throughout
   the environment.*

Our lives pattern historically in ways that profoundly shape the Earth's environment. The most recent example of this is the strong likelihood of global
warming.[5] Global warming is not definitely *caused* by human fossil fuel emissions, cattle methane emissions and a host of other gases our industrial and
consumer activity releases into the atmosphere. However, it is *correlated* with
that activity, and the likelihood is strong that causality is also there. Provided
it is, global warming is a result of our action across the entire space of the
globe that will affect many future generations, other living beings, and nearly
every ecosystem on this planet. Moreover, it has come about because of the
way our actions travel through ecological pathways toward distant effects.

A similar remark may be made about what Rachel Carson called "the contamination of man's total environment."[6] Our use of pesticides since World
War II has managed to place chemicals in our water cycles and land globally.
The level of toxins in the human body has increased dramatically in the last
half century, and DDT is found, in small quantities, in the breast milk of a
great many women worldwide. We do not know to date what the effects of

this contamination will be, but we do know that the likelihood of cancers has increased greatly and that we have affected the lives of many nonhuman beings by poisoning the environment for them. Our actions extend around the globe, far ahead across generations, and travel through the Earth's ecology in complex and hard to predict ways.

So much for two facts. The question is why they matter.

*

Please recall the two examples from today's reading. I will illustrate them at some length, and they will illustrate the facts we've discussed:

Freeport Mining Company, Irian Jaya. The Freeport Mining Company, also known as Freeport-McMoran, Inc. and Freeport-McMoran Copper and Gold, Inc., operates the Grasberg Mine in Irian Jaya, Indonesia. The region, also known as West Papua, has attracted "some of the world's largest oil and mineral corporations . . . Mobil, Esso, Shell, BP, BHP and Freeport."[7] The region also has "one of the largest tracts of tropical rainforest left in the world,"[8] and many indigenous people, such as the Yali and the Amungme, live there. Freeport, based in the old colonial city of New Orleans, made the Grasberg Mine the largest gold and copper mine in the world.

The mine is located in and around the nearly 14,000-foot high Jayawijaya Mountain and stretches through a slurry pipeline to the Arafura Sea. The mine is well over 100 by 100 miles in size and is an open pit. It is leveling the mountain. Large areas of rainforest had to be cleared to make it, and daily some 100,000 tons of metal tailings are deposited into the rivers filtering away from the mountain. When the mining ceases, the nearby Wanagong Valley will be filled to a depth of five football fields with waste rock, and the large Carstensweid Meadow will be covered several hundred yards deep.[9] Finally, the tailings from the mine are made of heavy metals, including copper, gold and silver, so the rivers are highly toxic to humans.

The costs are severe. Tailings from the Grasberg mine pollute rivers where the Amungme bathe, wash their wares, and drink. The heavy metals contaminate fish and mollusks people eat, and downstream, severe floods occur due to tailing buildup.[10] The mine has displaced a way of life. Moreover, Jayawijaya Mountain is the head of the Sacred Mother in the cosmology of the Amungme. So the Mother has been decapitated, and the mine now burrows down into Her shoulders and chest toward Her heart. Illness, poisoning, carcinogenic exposure, deprivation of food sources and potable water, physical displacement and religious violation are some of the effects of the mine.

Is the mine unjust? It is hard to see how the people of the region are due such disregard. Under Suharto, tribal communities had no legal claim on their land.[11] But in 1997, Tom Beanal, a head of the Amungme Tribal Council, brought a three part case against Freeport through US courts, just before Suharto's regime fell. The Amungme didn't want the mine there. Beanal charged the corporation with environmental damages, cultural genocide, torture, and killing. Yet even international law failed.

To decide whether there had been environmental damages, a very old American law was invoked: the 1789 Alien Tort Claims Act. (By the way, when you're in a court, a "tort" is an old French word for a "harm." It's not a cake.) This act allows companies based on American soil to be sued for harm they've done abroad.

Yet in spite of this opening in American law, the act was judged as not applying. Here's why: the judge believed there was *no clear international consensus* for understanding the damages as violating the customary law of nations.[12] "The plaintiff failed to 'establish the existence of a cognizable international tort.'"[13] That is, *no* harmful damage was seen according to international common sense!

What was missing from the judge's mind? Or rather, what was missing among the collective mentality of "international consensus"? I think our ecological nature was missing. After all, there still is no international convention for understanding human rights abuses as ecological in nature—despite the 1994 *Draft Declaration of Human Rights and the Environment* or the summer 2003 United Nations *Norms on the Responsibilities of Transnational Corporations and Other Business Enterprises with Regard to Human Rights*. For the Amungme, cases against the Freeport Mining Company based on our current international sense of justice were dead in the water. Ecology was missing from our international sense of justice.

*

Here is the second example:

Zortman-Landusky Mine, Montana. In 1979, the Pegasus Gold Corporation established the Zortman-Landusky Mine in the Little Rockies of north-central Montana. The gold mine ceased in 1998 due to bankruptcy.[14] Before its end, the mine erased Spirit Mountain. For the Gros Ventre and Assiniboine tribes in the area, this was a great loss. Where Spirit Mountain was is now a large, open pit.

Besides this cultural devastation, the tribes also experienced "cyanide spills . . . water pollution from acid rock drainage" and other environmental problems.[15] It is not surprising, then, they didn't want the mine there even after Spirit Mountain was a void in the shape of a pit. The tribes tried to use Environmental Impact Statements to persuade the Bureau of Land Management that the mines were unjust, and across more than a decade, some damages were awarded to the tribes due to the state of Montana and the Environmental Protection Agency weighing into the suits against the company.

Yet the effects of the abandoned mines are still felt today. In 2001, the Bureau of Land Management issued a reclamation project for the cleanup of the mines. However, the project was underfunded given what the tribes requested, and it exceeded the state's funds. Under the present Bush administration, cleanup of the site is not a high priority.

Given this dismal history, I have a hard time seeing how a people are being treated justly, and important facts are not being considered. The feeling of muteness and invisibility experienced by the Assiniboine and Gros Ventre must be extremely painful.[16]

*

Those are our two cases. Now consider them. In the case of the Freeport Mine, ecological damage is occurring on a massive scale.

1. The spatial scale of the injustice is immense.

The injustice occurs also through many levels of the region's ecosystems, notably through how heavy metals interact with river ecology to produce toxicity that also appears in the fat of river fish. So:

2. Environmental complexity plays a significant role in the injustice.

The case of the Zortman-Landusky Mine augments the Freeport example through a legacy of poor health flowing from the region. At the Zortman-Landusky Mine:

3. The temporal scale of injustice extends far beyond the causing act.

Finally, the loss of a spiritual mountain was not significant for American courts, even though in the late 1990s, Bill Clinton signed a landmark executive order on ecological justice that generated some policy. The tribes were upset because a religious land was erased. This means that:

4. The injustice concerns people's identifications with the land as well.

These four points implicitly show how we are ecological. Each injustice shows humans in need of a healthy relationship with the world of life. I want to explore how in what follows.

*

Consider a very general point: *Humans have a natural history.* The natural history of something is the set of facts explaining what it is in terms of its way of existing in the order of nature. Rocks have a natural history. So do humans. The term is antiquated and does not emphasize history in the way we might think. For instance, we may study the natural history of a flower by paying attention to its stamen structure and the way it facilitates pollination with a variety of insects. In doing so, we are not studying the history of how the flower became a symbol for a town in Georgia and what this later meant to a poet who lived there. Natural history is not historical in that way. If, however, we studied how the flower was hybridized over generations by horticulturists, that would be natural history. Natural history is the history of species and ecosystems.

All regions of the Earth have a history we need to know in order to comprehend the natural order within them. A geologist, as much as a zoologist, needs to know how a specimen came to be. The person studying the flower also needs to understand how hybridization affected the pollinating possibilities of the flower, and which steps in the lineage of hybridization led to what developments. All that is history. So, too, to understand how human smell developed to enjoy the flower, we need to understand how our life form developed in an evolutionary and ecological history.

Our natural history is made clear through categorical claims about the kind of being we are. University of Pittsburgh philosopher Michael Thompson developed their logic in a famous 1995 article called "The Representation of Life." [17] What are "categorical claims"?

Thompson jokes that the mood of these claims is the mood of the nature documentary. "Look at the human being—it enjoys rest at the end of the day. Watch out! It does not enjoy the occasional transgression from another human, let alone the tiger. Now it is spring. All the *young* human beings have their hormones racing. They may try to make babies."

To take a simple example of such a claim, humans are living beings *who do not thrive when bodily integrity is violated.* This claim is important for understanding why we *could* have a right to our bodies—for instance, against torture. This right wouldn't make sense with, say, amoeba: they thrive when cut in two. When we make human rights claims, categorical claims about the human species are in our assumptions. They are not sufficient for generating rights, but they are necessary for them.

Here, the facts of a species concern such things as the species' reproductive form and patterns, its preferred habitat, normal diet, and so on. In short, we describe a species' biology and ecology.

Now we describe the *ecology* of species in addition to its biology, because living beings develop relationships with their ecosystems in order to flourish. These relationships can be constitutive of the species, as when a species develops an incandescent lure that works in areas of the sea devoid of light but which would be counterproductive in shallower waters. The relationships can also be provisional, as when birds take up nesting in the engine of a hanger-docked jet. In both cases, living beings form relationships with their ecosystems in order to flourish. With humans, these relationships are between humans and lands.

I speak of human to ecosystem relationships more narrowly as "relationships between humans and lands," because I want to capture the ecological relationships found in our mining cases. In a couple weeks, we will spend time thinking more generally about what relationships between humans and lands show us about our sense of humanity. For now, I want us to have a general idea of what they are.

Mostly, humans live on or from lands, even though water cycles from sea to sky are just as important to human health as fertile soil. We hunt from lands, farm from them, and live on them for the most part. While humans do live on the water, the materials for even houseboat communities come from lands. Forays into waters are highly important but for the most part secondary, and we have yet to live in skies, except for the special case of astronauts.

When I speak of relationships between humans and lands, then, I am drawing attention to our natural history as ecological beings and speaking from our primary location in lands. By speaking of our location in lands, too, I am not making any claims about land as property. Rather, *that* there has developed a tight link between land and property is made possible in part by the fact we have relationships with lands. Yes ... Eric, right?

*

Yeah. I'm from Montana, and I love the book by Norman Maclean, A River Runs Through It.[18] *Does that book explain what you call a relationship between humans and a land? Also, I don't get the point about property.*

Thanks. I was being overly compact. The idea of relationships between humans and lands is a powerful one, and it has scarcely been mined—no, I mean, *fielded*—in philosophy. A philosopher at the University of Kentucky, Avery Kohler, works on what he calls the "ontology of land," and you could look at his work on liberalism and global justice to explore my point about property.[19] All I'm basically saying is that we don't have to relate to land as property, but *because* we relate to lands, one way we have decided to do so is by making land property. Some world cultures, such as the Mori in New Zealand, think it is blasphemous to say you own the land.[20] That is a different relationship with the land.

Your point about Maclean is right on, too. For those of you who don't know the novella, it explores how two brothers grow up and share brotherhood across fly fishing the rivers of their youth. It's profound, because one of the brothers had a rough adult life and died tragically, and the other went on to become a revered English professor at the University of Chicago. The land is so powerful that it mediates the mourning the surviving brother still has to do. Thus, there is a powerful relationship between these humans and their land, so powerful that the land serves as the symbolic transcendence of a loved one's death. That is, the land accomplishes maybe the hardest thing to deal with in life for a human being. Does that answer your questions, Eric?

Oh yes, one more thing: at the same time, too, we are discussing more general relationships between humans and lands. Maclean's is a particular and personal relationship. The point about our natural history concerns very general relationships with lands, not these particular ones. You might say we are currently speaking about evolutionary relationships with lands. Yet it is also a fact about our species that we form particular relationships with lands. Thus, if we were to put the point about Maclean's love for his land in the terms of Thompson, we'd say: human beings are living creatures who can identify with the land as a spiritual source.

*

Eric's point about Maclean helps us make a segue from Thompson to the two mining cases. Sacred Mother and Spirit Mountain illustrate our relationships with lands. The tribes don't just get food or water from these mountains. They see them as divine sites. This means they have an ideological relationship with the land, in this case an identification with a land as sacred. What should we say of our species when our ecological relations are not simply biological? What are we to make of the ideological dimension to our land relationships?

Humans are living beings who form identifications with lands, waters, and skies. The facts about us are such that not only do we need fresh water or clean air, but also symbolic relationships that answer some of the questions our species has about *the meaning of life, the order of the world,* or simply *what makes us different from other people.* In the gold mining cases, the relationship with land takes the form of spiritual relationship answering questions and meeting religious needs people have. But identifications with lands need not be spiritual. When mountain climbers think that mountains like K2 test their mettle as human beings, they have formed an identification with lands. This is an ethical identification within an ethics of self-realization. Similarly, when a scientist sees a swamp as a source of great wonder, she has formed a scientific relationship with a land. Or when people in Colorado Springs think of themselves as part of the Pikes Peak community, they have formed a communal identification with a land.

It's a fact of our species that we form ideological relationships with lands and that we can do so in a number of ways to flourish. At some level, such identification is necessary for our humanity. While we don't need to climb K2, having no cognitive relationship of wonder with the order of nature would not allow children, let alone scientists, to develop well. Imagine if our children did not express wonder except in artificial surroundings?

What questions did Spirit Mountain or Sacred Mother once answer for people? How did these mountains form people's transgenerational sense of who they are? What formative memories did the mountains and the rites associated with them give to children? My overall point here is that in order to give justice to the Amungme, Gros Ventre or Assiniboine, we should perceive how questions like these are at home in our natural history just as much as the question about what it means to respect our bodily integrity. Destroying these mountains dehumanized people, just as selling the Wailing Wall to a food franchise would.

Humans are both environmental and ecological beings. We affect and are affected by the world of life, and we form relationships with it so as to flourish. In a sentence:

We care about lands, and we depend on them for life.

Detailing our natural history for the sake of justice entails detailing how human needs and important, human interests are embedded in both kinds of relationships.

Now we've begun to see how these relationships are ideological and how little they seem to be recognized by courts. You might think that whereas courts might have trouble seeing this kind of relationship, they wouldn't with material relationships such as the need for a nontoxic environment. But recall the ruling on the Beanal case. No damage was seen! As it turns out, there is also a blindness to the material dimension of where we live in nature.

For example, we need nontoxic, nonviral water; clean air; temperatures that are not too extreme; and food sources. When the Working Group II of the Intergovernmental Panel on Climate Change (IPCC) issued its 2001 report on global climate change, it was reporting on human flourishing. You read this report for today along with our case studies, and I referred to it earlier when speaking of the likelihood of our impact on the planet. Global warming will affect all the basic human needs just mentioned—water and air quality, temperature, and food. Furthermore, it will do so on a vast scale, over many generations and through complicated ecological processes. Humans are such ecological beings that the possible effects of global warming listed by the report seem apocalyptic at points.

How well does our legal system see the material dimension of our natural history? If according people their basic human needs is a matter of justice, our ecological needs will become matters of justice under global warming. Yet as we saw, international law is not currently in a position to agree, even when it *does* agree. Let me explain.

In today's reading, you read about the famous 1994 case brought against the Spanish government through the European High Court of Human Rights—the case of Ms. Lopez-Ostra.[21] Ms. Lopez-Ostra brought a case all the way to Europe's highest court of human rights, a symbol of the new political structure of the European Union. Her complaint was that waste treatment plants near her home had made the air so noxious that it had crippled her life in many respects. She had to daily breathe this noxious air, and few friends or family wanted to come visit her. She felt depressed from this environmental strain. Ms. Lopez-Ostra's case would seem to be promising for ecological justice. After all, Ms. Lopez-Ostra won. She was successfully awarded damages for the noxious effects of sewage treatment plants near her home. Yet she won these, only because the Court interpreted the right to privacy in a broad way common to European legal traditions. The Court decided Ms. Lopez-Ostra's privacy had been violated by an awful and pervasive smell. They did *not* think she had a right to a healthful environment. Her victory was not a victory of ecological principles but a fortuitous loophole in the law. In our courts, by contrast, even a right to privacy wouldn't protect her, because we interpret it differently.[22]

But if human rights were squared with our ecological nature, having to daily breathe stinking air that impedes your taste, your socializing, and your kinship relations through patterns of irritability and depression *would* be protected by an ecological human right: the right to a healthful environment. Ms. Lopez-Ostra's home was troubled *only because* her ecological nature was. Thinking of the IPCC report on global warming, then, can we begin to raise the issue of global justice, emissions restrictions, and technology transfer to head off global warming when the potential ill effects of warming on—for instance—Bangladesh's flood plains do *not* show up as possible infringements of human rights?

Returning to the case of Freeport Mines, one of the great problems for ecological justice is that we do not have the legal understanding allowing us to assert how human rights are violated in rendering a whole people's rivers toxic and full of death. Yet the common sense understanding of that threat is clear. Nor—returning again to ideological relationships—do we have a vocabulary for seeing the relationship violated by beheading Sacred Mother or leveling Spirit Mountain. If we *were* to start articulating human rights claims in terms of human natural history and our relationships with lands, we could develop that vocabulary and the legal understanding needed for justice. Yet to do so, we must understand our natural history's relationships as both ideological and material. Otherwise, we will not be able to grasp how justice involves more than just physical health, but also includes the decency not to humiliate people by violating their sacred space.

Moreover, once we do understand the thick sense in which we're ecological, we can begin to see how thoughtlessly using the world's resources and hastily transforming massive parts of the world's wilderness is seriously, in the long run, dehumanizing. It doesn't just make people sick. It makes people *lost*. Our natural history has co-evolved with the Earth. What is hard to appreciate about that?

I sense frustration in my voice. It's a good time to take our twenty-minute break.

* * *

Let's get into what ecological justice calls for. We've seen how we might miss it given our current legal system, but let's focus on why it should be there and how we can think about it. As we do, we'll have another argument too for why we should be citizens of this world.

To begin, imagine standing in Tom Beanal's shoes as he argued for the Amungme as a tribal leader. The way he was seen by our nation's courts must have seemed irrational, ignoring the facts of our species and what it is to respect who we are. International consensus was not seeing that human justice is ecological—that humans are ecological beings. When you consider who we are, that is just *weird*.

Here was a man-made disaster that leads across ecosystem pathways to the illness and death of your kin. It renders your land uninhabitable, and on top of that, it erases the historical and psychological connections your people have made with the meaning of the land. It destroys your religious being expressed in a land religion. The mining operations would seem a serious candidate for a very bad injustice against a people. What has gone wrong in our culture's way of seeing?

Perhaps something very simple is at work. Perhaps our culture has not fully realized that justice can be ecological. Perhaps it is as simple as that. Yet the facts of our natural history help ground such a conclusion about justice, and the argument for why is straightforward. It has five steps. I'll put them on the board for you:

1. If we have justice, then we accord everyone her due.
2. If we accord everyone her due, then we honor people's human rights.
3. If we honor people's human rights, we support people having all capabilities necessary for exercising human agency.

For example, we have a human right against torture *only because* we require bodily integrity to be able to exercise our agency. Even if we choose to give up our bodily integrity, we must have that integrity to be of sound agency in the first place.

The next one is the key step:

4. Yet ecological conditions are some of our capabilities necessary for exercising human agency.

These conditions include ideological relationships with lands, for being able to have them is necessary for humans to live with *meaningful* agency. This may not be so for all humans at all times, but is so in a pervasive and recurring pattern among humans, including intensively at different times in life (e.g., during childhood).

Our ecological conditioning explains why, for instance, we often hear social justice documents arguing for a right to shelter, such as in article 25 of the Universal Declaration of Human Rights.[23] Ideological relationships also apply here, because being able to practice one's religion or live a meaningful life are necessary conditions on being able to exercise *human* agency. For instance, the Universal Declaration protects freedom of religion.[24]

Moreover, lest you think ecological conditions are out of our control (and so are not proper objects of justice), ecological conditions can in many cases be provided or at least protected from human infringement.

Here, then, is the conclusion:

5. If we have justice, we support ecological conditions for people.

This form of argument is a hypothetical syllogism. It is a string of conditional claims that interlock. In addition, we can use the argument's conclusion to run another argument form called *modus tollens*.[25] The specific argument would go like this:

i. (Same as 5 above) If we have justice, we support ecological conditions for people.
ii. Suppose then we do *not* support ecological conditions for people.
iii. We can conclude that we do not "have justice"—i.e. are not being just.

Thus, using *modus tollens* on the conclusion of our hypothetical syllogism leads us to the valid conclusion that:

iv. *If* we are *not* supporting ecological conditions for people, then we are *not* being just.

But since the consequent of a conditional statement (the part after the "then") is *the necessary condition* on the antecedent (the part after the "if" and before the "then"),[26] we know:

v. Ecological conditions are a necessary condition on justice.

That means justice is ecological. The courts were being unjust.

*

As we've seen, we cannot understand ecological conditions without understanding relationships between humans and lands. As we've further seen, these relationships include ideological and material kinds. For our species, ecological conditions include both healthful biotic conditions and cognitively important identifications with regions of nonhuman life. That the Gros Ventre and Assiniboine have a Spirit Mountain helps explain why the ecological condition of the Zortman-Landusky Mine is *sorrowful*.

That the rivers along the Amungme lands are toxic helps explain why they have relationships with the river *no more*. You no longer wash your children there, for example. In that case, the lack of a relation once made helps us understand the loss of an ecological condition. The rivers conditioned the Amungme's lives in healthy ways when they could bathe in them, and Spirit Mountain articulated two communities' sense of ultimate meaning when they could revere it.

Overall, what the argument makes clear is that without attention to the natural history of our species, we cannot be fully just. The argument also hints at something that will develop over the next month and a half. Radical environmentalists may worry that the account I've presented leaves no room for injustice to other animals or for explaining the great violence we can do when we destroy whole species or ecosystems. Yet I have left room. One of the advantages of seeing the natural fact that we identify with lands is that we also place ourselves in a position to see that we are a species that has moral relations with regions of life, including other life forms. These identifications, for example, involve even *sacred* obligations. Thus, the concerns of radical environmentalists are contained within what we've been discussing. Because we can have identifications with nonhuman life, we can have moral relations with nonhuman life. I will explain this point over the next month.

*

For now, we know that there are ecological injustices. What form do they take? Ecological injustices take place across vast spatial and long-term temporal scales and via much ecological complexity. We had better not miss these facts either.

Consider someone who sees the natural history of our species. This person is also just. She wants to respect people's ecological needs. She's also an average, middle-class American. For her, time is money, as much as she dislikes being rushed. With three kids to send off to school in the morning, she drives to work to make up time. It's just a few blocks. Also a whole lot of people do as she does: driving a few blocks to work, going to Blockbuster Video down the street at 8:50 so as to get back before 9 at night. Cars are convenient.

Pattern her behavior across populations and across time. Combine shortcuts cities make—for instance, in not having to convert a power plant this year or fix a chimney scrubber next year. Spread the years out and add in developing countries adopting coal-burning infrastructures for electricity. These countries often don't receive technology transfers from wealthier countries or lending agencies, and they rarely have free funds to develop alternative energies.

Meanwhile, Americans like our just person go driving on nights when, as in the words of Jaroslav Seifert, the city is a golden harp, a "desperate kingdom of love." [27] With your loved one next to you, and the kids with a sitter, you sit back and drive, down along the waterways, out past the neighborhoods where people lounge on the porches and front steps. The sun goes down, and you keep driving—everyone does—because the city is in twilight, and all its electric lights glitter across space.

Meanwhile, while humans dream, the atmosphere warms. Polar ice caps melt. Areas along the sea begin to lose ground in centimeters to rising water, and ecological processes are set in motion that may one day let both disease and displacement overtake whole populations of the poor in distant parts of our world.[28]

When our person with just intentions in her heart dies, none of the disasters will have happened. These disasters do not occur within her lifetime, and if they did, they would not affect her. She is a fortunate American. She senses her life and actions pattern into larger processes that could be— maybe—questionable. Yet, frankly, she's just one person, and time is money—as much as she hates being rushed.

What is missing from the example of this American life is attention to three more facts. These facts are ecological in nature. They should go along with the ecological fact we already determined, which I'll write on the board as number one:

F1. The natural history of our kind makes biotic conditions and ecological identifications part of what enables human agency.

Then, alongside F1 are three further facts. What our American is missing are:

F2. Many ecological processes important for enabling our agency occur on vast *spatial* scales.
F3. Many agency-enabling ecological processes occur on vast *temporal* scales.
F4. Finally, many such processes occur through *complex* interdependence with other ecological factors.

These are all three ecological facts—about the way our actions affect the biosphere and in turn members of our species. The facts can be illustrated simply by thinking about Mt. Jayawijaya. The mine does not operate anywhere near the scale of global warming. Yet its operations exceed the mind, let alone a mind formed by the lesson that time is money. I'll add up details to express the cognitive stress in grasping the situation:

> In the area below the mountain, as the rivers run toward the Amamapare sea-port and the Arafura Sea, 100,000 tons of heavy metal tailings sift into the rivers daily. An 80-mile-long slurry pipe leaks along its seams and joints into the ground. A whole mountain is being erased and shoveled over into a nearby valley. Miles and miles of tropical rainforest have been cleared, leaving an open pit of such a size that a mountain used to cover it. Trucks the size of build-ings and airlifts move to and fro, throwing exhaust into the air. Mangrove swamps have been leveled. The natural flora and fauna of the region have been impeded. Local subsistence economies have been affected. Ecological health has been hurt, not just in a single generation, but across many, as the Assini-boine and Gros Ventre case in Montana show with cyanide and ground water problems.

All that is a great deal. Without thinking of our lives in ways that pick up the scales and complexity of this situation, how can we grasp justice in it? When we use our computers with their gold chips inside, it seems incon-ceivable that we can reflect back to the slow erasure of a mountain, let alone the poisoning of river fish and people. Yet our economic patterns act as in-vestments in such injustice.[29] Only if we see how *a small golden chip* partakes in *the facts of justice* can we understand why the call to regulate the gold in-dustry is so important.

If you assume future generations deserve justice as do people outside our society, then the three new ecological facts bear importantly on justice. And it isn't unreasonable to assume humans around the globe and up ahead on the timeline of generations deserve justice. They are or will be actual members of our species, and every human deserves justice. Of course, there are a num-ber of complicated questions to ask when it comes to global and especially cross-generational justice. Yet I think we can avoid them here. I'm not de-termining how much or what kind of justice distant others deserve. Instead, we can accept current human rights dogma and assume people globally are owed human rights. Moreover, we can assume it is a matter of justice to think ahead to how humans like us will be able to live in the future. At a minimum, caution and sustainable practices seem fair to them. In this way, we can say all people around the world deserve at least *minimal* justice—human rights and our sustainable precaution—now and in the future. Beyond that, we can remain agnostic.

The injustices filtered through our three new facts do not fit easily into sound bites on TV. Nor do they come to mind easily when one is focused on one's self-interest in a competitive economy. Yet our lives and actions pattern in ways that support injustice where distant people or future generations are denied ecological conditions that are their due. We academics support the gold economy with our computers and their chips. Our country burns fossil fuels in defiance of a world consensus we should limit ourselves, and it is very hard to go to conferences or even to work without participating in these patterns. The facts of ecological justice are not well situated in the common sense of our society or its institutions. Yet facts shape reality, and as our examples show, we can support injustice when we act in ways blind to the spatial, temporal, and ecologically complex reach of our lives. It is for this reason that we should develop modes of moral attention that keep us focused as citizens. The conclusion of today's lecture will examine these modes of attention.

*

At the beginning of class today, we discussed how Mark Rudd realized a fact about America and then went to immoral ends as a desperate response. What should his fellow citizens have had in mind to make an America that was not in a bubble? I think modes of attention.

By a "mode of attention," I mean a form of thoughtfulness. By saying I am considering modes of *moral* attention, I mean to articulate forms of thoughtfulness that should be part of moral life. I will try to explain four of them, one for each fact we encountered today, and suggest why they would be good habits for a citizen. These are modes of attention to keep us from being in an anti-ecological bubble like the international consensus that ruled against Tom Beanal.

M1. The first mode is *attention to relationships between humans and lands*. Here, we need patterns of thought that search for (a) material and (b) ideological relationships humans have with lands, waters, or skies. Such patterns of thought will be questions. The questions need to search for biotic conditions and cognitive identification with lands. For instance:

- Do the people in that part of the world depend on rivers for cleanliness, drinking water, or fish?
- Do the people near those mines have an important identification with their land?
- How constitutive is that identification of their culture and sense of home?

Questions like these, made a habitual cast of mind, will keep people searching for relations.

M2. The second mode is *attention to vast spatial scales*. Here, we need questions that open our perspective to the magnitude of potential ecological harms, especially through the way those harms can occur as either (a) remote or (b) diffuse effects of actions. The effects of Freeport mining are of great magnitude, are remote from our gold purchases, and are diffuse in relation to our individual purchasing. One ring is only a small piece of mountain. Much the same could be said of the relation between global warming and individual driving, provided the causality is well established. Forming the mind through questions, attention in these cases can be expressed as follows:

- How will my lifestyle pattern affect people on the other side of the world?
- Do I support regulation hemming in the remote damages of major industries, such as the mining industry?
- Do my consumer patterns add up across my society as an unsustainable practice?

The frame of mind here is broad-minded, seeing ourselves as part of collective action and chains of economic causality.

M3. The third mode is *attention to long-term temporal scales*. Here, we need to think counter-factually and with foresight, in terms of what you might call (a) counter-factual caution and (b) investment. Think of the history of dealing with poorly stored nuclear waste. A good example of this history of mistaken storage comes from the Hanford Reach Area in the American Northwest, where many of the Northwest's salmon swim and spawn. Engineers assumed technology and government spending would keep ahead of the problem of radiated water. But that wasn't the case.[30] Today, the area has serious seepage problems where ground and river water are radiated by mistake. As a result, salmon become radiated as well. Some counter-factual caution would have helped, asking, for instance,

- But what if technological development or government spending will not catch up with our makeshift pools for radiated water?

Think too of the foresight of current attempts to preserve biodiversity through no-catch zones in ocean waters. These are off-limits marine preserves where no fishing is permitted. Such zones express an investment in the future, and it is this kind of investment that shows thoughtfulness. Moral attention shows in questions like the following:

- What of distant generations?
- What patterns are safe across generations?
- What if future generations see things very differently than we do?
- What of when humans are gone?
- Will we have ruined this planet for other living beings?

M4. The fourth and last mode is *attention to environmental complexity*. This mode has many dimensions, but we might start with how (a) synergistic or (b) indirect effects are frequent outcomes of environmental processes. For instance, air quality impact statements often do not consider how specific populations are at risk from multiple, not single, exposures to toxic elements and from the synergistic effect of those elements. Rather, the statements address single exposures to isolated elements and for one population, such as white males of average body weight. Yet different pollutants can interact with each other and form combined and new effects. And different people interact in different ways to the same elements, not least when some are pregnant or have allergies emerging from synergistic effects. The people of Chicago's South Side know that this oversight in how we measure pollution is harmful and sometimes deadly.[31]

Or take this example, made famous by Aldo Leopold. Culling wolves from the Rocky Mountain Front Range seemed a good thing to do for cattle farmers. Yet killing off wolves saved deer and elk from a major predator. They proliferated and in turn ate the countryside clean of its groundcover and first eight feet of foliage. This in turn made the land less capable of trapping runoff water, and so mountainsides began to lose soil at an alarming rate. The indirect effects of killing wolves had serious ecological consequences affecting farming and native habitats.[32]

How should we attend to such complexity? This last mode of attention requires education, more so than any other, and is needed to develop all the others. The education should include both formal and informal schooling and will be a dimension of what I will call "ecological maturity" six weeks from now. Ecological literacy is found in local communities and oral traditions, often more sensitively than in university textbooks. Yet careful analysis and scientific work are needed for sorting out the many and varied causal claims made within the context of environmental issues. For the sake of justice, we need to ask questions such as:

- How could my use of a sports utility vehicle contribute indirectly to loss of land along coasts in poor communities?

But we also need to ask:

- How clear are the causal connections between patterns of action and purported indirect effects?
- Are there real causes or are effects (e.g. ice-cap thaws) merely correlated with other occurrences (e.g. atmospheric warming) behind which there is a cause of which we are unaware (e.g. internal warming of the Earth due to geologic cycles)?
- Is there sufficient likelihood of causality to warrant precaution?[33]

However difficult the going is with environmental complexity, we should be able to ask questions like:

- How will releasing heavy metals into rivers affect river toxicity and, indirectly, the Amungme?
- What will be the synergistic effects on their children when the children bathe in toxic water and eat fish with high levels of toxicity?

These are merely outlines of four modes of attention. The four are necessary but not sufficient conditions on ecological citizenship, because people who do not cultivate these modes of attention cannot be just concerning ecological matters. Moreover, all these modes of attention show us once again why citizens today should be citizens of Earth. All these modes extend our minds to a global scale intertwining humans and our ecology.

Is it reasonable to make these four modes of attention necessary conditions on ecological citizenship? Let me hear what you think. Your questions will end today's lecture.

*

Please tell me your name when you ask your question. I'm still trying to match my roster with faces. Yes:

I'm Frank Minner. Professor, maybe your account of justice conflates an institutional problem with a personal one? Why think we should be personally responsible for these vast environmental, economic, or cultural blindnesses?

You're asking, by focusing on personal modes of attention, am I mislocating a problem occurring at the level of economies? Justice would be better served in cases of global warming by instituting the Kyoto Accord than by asking individuals to be more aware. Given, too, that the science of global warming is both highly contested and complex, it would seem easier to turn the matter over to well-structured technocratic administration. Furthermore, we are dealing with collective action problems, and the question of individual responsibility for global warming or gold mining is highly difficult to determine. Many think, for example, that states, not individuals, are responsible for global warming, to the degree anyone is responsible. For multiple reasons, then, perhaps states—not individuals—should adopt these modes of attention, and the justice of individuals shouldn't require them. In fact, the corporate nature of state agencies is much better suited to our modes of attention, because large organizations divide complexity into departments, are already cross-generational and are capable of diffuse data collection.

Here's what I can say in reply. First, can we expect states to think in ecologically enlightened ways unless citizens begin to think so? Who will hold states accountable? Second, our individual actions do have some effect on the problems of justice mentioned, even if corporate agents are the more useful sites of regulation for limiting injustices. Finally, modes of attention can be the practical thoughts of institutions. You can see the questions listed earlier in boardroom discussions, judge's decisions, official platforms and, as imperatives, in regulation policy. I have made attention personal through an example of an American life, but it can apply to corporate agents. An entire boardroom can ask the questions I outlined a few minutes ago, and they can even send those questions as a memo to the whole corporation! So we don't have to think the account conflates problems. Rather, it is open to both the personal and the institutional, and its conclusions apply equally in both instances. Thank you for your question.

Yes, in the back:

How can I live with these "modes of attention"? They are a lot to deal with! . . . Oh yeah, I'm Tina.

Your question reminds me of a concern used effectively by the Berkeley philosophy professor Samuel Sheffler to question some influential moral theory from the 1980s. The idea is that moral philosophies can be overdemanding.[34] They can ask us to dehumanize ourselves for the sake of what is right. Think of conscientious people who, with justice burning in their hearts, find themselves paralyzed by the global economy. That's you sometimes, right? Shopping *anywhere* seems to support injustice, as does using energy on the grid. Given few options seemingly free of injustice, people throw up their hands and shop regardless of fair trade, sustainability or what have you. If we are to see our lives and actions in the ways advocated by this paper, how are we to flourish? Our society is unsustainable, to start with the obvious.

That's how it feels, and it really is how it is once life gets busy and complicated with families and careers or multiple jobs. Later in this course, this problem will be so obvious that I'll argue creativity is a feature of maturity. For now, the way moral attention fits within moral life should be determined. Let me note two directions we could take.

First, institutions can deal more effectively with ecological problems than we can individually. It would be over-demanding to ask that we micromanage every bit of our energy use, but it would not be over-demanding to require we support institutions regulating energy across societies or screening our investments. Pragmatic considerations often take us to institutional answers. We will often not get the consequences our attention seeks unless we go through institutions. This answers Frank's question too.

Second, moral attention enriches life. Our lives are structured by moral choices we make every day, mostly through habit. Human beings are creatures who live and breathe moral decisions. To rethink one's life in light of moral discovery is both human and fulfilling. Certainly, it takes patience and much deliberation to resolve tensions and trade-offs, but the project of moral revision is rewarding. We become more competent with our lives and in tune with what we want out of life. Also, the attention advocated here is done for justice. It connects us with common humanity. We might remember stories activists tell in this regard: acting for justice lets them share in the human community. Changing one's life for the sake of justice can be a way to connect with fellow humans and to share in time across generations and continents. So while it might be overwhelming, patiently working on what one can handle should be seen as rewarding, increasing our sense of autonomy and our community with others.[35]

The American can live in light of the facts of justice while lobbying our government to adopt the Kyoto Accord, the International Criminal Court, the *Draft Declaration on the Human Right to the Environment*, while figuring out how to use public transportation more often and to screen her retirement investments from unregulated gold corporations. Doing so, she will find herself more connected to her fellows than when she drives across town in the darkness on Saturday night, because she can know that through justice now, some three-year-old like her own daughter Amina, in a distant place or time, has a better chance of growing up without a respiratory malfunction or malaria. That Earthly connection is established by justice and only by justice.

You're George, right? A philosophy major?

Yes. Aren't you glossing over the way unintended consequences are central to your examples? We do not intend to erase Mt. Jiyawijaya when we buy computers. Why suggest we may support injustice by logging in every morning?

The full answer to this is complicated and so we should discuss it in office hours. The part that is simple goes like this: not intending to do injustice is not a sufficient ground for not doing injustice. To take an example, the careless driver is still held accountable for going down the wrong lane. He didn't intend five collisions during rush hour, but he should have been more careful. It is careless to use the Earth's resources in such a way that people elsewhere in the world or future generations suffer. Provided it is, we should be responsible to exercise minimal care to avoid what unintentional harm we could readily avoid. And we can readily avoid such an injustice: with the internet, we now have access to numerous monitoring organizations that can help us track our basic consumption and its source in potentially unjust production zones. That's a first answer to your complicated question, but I see we're running out of time.

Elizabeth?

This is quick. How should these modes form public education?

I'd like to hear *your* thoughts. After all, I hear you are a Free School advocate.[36] When we log into our computers without making sure gold is regulated by human rights and environmental standards, we might support patterns of injustice. What should we know to deal with such situations? Do we need more facts, or do we need internships, experiences? Also, how can we develop a new international consensus so judges see ecological damage?

There's another dimension to this too: the dimension of real political influence. Given the way power corridors work around the judiciary and the legislature, simply seeing facts seems necessary for justice, but hardly sufficient. The justice might have listened if the Amungme plaintiffs were powerful, hard as that is to know. For truly effective modes of attention, we may seem to need know-how: law degrees, lobbying experience, media connections, guidance on Capital Hill. Have the modes of attention gone far enough then? How should education develop them?

These are open questions. One purpose of a course is to produce questions we have yet to answer. It's late. You've been patient, and I'll have to leave these questions to you.

Modes of attention can help us live clearer lives. Around us are the facts of our lives. When we have questioned and carefully studied them, when we have given them the attention they deserve, we will be more connected with our fellow humans.

Notes

1. The Daily Caffé was a "mom and pop" (locally run) café in New Haven, Connecticut which sadly closed in lieu of a more corporate restaurant to gentrify the area around Yale University. The Daily Caffé allowed New Haven kids to mix with Yale ones.

2. Rudd is interviewed in Sam Green and Bill Siegel, *The Weathermen Underground*, Sundance Film Festival, 2002.

3. Rudd spoke at Fort Lewis in April 2004, as part of a coalition opposing the war in Iraq.

4. This point is illustrated well in Gary Snyder's essay "The Place, the Region, and the Commons" in his *The Practice of the Wild*, San Francisco: Northpoint Press, 1991.

5. On this likelihood, see the *Summary for Policy Makers: Climate Change 2001; Impacts, Adaptation, and Vulnerability*, sixth session of the Intergovernmental Panel on Climate Change (IPCC) working group II, Geneva, Switzerland, Feb. 13–16, 2001, and the commentary on this by Peter Singer in his *One World: The Ethics of Globalization*, New Haven: Yale University Press, 2003, "One Atmosphere."

6. Rachel Carson, *Silent Spring*, New York: Mariner Books, 2002, 8.

7. "The Australia West Papua Association," at *au.geocities.com/awpab/environment.htm* (accessed December 2003).

8. "The Australia West Papua Association," at *au.geocities.com/awpab/environment.htm*.

9. "The Australia West Papua Association," at *au.geocities.com/awpab/environment.htm*.

10. "The Australia West Papua Association," at *au.geocities.com/awpab/environment.htm*.

11. "The Australia West Papua Association," at *au.geocities.com/awpab/environment.htm*.

12. Jean Wu, "Pursuing International Environmental Tort Claims Under the A.T.C.A.: Beanal vs. Freeport-McMoran," *Ecology Law Quarterly*, 28 (2001): 487, section III. See also Elizabeth Pinkard, "Human Rights and the Environment: Indonesian Tribe Loses in Its Latest Battle Against Freeport-McMoRan, Inc., Operator of the World's Largest Gold and Copper Mine," 1997 *Colorado Journal of International Environmental Law Yearbook* 141.

13. See Pinkard, "Human Rights and the Environment," herself quoting *Beanal v. Freeport-McMoRan, Inc.*, 969 F. Supp. 362 (E.D. La. 1997), 382.

14. My source for this case is Kathryn Munz, "Mineral Development: Protecting the Land and Communities," in *Justice and Natural Resources: Concepts, Strategies and Applications*, ed. Munz et al., Island Press, 2002, 309–311.

15. Munz, "Mineral Development," 309.

16. Without Phil Kannan's co-teaching, I would never have encountered these two cases. My thanks go to him for our fall 2003 seminar on environmental justice at Colorado College.

17. Michael, Thompson, "The Representation of Life," in *Virtues and Reasons, Essays in Honor of Philippa Foot*, ed. R. Hursthouse, W. Quinn et al., New York: Oxford University Press, 1995.

18. Norman Maclean, *A River Runs through It, and Other Stories*, Chicago: University of Chicago Press, 2001.

19. See for instance, Avery Kohler, "Valuing Land and Distributing Territory," in *Geographies and Moralities*, ed. Roger Lee and David M. Smith, New York: Blackwell, 2004, 135–148.

20. Brian Miller, a student in my winter 2004 course on justice at Colorado College, taught me this point in his term paper. See his "Justice and the River," at *studentwebs.coloradocollege.edu/~B_Miller/justice%20and%20the%20river.htm* (accessed May 3, 2005).

21. See Richard Desgagne, "Human Rights in *Lopez-Ostra vs. Spain*," *The American Journal of International Law*, 89 A.J.I.L. 772, 1995.

22. Again, my thanks to Phil Kannan for teaching me this case.

23. *Universal Declaration of Human Rights*, New York: United Nations General Assembly, 1948, Article 25 (1).

24. *Universal Declaration*, Article 18.

25. Both the form of a hypothetical syllogism and of *modus tollens* are argument forms of elementary logic. A conditional claim is an "if P then Q" (i.e., it shows a consequence of asserting P; on the condition that you assert P, you can infer Q). When you put several of these claims together to interlock, you develop a hypothetical syllogism (if P then Q, and if Q then R; so given P, then you can infer R). The conditionals interlock to allow you to validly run down the piano keys of them along their implications.

Modus tollens is a valid argument form that goes like this: if P then Q. Given the negation of Q, you can therefore infer the negation of P. That's it. It depends on a grasp of what is called a "necessary condition." The second part of a conditional claim is a necessary condition on the first part. When I say, "If it rains, then there is water in the air," there being water in the air is necessary for there being rain. Accordingly, if there is *no* water in the air, there is no rain. *Modus tollens* works off the idea that when you negate a necessary condition on something, you can negate it. See the argument as we proceed!

26. It is important for the reader to take time to imagine the lecturer pointing out each part of the argument and the conditional on the blackboard, using the written out argument steps.

27. "Wet Picture" in Raymond Carver, *A New Path to the Waterfall*, New York: Atlantic, 1990, frontispiece to his own poetry.

28. These predictions have high probability according to the IPCC summary report on climate change cited earlier in this lecture.

29. On economic citizenship and socially conscious investing, see Johann Klaassen and Jeremy Bendik-Keymer, "Of Blood and Money: War, Financial Collusion and Economic Citizenship," manuscript, 2005.

30. This case is discussed thoroughly in David Oates's *Paradise Wild: Re-imagining American Nature*, Portland: University of Oregon Press, 2003.

31. See Robert Kuehn, "The Environmental Justice Implications of Quantitative Assessment," *University of Illinois Law Review* 103 (1996): 116–149. In reference to Chicago's South Side, see also Jonathan Kozol, *Savage Inequalities: Children in America's Schools*, New York: Perennial, 1992, chapter 2.

32. See Aldo Leopold, *A Sand County Almanac and Sketches Here and There*, New York: Oxford University Press, 1989.

33. The answer is: yes. See Singer, *One World*, 16.

34. See Samuel Sheffler, *Human Morality*, New York: Oxford University Press, 1993.

35. This reply was suggested by Nikki Vangnes.

36. The World Free School movement is a movement to establish community-based schools with a great deal of attention to the autonomous development of the child. Elizabeth Baker, an actual Free School intern, is the model for this questioner.

LECTURE THREE

~

The Idea of an Ecological Orientation

For Breena

In the course of years the ospreys had woven or worked into the nest a twenty-foot piece of haul seine with ropes attached that they had picked up on the shore of the sound, perhaps a dozen cork floats from fishing gear, many cockle and oyster shells, part of the skeleton of an eagle, parchment-like strings of the egg cases of conchs, a broken oar, part of a fisherman's boat, tangled mats of seaweed.

Rachel Carson, *Under the Sea Wind*, 1941[1]
(Written on the chalkboard before class.)

Welcome back to the morning. Today we will have a shorter lecture, because you're splitting into groups to work on your projects on ecological justice. I like what I've been hearing about them. My main hope in assigning them is to let you realize concretely how common humanity is ecological when it comes to justice. I also want you to realize how being a citizen of the world is urgent given the way our actions relate to global processes. Finally, I want you to know you can make a difference if your conscience calls you.

The reason that guides conscience, by the way, is often thought of as the light of the soul. I have been enjoying how the different times for these lectures allow us to experience varied qualities of light through the windows of this hall. The morning is a time when the sun excites the room with industriousness. We leave our rooms early and are brought into a day filled with life. In the afternoons, however, we have to struggle to stay awake at first. Yet the sun is usually alive through the leaves outside, and the colored glass casts shapes on the shirts of the people in front of us. After break, our discussion becomes the afternoon: the main task. Then what was sleepy becomes a worked event. When we leave, we go to play sports, see friends, or move around the library until dinner. All the time, light settles through our unconscious. Why is light a metaphor for reason?

I put the quote from Rachel Carson on the board. You read her for today. As you may know, she is one of the twentieth century's most important environmentalists. The quote is from the book of which we read extracts for today, a lesser-known book than her others, but one I enjoy for the way it can give you a sense of ecological relationships. The book was her first, and it prefigures some of the most important nature writing of the twentieth century, including her landmark critique of pesticides on birds: *Silent Spring* (1962).[2] In *Under the Sea Wind,* Carson shows how land, air and water ecosystems interact, focusing especially on coastal areas. She shows her hallmark ability to explain science to non-scientists and makes coastal ecology interesting. I will not explain at this moment why I have put this quote at the head of our class or why you read part of this book for today, but both will be clear by the end of the lecture.

To begin, let's review where we are. These lectures contain a lot for meeting just once a week. I hope I spark conversations among you and your friends, for a course is designed to generate thought. Last week, we argued that justice is ecological and saw how that ecological dimension is global in today's economy. Out of a sense of common humanity, we ought to be aware of how our consumption in a country like America unintentionally supports an injustice across the Pacific Ocean in Irian Jaya. That was the point of talking about human rights and our categorical features. When we drive our cars heedless of how much carbon dioxide they throw into the atmosphere, we engage in an infinitesimal part of a potentially massive injustice against future generations. Our sense of justice ought to make us more economically aware, ecologically cautious and sustainable with an eye to the global dimension of our actions.

In realizing how common humanity and its sense of justice took us to ecological issues and global dimensions, we concluded one argument for why becoming a citizen in today's day and age is both an ecological and a global matter. Accordingly, to become a true citizen is to become an ecological citizen of the world. Is it acceptable to consume unaware of how we affect people made invisible by distance, culture, and powerlessness? Yet if it is okay, the sense of common humanity has to be given up. The belief that every human should have her capacity for human agency protected has to be given up. We can't keep our common humanity consistently and consume heedless of ecological facts. And we can't be socialized humans without a minimal sense of common humanity.

So last week's lecture left us with one ecological dimension to our humanity. What I want us to do this morning is think differently than last week. I want us to probe further what is ecological about our humanity. My argument today will rely on what is prudent. I mentioned prudence in our first lecture and said it was a dimension of a sense of humanity—what some people call "self-interest." What is prudent is what is in our own self-interest as humans. At the same time, I also noted that our sense of humanity involves a moral dimension that is not self-interested. I will begin today to hint at the moral side of our humanity, although prudence will be my focus. The aim will be to give an argument for earthly humanity that is *from prudence*, rather than *from justice*. The new argument can then supplement our argument last week. And along with this week's argument will come further dimensions of our sense of humanity.

Sometimes what is prudent is what is moral. After all, it is immoral to thoughtlessly endanger your own life as if it doesn't matter or to rashly endanger the lives of your fellows. But what is prudent can also come into tension with what is moral. Often, it is not in your self-interest to stand up to injustice. People who do so get fired, shot at, ostracized from their communities, and so on. Doing what is right can have a high price. Yet it is right, the moral thing to do. Moreover, respecting life often seems in tension with what would serve our interests. Why should we protect that endangered species when we could use its habitat for a new shopping mall or for grazing land to feed cattle destined for hamburger meat? So an argument from prudence appears different from a moral argument. That's why we are handling it separately this week.

Look at the international documents I had you read for this lecture. These were the Universal Declaration of Human Rights (1948), the Rio Declaration on the Environment and Development (1992), and the Earth Charter (2002).[3] The first document is the landmark document that helped form the moral charter for the United Nations directly after World War II. Formed as a response to fascism and in the hopes of stabilizing the emerging Cold War, it became the major document for the human rights movement's rapid growth in the second part of the twentieth century. It has thus been a highly influential document and is becoming more so as human rights institutions like the International Criminal Court emerge.

The Rio Declaration is a much less influential document, although it is a small and ambivalent landmark in recent environmental history. This document was perhaps the first officially widespread acknowledgment by global powers that sustainability is a serious issue, even though the document does not commit anyone legally to ecological initiatives. Nonetheless, it makes the claim that developing a sustainable society is something to which we should aspire.

Finally, the Earth Charter is not yet a landmark document and is unlikely to become so. Frankly, it's utopian and uneven in its writing. Still, I think it's important as a sign of the work to be done. The Earth Charter is a document shaped by religious leaders, social justice workers, and environmentalists from all over the world. They hoped the United Nations and other major organizations would adopt a long-range vision of integrating social justice, the lessons of peace studies, and ecological imperatives under the banner of respect for life on Earth. There have been a series of attempts to have the charter build up steam, but as of yet it appears the product of idealists more than of an emerging international consensus. That doesn't mean it's not educational or admirable, though.

I wanted you to study these three documents, because across them *we see thought become more ecological.* In the Universal Declaration of Human Rights, there is no mention of ecological problems, nor is there acknowledgment of the fact that access to nature might be a basic human right. The Earth's environment is left out of the picture. Then, in the Rio Declaration, there are moments when the environment figures centrally in human flourishing. For instance, we are told the Earth is our home. For the most part, though, this document is concerned with marking how important enlightened foresight will be for the long-term interest of humanity. The environment is then important for our well-being, but only indirectly, by way of the obstructions it can create for our pursuits if not managed well. However, in the Earth Charter, human well-being is seen as part of the vitality of the Earth's biosphere. On the flip side, the vitality of the biosphere is seen as directly important for human flourishing not just because it may impact what we can do and become, but also because a form of moral identification between us and the wider universe of life is proposed. Between the point A of the Universal Declaration and the point C of the Earth Charter, we see our common humanity greened. It is made more earthly.

Thinking of these documents, I want to ask two questions:

Two Questions for Today

1. How should we understand the changing relationship to the environment?
2. How should we justify it?

Here's what I will claim:

Two Answers

1. The shift in self-understanding involves a shift in what it is to be human. At the center of this shift is an *ecological orientation* (I will explain the new term in a moment).
2. The shift is justified by the good it brings to human life.

In later lectures, we will see how the shift is morally desirable, but I want to bring us to an ecological orientation through a form of self-interest, first. That way, we enrich our argument and also have some grounds for people who are hard-pressed to follow the moral argument later.

*

Let's take question one and answer it. Across the three international documents, we see a shift in being human. Of course, you may not understand your humanity in the ways suggested by the documents. And clearly, there are world cultures that already do understand what it is to be human in tight connection with the ecological vitality of the Earth. Australian aborigines or American Indians are often cited in this regard. What the documents do is show us a change in a dominant cultural conception—the international common sense we criticized last lecture. The documents don't speak for everyone nor do they need to. And we should note that whatever change the documents do show, it isn't a very deep one. After all, it didn't penetrate into international law when Tom Beanal made his case. The shift across these documents is more symbolic than actual. Still, it is significant.

What we can claim is that the progression of these international documents discloses a *desirable* way to understand ourselves as humans. The understanding can still be desirable even thought it's utopian. We will see why when we turn to the second question and answer it.

Think about this, then. In the Universal Declaration of Human Rights, being human is conceived against the background of what enables human dignity, but this dignity isn't ecological or ecologically enabled. Hence, we see a large version of what we saw last week: our ecological humanity is invisible. In this enormously important document, human rights make sure the conditions of our dignity are met. Yet these aren't ecological conditions, not exactly. Of course, some of the rights can be shown to *indirectly* entail ecological protections. For instance, the right to life implies the right to healthy living conditions, including ecological conditions. But such moves are clever ways of twisting the document for the sake of ecological justice. We heard about one of them last time in the case of Ms. Lopez-Ostra who lucked out when the European High Court of Human Rights interpreted the right to privacy broadly. All in all, the basics of what it is to be fully human are stated on the Universal Declaration apart from ecological health. That seems an oversight.

So it's good the Rio Declaration acknowledges we need a healthy ecological context. The reasoning is simple. If we undermine the ecological conditions that allow us to be healthy, we thwart our health. In this way, waste-siting practices that overburden the Earth's natural sinks or consumptive practices that seriously alter (e.g., warm) atmospheric conditions indirectly attack the conditions of our agency and so are undesirable according to the declaration.

This acknowledgment of our ecological condition marks a big change. What it is to be properly human is understood in *relation* to Earth ecology. The relation is one of dependence. We are dependent on the Earth's ecology for our health and agency. In this way, our humanity involves a vital relationship with the Earth—at least insofar as we need certain natural conditions to have agency and cannot supply them for ourselves via technology and commerce. The Rio Declaration fills in the gap left open by the Universal Declaration.

The Earth Charter goes farther, though. Not only are we dependent on the Earth's ecological vitality. We are morally linked to it. What can that mean? If I understand the idea permeating the charter, just as we acknowledge the life in us as worthy of respect, so we should acknowledge the life without us as worthy of respect. Doing so is humane. Humanity participates in the Earth's life. We are one among many life forms, and just as what is best in us is thoughtful about our own lives, so should what is best in us show consideration for the world of life in which we participate. The form of moral identification the charter supposes, then, is one by which we, living beings of a life form, identify with other life forms in the biosphere as also being worthy of respect. What it is to be fully human includes a moral relationship with the Earth's life. We do not only depend on a health-enabling environment—we should be morally committed to respecting life.

What I think this shift shows is the discovery of an ecological orientation. It's the ecological orientation that is desirable. What is an ecological orientation? It is, at least, a way of viewing human action so that our prudence is contextualized within what is ecological. That is, it's a way of viewing human flourishing as ecological.[4] Finally, it assumes being human includes identifying morally with the universe of life. So the contextualization is not merely instrumental, that is, aiming only to use nature. The contextualization is moral too.

When you are ecologically oriented to life, you try to flourish as a human, yet do so without sacrificing moral identification with the wider universe of life. Oriented ecologically, you don't think you can truly flourish if you don't respect life. Put in different terms, you are what Aldo Leopold called a "plain member and citizen" of the biosphere.[5]

An Ecological Orientation?

- Human action is contextualized within what is ecological.
- Human flourishing is ecological.
- Our humanity includes moral identification with the universe of life.
- You don't think you can truly flourish if you don't respect life.

According to the Earth Charter, people without an ecological orientation live flawed human lives. They can't flourish. By the way, there's some poetic justice to this idea. The word "flourishing" already suggests an ecological orientation. "Flourishing" is a botanical term, and so when we use it for ourselves, we identify with plant life. Moreover, we use it to describe what all life forms do when they thrive. "The pepperwood beetles are flourishing in this climate!" Human flourishing is an instance of what flourishing is generally, what life forms do when healthy. The word "flourishing" connects human life with the universe of life.

*

The preceding overview explains more concisely what the shift in self-understanding, the shift in our anthropology, involves. We can now turn to why it's desirable.

First, though, I should clear away an obstacle. At the beginning of class, I said my justification today will rely on how the new self-understanding serves our interests. I said I would not be arguing an ecological orientation is morally required. But didn't I just say an ecological orientation has a moral dimension? If so, it seems I'll be justifying a moral dimension through self-interest! Can we do that? And why not go straight to what is morally required, since I'm concluding we will have some moral responsibility to respect life?

Here's why I'm proceeding today through prudence, and in about twenty minutes I'll say why we can do that even when justifying moral attitudes. Arguing an ecological orientation is morally required would involve showing that the Earth's ecology of life *must* be respected. Of course, we could help ourselves to some of what we saw in lecture one. There, I claimed if an entity is alive, it must not be the kind of thing that does not deserve any respect. Everything alive deserves some respect. That would get us a moral requirement: if some X lives, X must be respected to some extent.

We might then let this conclusion shape the core reason for why an ecological orientation makes sense. The moral dimension of an ecological orientation would draw along the rest of what goes into an ecological orientation. Thus if we were morally required to respect life, acting in accordance with that requirement would require us to act so that the flourishing of our lives is integrated with the flourishing of the rest of life on Earth. Our participation in the Earth's life would then be a fitting and natural way of expressing our central moral commitment.

But the problem is, it takes a contentious argument to show life as such requires respect, and so I want to wait until a later lecture to ease us into it. To begin, it may seem life as such need not in all instances be respected. For example, given that freedom is often more important than life, we are not required to respect life when freedom looms more important. It is often right to brave death to remain free. So why think life necessarily deserves some respect?

Well, you might reply that life is to be respected categorically, and yet admit that freedom's conflict with life is an exception. For instance, we might note that for the human life form, freedom is so essential to life that without freedom life is often not worth living. Hence, freedom is the dynamic principle of the being—that is, the being's "life"—even when freedom comes in conflict with continued brain activity. Call that paradoxical, but no one said human existence was a stranger to paradox. Moreover, just because freedom is more important than life does not presuppose that respecting life isn't required. It just supposes that in cases where freedom conflicts with life, what is required is to respect the more important good. So perhaps respecting life is still required.

It is here, though, that a second problem appears. Many people would refine the claim about life to state that respecting human life is, all things considered, morally required. On the contrary, they might say, respecting *other* animal life is not required. Or even if they think all sentient beings deserve respect, they still might say that respecting plant life is not required. In fact, those who claim that respecting plant life is morally required seem a minority worldwide, depending on how demanding that respect is thought to be. This does not mean they are wrong, of course, only that it is hard to argue there is some reason why there's a moral requirement for us to have an ecological orientation toward all life. What about lichens, microscopic life, and killer mosquitoes?

I think it is best for starters to argue for the desirability of an ecological orientation through the good it brings to human life. Here's why. First, although I am not an historian, I suspect that the reason there has been a shift in our self-understanding over the past fifty years toward a more ecological humanity is due to the benefits it will bring us as our technology, productive activity, and population soar even higher into risk. The collective mentality behind those documents is sensing an increasingly likely danger.

Second, arguing for the good an ecological orientation brings does not entail we are morally required to have an ecological orientation toward life or the self-understanding of which such an orientation is a part. Rather, it entails that there are strong prudential reasons for having an ecological orientation and the self-understanding of which it is a part. Justification for an ecological orientation then proceeds in terms of what such an orientation adds to human flourishing and succeeds when it shows that having an ecological orientation is a significant gain for us. Justification need not show us we must have an ecological orientation, only that it would be a good idea to have one. As a first go at an earthly sense of humanity, that will do for more people than if we started moralizing straight off.

*

So what are the reasons that an ecological orientation is beneficial to our lives? I will discuss six reasons, each invoking a good given by having an ecological orientation.

Reason 1: The good of self-preservation. The first reason for having an ecological orientation is that it helps us ensure the health of our species in the future. When we have an ecological orientation to life on Earth, we do not act in a way that overburdens the limits of life on Earth, nor do we unsustainably pollute or radically alter the Earth's biosphere in a way that could create ecological instability. We don't do these things, because they would destroy our identification with life.

Thus, an ecological orientation makes wantonness not merely a failure of prudence but a failure of humanity. And yet *that* is most prudent, because it drives prudence into our self-understanding. Those who want the Rio Declaration to grip us, then, might better turn to the deeper environmental formulations of the Earth Charter, because these deeper formulations actually make it more likely we will be sustainable. An ecological orientation increases our safety and time with life.

Reason 2: The good of relationships. A second reason for adopting an ecological orientation is that it makes human life richer in relationships. With an ecological orientation toward life, you exist in a world filled with relationships to fellow lives. These relationships are structured in part by moral identification and in part by the spirit of participation in life so important to moral identification. As such, they are vital sources for the goods relationships bring—for instance, experience of other forms of life, self-understanding, complex belonging to a larger world, and so on.

In this way, having an ecological orientation opens up many benefits through the way of relationships. It's rewarding to live in such a way that the world is alive around you and connected with you in being alive. An ecological orientation increases our quality and depth of life.

Reason 3: The good of education. A third good obtained through an ecological orientation is the good of education. The ultimate goal of education is development into maturity. All human children must be educated if they are to live, let alone live human lives. Early childhood education and child psychology have long been aware of how important elementary interactions with natural elements, such as water, and natural objects are.[6] Children across cultures develop better when they can experience nature, inquire into nature, and draw connections between themselves and other forms of life or natural objects. Relationships with animals tend to be beneficial for children, too—one reason, perhaps, why so many children's stories use animals.

Exploring nature fills children—maybe not all, but most—with wonder. Children want to know where they live and who they are, and they need to wonder so in order to develop. When they realize who they are, they mature. An ecological orientation is supportive of this dimension of childhood development. By respecting life and seeing our dependence on it, we can better teach children who they are and what nature is. An ecological orientation brings development and maturity.

Reason 4: The good of discerning reality. The fourth benefit of an ecological orientation is found in discerning reality. Much as a zoologist, botanist, or molecular biologist can discern the wonder and strangeness of the world of life around her, so someone with an ecological orientation will discern the world of life around her. After all, she must do so, as such discernment is a part of moral identification. Without seeing what we respect, we don't truly respect.

An ecological orientation entails a practice of paying close attention to our ecological context. Such attention leads one outward *to the lives them-*

selves, to echo a phrase from the Jewish-German philosopher Edmund Husserl.[7] That being so, one with an ecological orientation will be practically required and disposed to discern the reality of life. Such discernment, in turn, is rewarding, or at least helpful. And it can also contribute to good science. An ecological orientation increases our knowledge of life and sense of reality.

Reason 5: The good of human history and culture. An ecological orientation is also good for letting us appreciate human history and culture. All of the world's cultures have had to deal historically with their ecological contexts. Their struggles are woven into their art, customs, and legends. Also, many of the words we take for granted draw on their ecological relationships— "culture" itself comes from a Latin word meaning the tending the plants in a field. Furthermore, many cultures historically and today hold that respecting nonhuman life is a matter of common humanity.

We cannot understand our history (and so who we are), nor other cultures (and so who we all are), without appreciating an ecological orientation. If we have one, it is more likely we can understand such history and culture. In this way, an ecological orientation is good for developing our historical consciousness and cultural awareness.

Reason 6: The good of a complex aesthetic sense. Beauty, of course, is in many ways subjective, although many studies point to large commonalities across perceptions of beauty. This much, though, is sure: finding beauty in life makes one's life more meaningful, and finding patterns in life is important for all areas of human intelligence. There is no thing except perhaps human language and symbolism that is more complex and yet patterned than nature. Nature has given rise to as many judgments of beauty as art and to almost as many as someone one loves. People find nature ugly or terrifying, though, too—and such views make sense. Yet this much is sure: appreciating the diversity of nature opens the human mind and makes our aesthetic sense more complicated.

A person who can see how a beetle might be beautiful has a more complex aesthetic sense than someone who cannot even seriously attempt such a judgment. A person who can draw connections between the fissuring of rocks and a painting[8]—or between the movement of waves and music[9]—has a more developed aesthetic sense than someone who cannot. An ecological orientation helps provide us an appreciation of nature that leads to greater pattern recognition and appreciation of other forms of life. An ecological orientation gives us uncommon beauty and aesthetic complexity.

An ecological orientation gives us at least (let me write these on the board):

1. safety
2. time
3. quality of life
4. depth and breadth of relationships
5. childhood development
6. maturity
7. knowledge
8. a sense of reality
9. better science
10. historical consciousness
11. cultural awareness
12. uncommon beauty
13. aesthetic complexity
14. . . .

I hope these benefits spell out the groundwork for (a) how an ecological orientation is good, and (b) how one might continue to justify it. An earthly sense of humanity might *not* be a bad thing.

I want to reiterate one last time that while an ecological orientation includes moral identification, I have not argued directly for identification, but indirectly by saying how it would benefit us. That is a tricky way to argue for a moral attitude. It's like saying: "You shouldn't lie, because if you lie, people might not trust you anymore, and you want them to trust you." You are then honest because it will benefit you, not because lying to another is almost always a way of disrespecting him or her. This might trouble some of you—yes?—and so I want to field this objection, which I said I'd answer about twenty minutes ago.

You could object that while I have argued for how an ecological orientation benefits us, this manner of argument is not what one would use from within an ecological orientation. Within an ecological orientation, one would think that one should respect life, because life just deserves respect. An ecological orientation supposes a form of moral identification with the Earth's ecologies of life. Wouldn't one arguing from within such a perspective begin by showing that life should be respected? Shouldn't we pursue moral requirement again?

To answer this concern, we could say, first, that our moral identification could simply suppose there is a *loss* when life on Earth is disrespected. An ecological orientation might just as well urge respect by acknowledging loss or inversely benefit. Those do not necessarily entail requirement.

Second, it is not inconsistent to argue for the good an ecological orientation brings as well as the respect for which it calls. Nothing about respect for life precludes as morally or logically inconsistent showing how respect is good for us *also*. I will argue later that respect is called for even when it does not immediately benefit us. Here I'm arguing it is also good for us.

We know in raising kids to be respectful of others that it will benefit them to do so. They become better humans. You can point out that being honest has benefits. But that doesn't imply that if being honest does *not* benefit us, we are permitted to be dishonest. Requirements can be beneficial even while they are requirements. If we want a good life, an ecological orientation will help, and it just might be something we must have as well. Thus it's neither inconsistent nor unfaithful to argue as I have.

*

I want to close today's lecture by marking where our exercise in justification stands in environmental ethics, since this is a course that involves a good deal of environmental ethics. Today, I interpreted a moral possibility as it arises across several international documents. Second, I gave reasons why that possibility should be developed in our lives. Finally, I suggested a style of argument for furthering that possibility. In short, I found an ecological orientation in a text, gave reasons why the orientation is good, and suggested we can argue for moral identification on prudential grounds. My strategy would seem odd to many environmental ethicists who advocate moral identification, however. But I think this oddness is important.

Over the past twenty years, much of environmental ethics has tried to show that we are morally required to respect nature. This exploration of moral standing has been worthwhile, but it has remained at loggerheads, I think, because it must deal with such basic, and as such contestable, moral intuitions. In the meanwhile, many other ways of showing the good in an ecological life have gone missing, and this has marginalized the field, making it seem overly extreme.[10]

I agree that nature should be respected, period. Next week, we will begin an argument for why this is so. Yet we would do best to fill out the good in living an ecological life as much as possible. Not only do we thereby stand to win the most to the side of good sense, but we also gain a fuller picture of what living an ecological life does and of how it changes our humanity. This is a somewhat different but worthwhile approach to environmental ethics.

In general, I like to think of being ecological as a chance to discover and then articulate a new poem in human existence. Poems have many sides, and we need to get to work interpreting their richness if they are to shine as beau-tifully as they can. That is why I opened today's class with the quote from Rachel Carson. Her quote shows the activity of an osprey making its nest of scavenged parts, many of them human artifacts or the parts of other species. The osprey's activity should seem poetic, even beautiful. In making this claim, I am making what the modern philosopher Immanuel Kant called a "judgment of taste."[11] The judgment is subjective, yet it suggests (and can only suggest) something we should take as universally true. This osprey's nest is beautiful because it is ecologically integrated with many other kinds of life, even while it lays a future for its young and so benefits itself. That is what we humans should be doing in our time. As we do, we can let our earthliness weave us in, piece by piece, to a fuller and more decent existence.

Notes

1. Rachel Carson, Under the Sea Wind, New York: Penguin Press, 1996.
2. Rachel Carson, Silent Spring, New York, Mariner Books, 2002.
3. These are all listed in the bibliography.
4. "Human flourishing" is an expression emerging out of a tradition many trace back to Aristotle in his lectures Nicomeachean Ethics, named because Nicomachus took the lecture notes that were later transmitted. Aristotle thought that the proper end of ethical action is the human good, and he understood the human good as the realization of one's morally structured and social humanity in a healthy and materi-ally sufficient life. If I were to locate my imaginary lectures in a tradition, I would say they attempt to explain why we should notice the ecological dimension of what Aris-totle first attempted to explain about our ethical nature.
5. In his "Land Ethic" in The Sand County Almanac.
6. See Leila Gandini et al., eds., The Hundred Languages of Children, Englewood: Axel Publishing, 1999.
7. "To the things themselves!" is a rallying cry of Husserl's work. See, for in-stance, The Idea of Phenomenology, Dordrecht: Kluwer Academic Publishers, 1994.
8. As in a painting by Willem De Kooning, Excavation, 1948, oil on canvas, Chicago: Art Institute of Chicago General Collection.
9. As in Steve Reich's Music for 18 Musicians, 1976, New York: Nonesuch, 1996.
10. Some of these concerns and their history are explored in the volume edited by Andrew Light and Holmes Rolston, Environmental Ethics: An Anthology, Oxford: Blackwell, 2003.
11. Immanuel Kant, "Analytic of Aesthetic Judgment," in The Critique of Judg-ment, Indianapolis: Hackett Publishing, 1987.

~

Rooted in Our Humanity

For Steve

Hey you all. I hope you don't mind the rain. If you want, open up your umbrellas and put them along the wall by the door there.

Today we have our work cut out for us. I guess it's a good day to work hard. (Don't worry. We'll take a coffee break in the middle.) Last time, we explored why it is a good idea to have an ecological orientation. We looked at a shift occurring in international documents arising in the last half of the twentieth century, all with the aim of operating globally. Strictly speaking, it was an anthropological shift, a shift in our account of being human. What shifted was an understanding of what it is to enable human life properly, and it seemed to move toward an ecological orientation.

An ecological orientation is a habit of contextualizing our lives and action within our human dependence on a life-supporting ecological order, and it is a habit of morally identifying with the wider universe of life. I said there may be straight-up moral reasons why we should so identify, but I left them until later. Last time, we argued simply that an ecological orientation is good for us. It helps us flourish. Not only from considerations of *justice*, then, but also from *prudence*, we should become citizens of Earth.

Today, however, I want to begin the moral argument, for I believe we should respect life beyond humankind for direct moral reasons. Making a successful argument as to why we should is one of the highest aspirations of environmental ethics, and it has proven to be a difficult endeavor. I do not think

I will solve deep mysteries in the argument I'll give, but I do plan to give an argument that is not standard in the field. I will be arguing that our sense of humanity ought to commit us to respecting nonhuman life and its biotic conditions. In this lecture and the next couple, I will show how. Once we get such an argument—provided it is successful—we will have a clear reason for why having common humanity commits us to becoming ecological and so why becoming a citizen of the world commits us to becoming an ecological citizen.

As we head into this several-week-long argument, it might be helpful to understand why arguing for respect for nature from our sense of humanity may seem disturbing to some environmental ethicists and environmentalists. There's a long-standing view among environmentalists that goes back at least a generation. This view claims our present ecological crisis comes from human self-centeredness. Environmentalists in this tradition hold that when we act out of our sense of humanity, we assume human life comes first or that human life deserves more of the Earth's resources than other forms of life. People call this view "anthropocentrism."

As I noted three weeks ago, "anthropo" comes from the Greek word for "human." Anthropo*centrism* is the view that our lives ought to be *centered* around our own interests and that we do not have to respect other forms of life or care for other living beings for their own sake.

Anthropocentrism (Human-Centeredness)

The view that our lives ought to be centered around human interests and that we do not have to respect other forms of life or care for other living beings for their own sake

When we say someone is self-centered, we mean not only that he is selfish, but also that he thinks of his whole world in terms of himself. His habits don't manifest an understanding that other people have lives too and that the interests of others matter. So, too, with anthropocentrists. They are selfish on behalf of humans and act as if the whole world revolves around human interests.

Imagine, then, you are an environmentalist who thinks our current ecological crisis comes from a cultural human-centeredness. You will think the idea we have reason to respect nature *out of* our sense of humanity is absurd. You think our sense of humanity urges *dis*respect for nature.

Yet these views of our humanity are hasty. In different contexts being human-centered means something different. Someone human-centered is *humane*. A human-centered person is not money-centered, status-centered, fame-centered, or ethnocentric. Rather, she is centered on the humanity of people. This means she organizes her life around our common human struggles and fate, on what we really feel, on connecting between people of different backgrounds and social positions. In this manner of speech, being human-centered is a virtue—a sign that someone hasn't lost what matters in life. It's a testament to everyday human things, rather than to pretentious or dehumanizing things.

Saying someone is human-centered usually implies she has compassion and perspective on who we are and what really matters for human life. Commonly, she has a certain kind of wisdom: a sense of psychology, development and of the most meaningful parts of the life cycle. More than anything, she tends to have a knack with relationships.[1]

A human-centered person also has a particular view of human existence, because she viscerally understands our finite nature.[2] In the terms of Wittgenstein and Kierkegaard, two philosophers who argued passionately for being human-centered, to be centered on humans and in one's own humanity is to accept our limits while being astonished that we and this world are—as if existence were a gift or a miracle.[3] Accordingly, to be centered by our own humanity is anything but hubris and selfishness. It is a form of humility, and it is openness to the universe in which we live.

Being human-centered in this tradition also involves being aware of what Rousseau called our "frail happiness"—the fact that out of our vulnerable humanity, we can find joys by accepting our limits and also by supporting each other.[4] As Rousseau writes:

> I do not grasp how someone who needs nothing can love anything. I do not grasp how someone who loves nothing can be happy.[5]

Having a strong sense of humanity in this tradition—the tradition found also in social justice and human rights—is to be aware of the human condition and to be respectful of the fact we are alive. More importantly, it is to love out of the needs we have in being alive. Love is a far cry from self-centeredness, even if it responds to genuine needs and desires.

How strange, then, that environmentalism has not discovered this tradition. The human condition is ecological and so are our needs. Correspondingly, often our loves are too. We saw this when discussing natural history and relationships with lands, and I'll fill it out extensively next week. People centered on humans understand what it's like to sweat in the dirt all day. They also get that not having time to stand outside in the dark and look at the vast night, walk through the forest with its hatch-marks of sun and its waves of sound, or show one's children the lake when their feet can be seen in the clear water and salamanders sun on rocks . . . how missing that is soul-killing. Missing that is not what human life is about.

Moreover, human-centered people understand that suffering is miserable and are poised to feel that other creatures suffer too. By looking at our own species, they are better able to understand the existential condition of others (a point I'll explain later today). Many may not have drawn the connection between their compassion for humans and compassion for other forms of life, but they have better resources than someone who does not have compassion, and they should draw the connection. It is humane to do so (a point I'll argue in two weeks).

What I hope I've just done is to have switched the way you hear things enough to remind you of a different way of hearing what it is to be humane than that found in environmental arguments against anthropocentrism. What is perhaps most unusual about these lectures is that I began my argument for becoming ecological from what serves us—either through justice or prudence—and then will not give up on our humanity when we turn to respect other forms of life. The main animal liberationists and what are called "deep ecologists" never do this.[6] They say we need to abandon our humanity for something else. But close attention to what is best in our sense of humanity discloses a capacity for moral identification with non-human life. We do not need to give up on ourselves. We should be *true* to ourselves. That's what the next three weeks will argue. Is that clear as a general idea?

Yes, Kate?

I don't get what you are saying here. There is no necessary implication from the humanity we show each other to being humane with, say, other animals. We don't chastise a human rights activist for eating factory farmed meat on the grounds she's a human rights activist. She stops concentration camps from happening and doesn't have to think about factory farms. They are different. It's offensive to mention them in the same breath as if they were somehow on a par. Elizabeth Costello gets this objection in J.M. Croetzee's The Lives of Animals.[7]

That's true. To kill a human being is qualitatively different from killing another animal, because to kill a fellow human is to destroy our universe from within. Respect for each other is the essence of socialization, and we are profoundly social beings. So the old Jewish saying goes: "Every time you lose a life, you lose a world." It's not an exaggeration. But even if the cases are qualitatively different, we shouldn't assume our human rights activist oughtn't think about factory farms, *too*. And how do you know that the implication from respect for each other to respect for other life isn't strict once we clarify an assumption that grounds the inference? Perhaps we are missing an assumption or two.

*

That's a great question. Consider two quotations, which I'll write on the board. The parts I underline will be my emphases. The scripted part is the author's emphasis. The first quotation says:

> "The response to animals as our fellows in mortality, in life on this earth . . . depends on a conception of *human* life."

This is by the Palestinian-American philosopher Cora Diamond.[8]
The second quotation comes from Homer's *Odyssey*:

> "My heart was a storm in me as I went."[9]

Diamond's quotation suggests that the concepts we use when we respond to animals with fellowship come from our sense of humanity. Homer's saying shows that when we express some of the emotions most central to ourselves, we turn to nature to help us express who we are. Nature is part of our sense of humanity. The quotes show two different directions of relationship with nature: from us outward and from nature to us.

Through the ideas contained in quotes like these, I want to establish that respect for other life can come from our sense of humanity and that our sense of humanity can come from nature. That is, I want to establish the *possibility* of respect for life and other moral identifications being found within our sense of humanity. Doing so will show that an ecological orientation's moral dimension is not impossible. Then, next week, we'll explore how some people's sense of humanity already involves identifications with nature. Respect for nature is an actuality among many cultures. That will set us up for the following week, when I can show the desirability of respect for life coming from our sense of humanity. At that point, I'll argue we ought to respect nature, because it is true to ourselves, because it is authentically human.

*

Okay, then. We have to see it's possible to identify morally with nonhuman life. What do I mean when I speak of identification? What I will be calling an "identification" comes from forms of analogy. These analogies compose forms of reasoning, and the reasoning establishes identifications.

Now a strict identification is when some X is completely like some other X, except for their different instances or individuations. For instance, the number "4" is identical to the number "4," except that the first one was mentioned first. They are identical but for an instant. A new Kenneth Cole shoe in a store is identical to another version of its same kind, except for infinitesimal differences coming from individuation: the way this stitch was slightly different than that one. They are identical but for idiosyncrasy.

The way I'll be using identification is different from a strict identification, however. When we say people identify with each other, we don't mean they meet their exact clone. We mean they meet someone with whom they see likenesses in parts of their lives that they take to be important. Likenesses signal analogical reasoning. "Oh, he had to deal with a prejudiced community, too. I had an experience *like* his. I can identify."

Such a form of reasoning is analogical, because it goes like this:

Just as there is some X to some Y, so there is some W to some Z.
Or:
Just as a Jew had to fight an anti-Semitic community, so a Muslim had to fight a xenophobic one.

There are differences between the cases, but similarities enough that we can form identifications—not strict identification, analogical identification. This kind of identification will be the form of identification making possible respect for other kinds of life out of our sense of humanity. And there will be two kinds—one going *from us to nature* and one going *from nature to us*.

Two Directions of Analogical Identification

[Just as] Us → [so] other forms of life
(analogies outward)

[Just as] Nature → [so] us
(analogies inward)

Analogical identifications constitute parts of our sense of humanity. What is a sense of humanity, though? We've been mentioning it for a while. I'd like to approach it through one of its consummate expressions. According to Cora Diamond, one of the consummate expressions appears in matters of life and death.

*

In her article "How Many Legs?" Diamond discusses a moment of common humanity from Charles Dickens's story, "Our Mutual Friend."[10] In this story, a character named "Rogue Riderhood"—a most hated man—drowns in the Thames River. He is dredged up from the bottom not too long after he has capsized and is brought to a local, workers' bar. There laid seemingly dead on a rough, wooden table, he is surrounded by the very men who hate him, working people he's exploited time and again. Someone has called a doctor, and a doctor is there too. The doctor thinks there may still be some chance of bringing Rogue back to life.

In that moment between life and death, the whole bar silences. Everyone in the bar hangs on the doctor's effort under the circles of the lamp. Though the bar is silent, it's as if you can hear people hoping for the revival of Rogue, the man they would normally hate. An odd situation.

What Diamond learns from this episode is worth citing at length. It is on the handout you received when you entered today. Diamond writes,

> [Charles] Dickens is concerned with our sense of death as our fate, and with how that sense of death as common fate shapes our understanding of a situation, our conception of what counts in it. . . . For Dickens, . . . the sense of death as common fate is tied to the idea of life and death as solemn and mysterious matters, and to that of death as our common enemy, an enemy of a special and terrible sort. . . . The doctor and the rough fellows and the others in the pub see in Riderhood *a mortal man like themselves; nothing else about him comes into their understanding of the situation and its demands. . . . Death is something on which the human imagination has seized. . . .* For [Dickens], the fact we all die is not that fact and nothing more; it would be a failure of imagination to see it so, a failure with profound consequences for our capacity to live well. To understand its significance is to be able to make connections between a sense of who we are, what kind of being, and the way we live. These are the connections not only between the imaginative understanding of ourselves as sharers-of-mortality and a willingness to set to to save even a man like Riderhood; they are *connections between our common fate and our capacity to enjoy life and to live compassionately.*[11]

I think this is an amazing passage. If it is unclear, focus just on the underlined phrases and sentence. *Facing our mortality gives us a sense of the human condition and what matters in life. It allows us connections with each other and perspective on when to enjoy life and when to be compassionate.* Diamond writes: "The others in the pub see in Riderhood a mortal man *like* themselves." This fellowship is so basic as to strip away the antagonisms these men had with

Rogue around business and neighborhood life. Diamond says, "[N]*othing else about* [Rogue] comes into their understanding of the situation and its demands." Struggling against death is so basic to the meaning of life that nothing else matters in this instant. That's what it is to be humane: sharing life's struggles to flourish with another doing the same. "We all do what we can."[12]

How is our struggle against death basic? It is not basic in the sense of our being programmed by evolution to try to survive. Diamond is addressing the meaning of human life, what gives our lives a purpose and makes sense of our struggles as an everyday human. She is not talking about what we automatically have to do. A sense of humanity is *imaginative*.

She suggests that when we have humanity our imaginations get a grip on ("seize on") important dimensions of human life and make something significant of them, significant in such a way that they help us "make connections between a sense of who we are, what kind of being, and the way we live." What she means, I think, is that as humans, our sense of humanity appears in the way we've imagined the most basic constituents of human life's meaning. These imagined constituents image life's unavoidable contours: what we have found so gripping that without it we cannot make sense of who we are and why we live. We shape the meaning of our lives around what allows us to understand who we are and what we live for. These shapes of meaning give us a sense of what is important—an image of life as it goes when rich, deep or meaningful or when tragic, empty or blunted. Her point is that *it is hard to make sense of who we are if we lose a grip on the shape of human life's meaning*, including such basic things as the way mortality shapes the meaning of life. Hold that thought for when we come to nature.

I can see blank looks. Let me give an example. *Without a sense of mortality, whole areas of human life make no sense*. Take work. For what do we work? Why is work a problem when it takes over all of life? Why is it sad or unjust when people have to slave away day in and day out? A big part of all the answers is that *life is temporary. Life is temporary, because we will die*. We don't have all the time in the world. In fact, when we remind people that they have "all the time in the world," we do so to slow them down enough to accomplish or enjoy something meaningful. Because they shouldn't *waste* their lives, we try to relax them. They *can* waste their lives, though, because humans have limited time. In other words, when we tell people they have "all the time in the world," we do so precisely because we do not! Work *and* open time do not make sense without mortality.

Or take personal relationships. When we love people, we know that because humans die, we have to be sure to show them we love them, and we don't want to be out of sorts with them. To love someone is to want her to know she is loved and to be in a right relation with her. Because we are mortal, it is possible that someone could die without knowing she is loved or while alienated from you. That would be tragic. Mortality pressures our loves and gives them urgency, a longing for harmony that would not be there if we were immortal. Also the act of sacrificing oneself for someone one loves loses its meaning if we forget our mortality. A sacrifice is one of the most meaningful gifts, because we give up some part or all of our limited life for another. Finally, realizing you love someone is honed by the whittling knife of death. One sign of love is that you don't want to miss this one chance to form a relationship with a person: it does matter if this trial doesn't work out; there aren't just other women to date. There is this one chance because we live only once, and it is temporary. She's here now, and you may never get the chance again.

I hope these examples show how mortality shapes our sense of humanity. What would human life be without work, open time, and love? It wouldn't be much, and it wouldn't be human. Only thoughtless people—whether from their own fault or from some trauma or burden—fail to appreciate that work can eat up one's life or that love is fulfilled in time, even if it is significant eternally.

*

How is it that an imaginary grasp of mortality provides moral guidance? The answer is simpler than you might expect. Our mortality is basic to our sense of humanity. It should be basic. Knowing it is the kind of knowledge the philosopher Raimond Gaita called "knowledge in your guts and in your bones."[13] A person whose life is not oriented in large ways by a sense of her mortality is a person who lacks perspective.[14] It's as if she's abstract from life. Only when you live with a sense of the finiteness of time can you live with a sense of what matters for humans in general. In short, you lose touch with the human good. A sense of mortality is a necessary condition on acting in light of the human good.

It is more than that as well. A sense of mortality clues us into what matters in a situation where humans struggle with life and death. It provides a form of analogical identification with the plight of others. Just as she has to deal with her mortality, so I have to deal with mine. And just because I also have to respect my fellow humans, I know I should empathize with her on such a basic matter and respect it. A sense of mortality provides moral guidance *when joined to other dimensions of our sense of humanity,* such as our socialization into respect for each other. Put briefly, our sense of humanity gives us sufficient reasons to have fellowship or solidarity with others.

At the same time, the fellowship provided by a sense of humanity is the kind of thing that is imaginatively open, as I hope Diamond's descriptions evoked. There are many different ways to face death. Imagine a culture in which the way to face death is to chant harmonically. The barroom roughs start chanting as the doctor works on Rogue! A sense of humanity both respects and perceives this difference, as part of the human struggle with death.

There is a larger point here, too. When we are aware of the imaginative way we have shaped the meaning of human life around basic existential conditions, we can be open to a great many dimensions of human life as these come into action and are at stake. In the Rogue Riderhood example, death the enemy is at stake. You could imagine other examples. Imagine two people in love, dancing especially well in that same bar. The barroom toughs, not much for the lovey-dovey thing and often shady when it comes to whom they pinch and what jokes they tell, they nonetheless are captured by the zone of life in front of them—the *couple*. Here too, a sense of humanity comes out. There's fellowship around human goods and ills. Now the good is love, and the ill is that they uneasily sense they have lost it in their lives. Quiet, quiet. Maybe it will come again.

Or to make one more example, there might one day be an especially good conversation going on. Perhaps political, or about the Church. The roughs, not usually much for talk and reasoning, get involved, each to his ability, and stand together in the work of reasoning. "Yes," they think, "people *should* be able to dance at Church, by G-d! And here's why."[15] Here, human fellowship opens up around an understanding that in human life all of us at times must make up our own minds. That is an existential fact. Freedom of thought is something on which the human imagination has seized. There are thus many aspects to life that are necessary to the meaning of a common humanity.

Maureen:

This sounds like Thompson.

Yes and no. We do seem to be in the neighborhood of categorical features of the human species. But Diamond's isn't a zoologist's judgment. She reads off the imagining points of our humanity from reflection on the meaning of our lives, not by looking at us as a biological species. The similarity is there, because we *are* biological and that shapes our meaning. But the two are coming at the categorical nature of who we are from different angles. Thompson, for example, wouldn't claim that categorical claims include ones like this: *Love is a chance because of mortality.* Diamond *would* and about how features of our humanity explain the human good and the meaning of life.

I sense there is a lot of good work that could be done answering you more thoroughly. Yet let me end here with this one point. My hunch is that categorical claims are *part* of some of the more basic features of our fate on which "the human imagination has seized." That is, Thompson's work could help explain part of Diamond's, but the kinds of claims in each are still different.

I hope you have a better idea of what a sense of humanity is when we speak of one. A sense of humanity should orient us toward the human good and respect for that good in each other. A sense of humanity is also an orientation toward life in which we are ready to have compassionate respect for others, and in which we are sensitive to our relations to others in terms that are potentially compassionate and respectful. A sense of humanity attends to our vulnerabilities, needs, and goods as members of our species, caring for and respecting the cycle of flourishing that sculpts human time. At the same time, a sense of humanity is an orientation of something not unlike wonder in which we see humanity with an open mind, realizing that the vast human universe includes many different ways of interpreting how the core dimensions of human life are to be handled and even what these core dimensions are. *Capiche?*

Now for a break!

* * *

The rain has lifted. Keep your good mood on, because we have a climb ahead of us. Before break, we eased up to what a sense of humanity is and earmarked the notion of analogical identification as crucial to how our sense of humanity can involve respect for nonhuman life. We now need the argument for how such identification can work. First, the idea will be simple. Other forms of life struggle with mortality, *too*. And then the idea will be subtle. *Our* form of life has woven the meaning of other forms of life into it already. Nature is something on which the human imagination has seized. Those will be our analogies *outward* and our analogies *inward*.

Let me begin my exposition of these forms of analogical reasoning from a philosophical story once again involving Professor Diamond. In the late 1970s, Diamond criticized the arguments of two animal liberationists, Peter Singer and Tom Regan. Her articles "Eating Meat and Eating People" and "Experimenting on Animals" opened a way of thinking of moral relations to other animals as extensions of our sense of humanity. "The Importance of Being Human," from 1991, further developed this reflection, and she has returned to it recently in "Injustice and Animals."[16]

Diamond argued that doing moral philosophy with Singer and Regan's mode of reasoning produces mysteries and mis-emphases in moral life. Their mode of reasoning is what might be called the "P line of thinking" (this is my expression). The P line of thinking looks to salient moral *properties* (the P's) to ground moral respect. The basic idea is that morality is the business of managing due attention to moral properties. With Singer, the property in question is *sentience* (feeling), and with Regan what's at stake is *being an experiencing subject of life* (awareness). For the P line of thinking, once you have the property in question, you're due—usually equal—moral respect. In terms of respect for other animals, the attempt is to show how both humans and other animals are *strictly identical* with regard to moral standing in virtue of possessing the relevant property. Our moral life with them is then an open and shut case. We must respect them according to their being strictly identical with us at the level of moral standing.

The problems with this line of thinking come up in a number of places. In her earliest work, Diamond used the example of the respect the dead are due to open her objection.[17] Anthropologists often distinguish *Homo sapiens* from other species by our cross-cultural need to symbolically mark death. We are a species with funeral rites. Such rites are as varied as hanging corpses in cocoons from trees, or eating part of the dead person.[18] Dead humans don't have sentience, though, and so Singer seems to render the moral dimension of funeral rites mysterious. He can't explain why we have a moral reason to respect the dead. For him, moral reasons flow from the ability to feel something, but if you are dead, you can't be a source of reasons to respect you. Nor, in a related example, can Singer account for many vegetarians' conviction that it is not okay to eat roadkill. Roadkill is already dead—it doesn't feel anything—but many vegetarians would still think it immoral to eat meat.

With these examples, Diamond wanted to consider how the P line might make mysteries of our lives. But the example of the dead wasn't her best choice, as Singer could easily argue that we ought to revolutionize our morality and teach the vegetarians better. He might also argue that we have reason to respect the dead, because of the psychological discomfort *we* might feel in treating them as mere things, or as food. He'd say our overall good feelings are promoted by acting *as if* the dead are to be respected, even though they are without moral standing, in truth.

So it's good Diamond took up another example in 2001. Consider the gorilla who has part of his brain removed in an experiment. He loses some of his body functions, and so goes to the bathroom on himself. Behind a one-way mirror, researchers roar with laughter. For the P line of thinking, what wrong is done by the laughter? The creature isn't hurt by it. He's clueless about it. So no sentience is occluded (we're focusing on the wrong of the laughter, not the wrong of the operation, and besides the operation happens under anesthesia). His capacity for experience isn't disrespected, for it's not as if the researchers disrespect his awareness in laughing without his knowledge. The laughter is not getting in the way of his consciousness. In fact, nothing in him, no property, is disrespected. The laughter was behind glass. You could respect all the complex moral properties in this creature, and still laugh out of sight from him. Yet this shows a failing to relate to this creature as having a life that's been deformed.

This last example comes from "Injustice and Animals." If we read it back into "The Importance of Being Human," more emerges. In the 1991 article, Diamond discusses some writing by D. H. Lawrence on the otherness of a gorilla's life. She links discovering how different a gorilla's life can seem with respecting the gorilla. There's a virtue, an habitual expression of humanity, in respecting the otherness of the gorilla's life, and respecting the gorilla is essentially respecting *its*—that is, not *our*—form of life.[19] This moment in Diamond's work poses a problem for the P line of thinking. There, moral regard is about respecting the way other animals are morally identical to us. Yet one might think respecting an *other* animal hinges on acknowledging its *difference* from us. Can difference be a source of respect?

Deeper still, reflecting on the otherness of the gorilla's life should open up questions about our own. Is it known and settled? A sense of humanity includes being open to what is unknown about, or surprisingly special to, human life, and this openness is part of being moral. Who are we, really? Yet for the P line of thinking, "Who are we, really?" is hardly a moral question. What is a question is how to properly manage determinate moral properties. This is a narrow and abstract view of what grounds respect.

Diamond's work urges us to reconsider the full dimensions of respect for other animals. It avoids doing violence to our moral fabric and seeks ways to have morality come out of our condition as a response to it. In this way, her view of morality is ecological already. And it has many specifically ecological potentials. For instance, it makes sense on her account how our moral orientation might be deepened through our openness to the differences and unknowns of other forms of life. The moral response *par excellence* for her view is fellowship around a shared fate, but part of that fate is to be thrown to sea amid many *other* struggling forms of life. They have that fate as well, even if they do not reflect on it. What other ecological relations might be pursued in this vein?

Humans and the other animals are not in the same moral community strictly speaking.[20] Respect is a matter between primarily humans. Furthermore, humanitarian respect—as we saw above in our Rogue Riderhood example—is shaped by what goes into leading *human* life. We have vulnerabilities, needs, and goods as a species. A sense of humanity attends to these, caring for and respecting the cycle of flourishing that sculpts human time.[21]

Yet at the same time, we can see how analogies between our condition and that of other animals place us on a moral continuum. Why couldn't we extend respect to other animals once we see that *having a life* and *having a good* can be seen in other life forms? They too have lives and a good according to their species. What is good for another species is different from what is good for ours, but analogies allow us to incorporate differences in a way that does not erase them.

There's a way to extend respect to members of other species while acknowledging their specific difference from us. Other animals, too, have lives to live, face death, and have the sort of existential independence we have when we're thrown into time to flourish or perish. They too are not just things. Given our sense of humanity centers around our having human lives to lead, could we open an analogous form of respect to other animal lives in virtue of their having an analogous lot as our own, for instance, a *gorilla* life to lead? To do so would creatively open our sense of humanity toward moral affiliation with nonhuman life. We would be drawn by analogy outward.

The point isn't that respect is at bottom just respect for a better property, say, having a life. Nor is Diamond blind to the fact that properties figure in moral attention. They do. Rather, what's at stake, first, is how moral life is not narrowly about managing properties, but is more commonly about such things as *relating to others, putting yourself in their shoes, appreciating what an indignity is for them,* and so on. In short, it's about all the things that go into such virtues as the virtue of humanity. The gorilla has a life, and, with one's sense of humanity open to that fact, it's an issue whether you laugh at him without his knowing it. That is not how one relates to a life marred by indignity. You might even think it's especially how you don't relate to a different form of life. Where is our hospitality?

The P line of thinking is about morally identical beings. But respect for the gorilla is respect for *its* life. We need a finer tool: analogy, not strict identity. The gorilla has a life different than, but just as, we do. This can count when we take our sense of humanity into the wide world. In fact, it allows us to reach our first form of analogical reasoning—a way of forming analogical, not strict, identifications. I call it "analogical extension."

*

"Analogical extension" is the extension of our sense of humanity to other forms of life across their analogously, which also means differently, being a life form with a specific good.[22] Brought out in practice, this mode of reasoning can create an ecological dimension to our sense of humanity, and it explains how such a dimension is possible in many world cultures or even in ordinary relationships like those humans have with pets. The mode of reasoning is (I'll write it on the board):

As some life form O is like us humans in life cycle salient ways C, B, . . ., so we can respect O like we respect each other in attending to C, B, . . .

For example:

As the gorilla is like us in having an integrity that comes with normal body functioning, so we can respect him like we respect each other, in light of our bodily integrity.

"Like" marks that respecting O both attends to salient aspects of life, as does a sense of humanity, and *translates* to O's form of life. Respecting our gorilla won't involve taking care he has, say, work opportunities. Respecting him is taking care he's free for his ends in a manner and habitat fitting his form of life. Additionally, the point of referring to "life cycle salience" is to keep in touch with the idea that we're extending a sense of the other animal having a life, complete with a specific good. Here, we look to the basic needs, vulnerabilities, strengths, and existential stresses of the life form, its life cycle.

Analogical extension draws on the fact that there's rational openness to nature in our notion of having a life to live. The notion is open to, and invites, wider application. Then the moral relations involved with such a notion are themselves open to wider application, given translation to fit the other life's form (*its* needs and burdens). Thus, we can respect other animal life out of a sense of humanity, if we attend to the ecological possibilities already in our sense of humanity. Those possibilities make it so that once you've seen the gorilla has his life, it's wrong *not* to have respect for him. We'll come back to this point in two weeks. Yet, Kate, I want to echo your question and say that here we may have the missing assumption that can open up an entailment from respect for human rights to respect for factory-farmed animals. Perhaps we have to accept that other animals have lives, *too*.

With analogical extension, one can relate to the whole universe of life with some form of respect, but what this entails needs further work. To begin with an extreme case, given we ought to kill some bacteria in us because they are our enemies, should we nonetheless respect them when they are unable to harm us? Of course, we aren't answering what we should do this week, but what we can do. So I will leave the question of harmful bacteria to the side until the eighth week. Note it nonetheless. (The notion of their being *enemies* is already an analogical extension!)

*

There is our first form of analogical, not strict, identification. Analogical extension provides a mode of reasoning at work in other-regarding ecological relations. The second resource we have available for developing a sense of ecological humanity is a mode of practical reasoning at work in self-regarding moral relations. This mode of reasoning could provide a check on our selfish behavior toward the Earth's life and resources, one whereby we, and not just they (i.e., the other animals), lose out when we are thoughtless with the Earth.

The mode of reasoning I've in mind also grows out of ecological possibilities already in our sense of humanity. The idea here is not that we need to open up our sense of humanity to something more. The idea is that nature is already woven into our sense of humanity so much that to respect ourselves can involve respecting nature. Consider this fact: humans commonly awaken to their humanity through nature. A very common way this happens is through going to a garden, woods, or shore to sit or walk. People get back in touch with themselves through going out near a zone of nonhuman life. In this experience, nature discloses our sense of who we are. Our humanity is thereby implicated in nature.

I propose this implication works through analogies we draw between nature and human life, analogies "inward" as I wrote on the board earlier. What I will call "analogical implication" is a mode of analogical reasoning whereby we can come to discover and respect humanity in ourselves through attending to nature.

The mode of reasoning is (again, I will write it out):

As we are like O, some other life form or region of life, in life cycle salient ways S, R, . . . so we can come to discover and respect our humanity through attending to O's life.

For example:

As we are like a tree in needing roots and a clear space to flourish, so we can discover and respect our humanity through attending to the tree's life.

Analogical implication appears often in everyday life, most often when we draw on nature to teach us about humanity. The example on the board of the tree draws on the complex analogical implication found in Andrey Tarkovsky's last film *the Offering*, where a tree becomes the icon of life after being a symbol of death suspended in life and fatherhood in the work of the son.[23] If generation and fatherhood and our lives themselves can reveal their shadowy essences through analogy with the tree's branched life, how much clearer can analogical implication be?

Children's stories also use analogical implication when they have children learn from nature about important values in human life. Think of *Charlotte's Web*.[24] In world civilization, most foundational myths use analogical implication. Hesiod's *Theogony*, for example, reads like an extended exploration of human life through nature. The very gods are often forces of nature appearing as human-like beings. Analogical implication also appears in songs and poems. Consider Irving Berlin's standard, "How Deep Is the Ocean?" comparing the depth of one's love to the depth of the ocean. It is the depth of the ocean that answers the question in this song, suggesting that we learn about love by seeing this source of our lives in the ocean's elemental silence.[25] Or in Rimbaud's "Par les soirs bleus d'été" ("With blue evening, all summer"), the lyrical subject discovers what it is to be young by being reflected in the late evening sky.[26]

Even in the example of the tree written on the board there, "roots" supposes analogical implication. In ordinary language, we speak of having roots, thereby being analogically implicated in the literal roots of plant life. Here, *the ecology of ordinary language attests to our implication in the Earth's wider ecology as a matter of common sense*. Being rooted is a mode of self-respect. We do not have to project our humanity toward nature. Nature can already be part of us.

On reflection, this might be surprising. Nature helps us discover and maintain the human. This suggests the line separating us from nature is questionable. Where are we? At the same time, the discovery occurs through analogy. Though we are like nature, we are also different from nature. Analogical implication rests on how we belong to, even while being different from, the varied life of the Earth. This acknowledgment of belonging, alongside an equal recognition of difference, can open a relationship crucial to ecological sensibility. With analogical implication, to relate to our life with full humanity is to relate to the varied life of the Earth out of respect for this astonishing source of ourselves, a source that raises questions about who we are, while leading us to see the articulation of our existence in relationship with different forms of life. We can lose out when we destroy the Earth, then, because we destroy our humanity's roots in the wider universe of life.

Analogical implication thus further explains how it is possible to have an ecological relationship with the differentiated life of our biosphere. This analogical form is another mode of reasoning that brings out ecological possibilities in the way we already think to suggest a deepening awareness of our identities. Humanity, in our very self-understanding, emerges in relationship with the Earth's ecology. The Earth is in the meaning of our culture, time, and love.

*

If what I've been explaining makes sense, then what makes up the heart of our moral life—namely our sense of humanity—is already open to ecological sense. We have simply to be attentive to our lives to see how much nature calls for respect, and to discover how that respect for nature is self-respect. You may have noticed, though, that the two modes of practical reasoning seem to be in tension.

On the one hand, analogical extension asks us to extend humanity to nature, whereas analogical implication moves by sleight of hand to show us that nature has already extended into us. If nature is already part of us, why do we need to extend ourselves to it? Or if we need to extend ourselves to it, how can it already be part of us?

These questions bring out an important point about the development of the ecological orientation I have been working for here. It is a fact that, in crucial respects, our Western, increasingly global culture does not forefront respect for the biosphere. In fact, such respect is often seen as unintelligible. We saw this in lecture two, with Spirit Mountain's invisibility to the eyes of the law. Yet there are places in our form of life where this view of things does not quite hold, or is on slippery ground. And it is to these places I have wanted to point. They allow us to know ourselves more profoundly as in fact ecological in some of the core understanding of our form of life. In this way, the resources I've been pointing to allow us to know ourselves better, and to show up a culture disrespectful of nature as in fact lacking depth of self-understanding. This, ultimately, grounds my continued suggestion that both analogical extension and analogical implication are potential modes of human flourishing. They get at the kind of selves we are when we flourish, at least in those crucial respects involving our humanity. The full argument for that will follow over the next weeks.

Each mode of reasoning can work from a different direction to unlock our lack of self-understanding from a disrespectful stance toward nature. Each of these directions, moving both from our humanitarian life outwards and then back from nature to our humanitarian life, sculpts a part of the *relationship* our human life form has with the wider life of the Earth. The answer, then, as to why we can at once reach out to nature and yet find nature reaching into us is that we are in relationship with nature and have been throughout our cultural history. Being in relationship, neither nature nor we are the sole conceptual origins of our sense of selves or of the moral concepts our selves should be guided by. Rather, what these resources show us are two ways to start re-establishing, or excavating, that respectful relationship from within a disrespectful culture.

*

I want to leave you this afternoon with a glimmer into next week's talk, a simple picture that is, to my mind, the core of these lectures. I want to tell you about a case of ecological creativity in New York City where caring for nature generates a sense of human dignity across analogical identification. You read this book for today. Open it up, will you?

During the late 1980s and early 1990s, Diana Balmori and Margaret Morton documented the temporary gardens of homeless people around New York's lower East Side. What they discovered is collected in their photo-essay, *Transitory Gardens, Uprooted Lives*. This starkly beautiful photo-essay shows how homeless people find dignity in makeshift gardening throughout the abandoned lots of New York City. I would like you to think about that essay for a moment.

Made out of recycled material, the makeshift gardens turn scavenging into an art form. Due to scarce natural resources such as fresh water, biotic conditions are scarce in the gardens, although every garden includes either some natural life or some representation of natural life. When the found praying mantis, chicken, rabbit, or cat is absent, stuffed animals or other simulacra of animals inhabit the garden.[27] Alongside the one bulb watered with what water there is, the box tomato patch or the incorporated bases of ailanthus trees, there's simulation of plant life: an inflatable palm tree, some plastic vines, a nylon flower.[28] A zone of nature is sought. Imagination approximates this aim. Artifacts are woven in along the way. Dolls, figurines, flags, toy trains, fake jewelry, containers—a landscape. The gardens don't waste anything. They make waste into dream-image.

If the gardens are astonishing, the gardeners' relations to them are even more so. Here's how James described his feelings about the garden he worked daily:

We got proud. . . . Man, you understand, we are homeless, we are not helpless.[29]

Why isn't he helpless? Perhaps the gardens give a sense of ownership and *rooting*.[30] The gardens also manifest care in a city where care for the homeless goes wanting. But I think the most fundamental reply is that the gardens are zones of *life*, where nature and humanity come together in a way that suggests their conjunct *flourishing*.[31] Another man, Jimmy, spent what money he had to make sure goldfish swam in his pond, a hole lined with black garbage bags to hold water while giving the illusion of depth.[32] When the fish were stolen or killed by neighborhood kids, repeatedly, Jimmy re-emptied his savings to replenish the pool. Why? Perhaps his life depended on it. When he took care of the pool, he took care of himself. In that way, he was not helpless.

What the gardens show is an interdependent relationship between nature and humanity where the respect of nature is the self-respect of humanity, and where nature serves as the source inside us from where order is spun. In these off-zones of the City, nature opens a way to humanity. Although New York discards people, nature, things, and chances, these gardeners recycle everything—even a first into a second chance. They allow nature to grow. Their lives and their neighborhoods grow alongside.

Here is analogical implication. The very form of gardening places nature inside creation, just as nature is placed inside self-respect. Jimmy picked a black garbage bag, because it mattered his fish have a pond. At the same time, he opened a zone of reflections in his life.

One of the most powerful pictures in the book shows Jimmy sitting next to his pond, lost in thought. The chair he sits on is outside in the elements, yet also a mark of his home.[33] Imagine him looking into the pool he has created. The sky mixes with the water and the shimmer of bronze-red fish swishing this way and that against the blackness. Light pours down through the water. As Jimmy looks into the pond, life shines back through his care.

Notes

1. A human-centered person is a *feminist* in the sense advanced by eco-feminism. *Care in relationships* is central to her way of being, as is a belief in the *moral equality* of humans. Of course, she advocates more than feminism, but she opposes all forms of nonconsensual domination over people and, as we will see, should be open to respect for nature. For more on eco-feminism, see Karen Warren, *Ecofeminist Philosophy: A Western Perspective on What It Is and Why It Matters*, Lanham, MD: Rowman & Littlefield, 2000.

2. It is arguable that this view of our humanity as articulated *around* our limits first takes shape in modern philosophy with Immanuel Kant's *Critique of Pure Reason*, New York: St. Martin's Press, 1965.

3. See Søren Kierkegaard (a.k.a. Ante-Climacus), *The Sickness unto Death*, Princeton: Princeton University Press, 1983. Kierkegaard talks throughout his work of existence as a gift. On this, see Rick Anthony Furtak, *Wisdom in Love: Kierkegaard and the Ancient Quest for Emotional Integrity*, Notre Dame: University of Notre Dame Press, 2005.

Wittgenstein wrote that—I am paraphrasing—the miracle is that the world exists. This comment was found in an unpublished paper by Irad Kimhi. I suspect it is from Wittgenstein's remarks on culture and value, or his remarks on religion. See Ludwig Wittgenstein, *Culture and Value*, Chicago: University of Chicago Press, 1984 and *Lectures and Conversations on Aesthetics, Psychology, and Religious Belief*, Berkeley: University of California Press, 1967.

4. This remark comes from book IV of Rousseau's *Emile*, trans. Alan Bloom, New York: Basic Books, 1978. See also Todorov's commentary on it in his *Frail Happiness: An Essay on Rousseau*, College Park: Pennsylvania State Press, 2005.

5. *Emile*, 221, translation slightly modified.

6. See, for instance, Peter Singer's *Animal Liberation*, New York: Ecco Books, 2002, or Arne Naess's or George Sessions's philosophies of deep ecology. (Arne Naess, "Identification as a Source of Deep Ecological Attitudes," in *Deep Ecology*, ed. Michael Tobias, San Marcos, CA: Avant Books, 256–270; George Sessions, ed., *Deep Ecology for the 21ˢᵗ Century*, Boston, Shambala Press, 1995.)

7. See J.M. Croetzee, "The Lives of Animals," reprinted in *Elizabeth Costello*, New York: Penguin Books, 2004.

8. Cora Diamond, "Eating Meat and Eating People," in *The Realistic Spirit*, Cambridge, MA: MIT Press, 1995.

9. Homer, *The Odyssey*, trans. Richard Lattimore, New York: Perennial Classics, 1999, IV, 572.

10. See Cora Diamond, "How Many Legs?" in *Value and Understanding: Essays for Peter Winch*, ed. R. Gaita, New York: Routledge, 1990, 149–178.

11. "How Many Legs," 170–173. I've added the underlining, of course. Diamond's exegesis of the passage from Dickens on the top of 172 is a model of the philosophical, close reading of literature. She explores how the *tense* shift in the story manifests the *sense* of shared humanity.

12. See Cat Power, "Maybe Not," on *You Are Free*. New York: Matador Records, 2003. I am being playful with Chan Marchand's (a.k.a. Cat Power's) lyrics in her spirit. In "Maybe Not," she sings that we all do what we can to get the next thing for our lives and don't consider how we can be free with each other. Yet at the song's end, she also suggests we can do what we can do to have freer minds, and her perspective throughout the album is humane in the sense described in this lecture, even down to her ecological identifications. It seems to me she wants to remind us of solidarity around what is elemental to a meaningful life, a point her minimal songs show.

13. In his *The Philosopher's Dog*, London: Routledge, 2003.

14. I am grateful to the senior citizens of the Pikes Peak Senior Citizens Center for bringing me to this point in a lecture they invited me to give in April 2004.

15. This was a topic my Grandpa Bendik used to discuss in his Elyria, Ohio Lutheran church. He was a coal miner and a machine-shop worker and would have studied to be a minister if he hadn't left school in sixth grade to support his younger brothers. His friends called him "Bishop." He thought that dancing with whomever

wanted to dance was not a sin, unless you were sinning inside yourself. Otherwise, people should not judge what's going on in your mind.

16. All these are listed in the bibliography.

17. Diamond, "Eating Meat and Eating People," 321.

18. The example of corpses wrapped in cocoons so that trees become graveyards comes from Apollonius of Rhodes's *Jason and the Golden Fleece* (*the Argonautica*). Our rites also can involve imagination as wild as Jean Genet's in his *Funeral Rites,* New York: Grove Press, 1972.

19. Diamond, "The Importance of Being Human," in *Human Beings,* ed. David Cockburn, New York: Cambridge University Press, 1991, 41.

20. Diamond, "Eating Meat and Eating People," 322–325.

21. Diamond, "Eating Meat and Eating People," 328–329, and "The Importance of Being Human," 43–44, 51.

22. Philippa Foot, in her *Natural Goodness* (New York: Oxford University Press, 2003), discusses the notion of a "species kind of good." That is a good relative to a species—a *specific* good. Foot has also learned from Thompson, her student. For reasons that may appear in lecture 8, my account of human flourishing is not well captured by Foot, although there are similarities with what she and a number of other writers have been trying to do in ethics by following Aristotle in light of analytic philosophy after Wittgenstein.

23. Andrey Tarkovsky, *The Offering,* Paris-Stockholm: Exile Production, 1986.

24. E. B. White, *Charlotte's Web,* New York: Harper Trophy, 1974.

25. Irving Berlin, *The Complete Lyrics,* ed. Kimball, New York: Knopf, 2001.

26. Arthur Rimbaud, "Par les soirs bleus d'été" in *Une saison en enfer,* Paris: Gallimard, 1987.

27. Diana Balmori and Margaret Morton, *Transitory Gardens, Uprooted Lives,* New Haven: Yale University Press, 1993, 52–55.

28. Balmori and Morton, *Transitory Gardens, Uprooted Lives,* especially 101.

29. Balmori and Morton, *Transitory Gardens, Uprooted Lives,* 70.

30. Balmori and Morton, *Transitory Gardens, Uprooted Lives,* 40, 85.

31. Balmori and Morton, *Transitory Gardens, Uprooted Lives,* 66. This reply is fundamental, because it makes possible the two previous replies. In order for the gardens to show care of the sort called for by humanity (what is lacking in New York with respect to the homeless), the gardens must be alive. In order for the gardens to be places worth owning and capable of giving one rooting even in the political order, they are likely to have to be worth caring for, but their being alive makes them worth caring for.

32. Balmori and Morton, *Transitory Gardens, Uprooted Lives,* 60.

33. Balmori and Morton, *Transitory Gardens, Uprooted Lives,* 61.

~

Relationships between
Humans and Lands

Good morning. I hope you had a restful week, and also had time to mull over both our notes from last class and the Diamond, Gaita and Balmori-Morton readings some more. Last class was dense. We defined what a sense of humanity is and saw that it's possible to have respect for nonhuman life flow from our sense of humanity. This week, I want us to pick up on the detail the gardens of the homeless left us and realize more fully how human culture has relationships with zones of life. I want us to realize how those relationships form our sense of humanity, too. This will add credibility to the claim of the next lecture that respect for life is something we *should* have.

Here's how I want to begin. Without knowing it last week, I indirectly criticized a movement in environmental ethics called "deep ecology." I want to tell you a story about that. The ideas for these lectures started in winter 2000, when I thought about how many students love deep ecology and about how misguided deep ecology can be. I wanted to re-articulate the intuitions people might love in deep ecology in a way that was less offensive to my moral sense and reason.

Here is the moral problem. There is a strand in deep ecology—not all of it, but a significant part of it—that is deliberately inhumane, hateful of people on the Earth. It is misanthropic. This became clear through some infamous incidents. One of them—perhaps the most infamous—took place in a popular American deep ecology journal of the radical group Earth First! An anonymous author named "Miss Ann Tropy" suggested that AIDS was a good thing, because it killed off people and so gave more room for nonhumans.[1]

This was supposed to be cute, because "Miss Ann Tropy" was being misan-thropic.[2] You might think such a view is rare, but in my experience teaching students passionate about the environment, views like this from Earth First! are fairly commonly expressed. They appear in popular movies like the one that first showed Brad Pitt can act: Terry Gilliam's *Twelve Monkeys*, where an ecoterrorist manages to release a super-virus that kills off most of the human race and forces the rest underground.[3] They appear in offhanded comments about how it wouldn't be so bad, after all, if a lot of us humans somehow dis-appeared, or, even more frequently, in a disgust at the human race and a feel-ing the planet would be better without us. How many people hold such views *unexpressed*, or in ambivalent, mixed emotions? Here were people who out of love for the Earth were filled with self-hatred.

This posed a moral problem for me. There are good reasons to be harshly critical of the way humans consume so much of nature. But it is quite another thing to indulge one's anger to the point of supporting human tragedy. Imag-ine standing in a village in Africa overrun by AIDS and explaining to every mother of every lost child and every spouse of every lost love that AIDS is a good thing. Tell them it all worked out for the best. People who say such things seem to me to have lost their grip.

I am not focusing on some rare deep ecologists, either. There is a *concep-tual* misanthropy to much in deep ecology. This is because deep ecologists see humans as selfishly taking over the Earth (they have some good reasons to think so) and then see the problem in what we called "anthropocentrism"— the view that our humanity inevitably leads us to be selfish with respect to the Earth. At bottom, when I thought about it, the root of the moral prob-lem is this conceptual misanthropy. Does our humanity inevitably lead us to be selfish with the Earth? I hope I showed last week that it is possible for our sense of humanity to be caring, not selfish.

The way deep ecology jarred with my reason is different. Deep ecologists advocate a psychology whereby we become sympathetically fused with the whole of nature—strictly identifying with its interests as the same as our own and on an equal footing.[4] They speak of the self "immersed" in or "one" with nature. But the conceptual problems with this idea are serious. First, there are problems surrounding moral responsibility. If we are one with nature, talk of each of us as individuals has to be suspended, and with it talk of moral re-sponsibility as we know it. Am I responsible for the otter's actions? Or the wind's movement? Is the tree responsible for my failure to respect someone? Second, there are problems concerning identity. If all is my self, where is the other in relation to whom I am a self? Are you myself, too? Third, if we are part of nature, we need to see the complex making us an organ in the greater functioning of the whole "self." But there is no single macro-organism of which we are a part, and even ecology suggests that the next largest biotic whole to which we belong—ecosystems—are chaotic.[5] Rather than being strictly identified with the whole of nature, then, it seemed more reasonable to me to understand how we are *like* other forms of life. We keep a discrete sense of ourselves, then.

Now my objections to some aspects of deep ecology may seem technical, but there is a simpler way to put it for those uninterested in conceptual problems. The deep ecological intuition is that humans form identifications with nature. The idea is that such identifications can run so thoroughly through our personalities that we lose the narrowness of our egos and become open to life around us. Life itself is astonishing and often beautiful—and the truth of the matter is that we are a part of it. We can live life with that understanding. To do so is to keep in mind a truth about the human condition that seems worthwhile, even essential, to self-knowledge and moral clarity. Yet here deep ecology takes a wrong turn, I believe, because it advocates oneness as the way to identify healthily with nature.

What is problematic about this turn can be seen by noticing who manages to be one with nature. According to deep ecology's classic texts by the Norwegian philosopher Arne Naess, maturity consists in widening identification experiences until one reaches the status of an illuminated person who identifies with "the whole."[6] Such a status is rare—a matter for the enlightened (I have not heard deep ecologists give an everyday word for such a person). But this vision of human maturity seems false and uncharitable to who we are. Nature already reaches into human life at the level of self-understanding. Analogical implication helped us see this. It seems to me that when we look at ecological identification, we are in the realm of common sense. It is not a common sense stressed by our current global economy, but it is there nonetheless. And that there are parts of common sense filled with ecological identification suggests that the psychology of such identification need not be limited to an almost mystical oneness. We are already greener than we think.[7] *The psychological availability of connections with the wider universe of life is more at home in common, human sense than deep ecology seems to admit.* In fact, we seem to need only to be true to ourselves, not to completely restructure ourselves, to reconnect with such identifications.

The personal confirmation I had for my intuition came through my memory of experiences watching the films of a Russian filmmaker named Andrey Tarkovsky. His film *The Offering* left a mark on me from when I saw it at eighteen in the Nordic Film Festival of Rouen, France, 1988.[8] That film manages to merge human emotional interiority with ecological identifications in a way

I—given my particular personality—found more intimate than any other work of art I'd seen. Moreover, it manages to explain such identification within a background reverence for life that suffuses the film's vision. This made me understand that *ecological identification arises out of reverence for life* and that *we need only attend to what is inside us to see how deeply the human condition's meaning is ecological.* In fact, so much of the beauty of human life arises around that fact. We are more nature-indebted than we think.

What I've tried to do in these lectures, then, is like some part of deep ecology, but is morally and conceptually clearer, I hope. As we will see next week, it is little more than a translation of what I learned through Tarkovsky's work of art. I think deep ecologists have been superficial when they look at our sense of humanity, and I think this superficiality has allowed them to become misanthropic. Looking carefully at what is best in us reveals a sense of humanity that is already ecological or potentially so. Humanity need not be divorced from nature, nor transcended in an almost mystical oneness. Nature is already inside us, and what we need to do is bring out what is best in us so that we recognize the ecological dimension of who we are.[9]

I think this kind of approach is deeper than deep ecology, if we have to go somewhere deep. Or, as I would rather put it—because all this stuff about being deep is pretentious—a nonalienating way to realize how earthly we can be is to develop the ecological dimensions of our humanity. The sedimented experience of human time on Earth has already made respect for nature part of our many cultural and physical dimensions, and what is best in us should respect life as an expression of our own humanity.

The way to be deep is to look at what is best in us. This is a way of being thoughtful and nothing more. It's like looking at the most evident thing in the world that people have forgotten to see, because they take it for granted. In a way, it's being deeply superficial, not superficially deep.

*

I think human cultures continually and repeatedly form analogical identifications with nonhuman life on Earth (and beyond Earth, too, in thoughts of the stars). In our second lecture on justice, we saw such identification in what we called "relationships between humans and lands." I would like to spend today's lecture filling out the category of relationships between humans and lands, because they provide a good way not only to see how we can respect life out of humanity, but how we already *do*. Our examples of the homeless gardeners and of the idea of the Earth Charter already intimated we do. Relationships between humans and lands show us how ecological identification is part of the moral structure of human communities.

The kind of relationship between humans and lands on which I will now focus is having a sacred place. By considering sacred places, we will focus on ideological relationships with lands. Depending on a river for clean water is a material relation, while depending on it for sacred immersion, as in the Ganges, is an ideological relation. Focusing on the sacred in land will show us to what extent ecological identification can constitute human morals.

The sacred is a consummate form of what is to be morally respected. When, for instance, we say a child is sacred, we mean that it is to be respected even more than we ought to respect each other. It is extremely evil to kill a child, and some of the most perceptive moralists—for instance, Dostoevsky—rightly claimed that the murder of an innocent child places all of existence on trial.[10] When things are sacred, they are at our moral core.

What, then, are sacred places? They are places in nature with spiritual significance. When we talk about something being "spiritual," we usually mean it invokes the divine. Many cultures throughout time have had sacred places at the center of their religious rites and shared meaning, and this is an important fact we need to consider, if only because people like the Amungme deserve it. We also need to consider this fact because sacred places manifest analogical identifications between humans and zones of nonhuman life where these zones reveal to us our own humanity.

I'll turn off the lights, and we can look at these images I've collected from different parts of the world. I wrote about these examples in an encyclopedia article I hope made it into some high schools. The examples aren't comprehensive, but were chosen to get us thinking about how much variety there can be among forms of sacred place—historically, globally or even in the very same country. Many cultures have sacred places.[11]

1. "The Aborigines of Australia have many sacred places in their culture. In their culture, relationship with the land is as important as kinship with one's family and tribe. The land literally is part of one's *kind* (or kin). In this way, places in the land are charged with high emotional meaning and are part of the relationships making up the life of the community. For example, near Ilpili, there is a place atop a hill. Elders take young men about to be initiated into adulthood to the rock formation there. The place is sacred, and must be approached in silence, slowly crawling. People do not talk *about* what it is like inside, but it is a place inside which one becomes an adult.

2. "Similarly, the Boy Scouts of America have an initiation into their honor core, the Order of the Arrow, named in honor of Native Americans. During this initiation, which is not spoken of publicly in detail,

young men "tapped" into the Order visit a place in the woods [that] summons love for the Earth. By visiting this place at the end of their initiation ordeal, they learn that hard work and discipline are rewarded by being worthy to experience the beauty in a natural place."[12]

3. As we discussed last time, "[r]esidents of New York City have noticed over the past [twenty] years that many homeless people in the Village make gardens out of whatever material they can find and on what little land they can temporarily enjoy. These gardens are sites of intensely meaningful activity and show how the gardener's concern with the most sacred values in life is found by integrating nature and human life. Each garden is a shrine made out of found materials, such as figurines, signs, and chairs from dumpsters and curbsides. Within these built shrines, plants and even animals are encouraged to thrive. These are urban sacred places.

4. "Around the world in Japan are Shinto shrines within which, no matter how developed the surrounding world is, one can find the presence of wild nature, often involving trees as old as 800 years. In the inner spaces of the shrine, people can commune with a world of select, archaic wilderness.

5. "Or, in fantasy, European Romanticism and the Russian Orthodox spiritual tradition combine in Andrey Tarkovsky's film, *Stalker* (best translated as *Searcher*).[13] There, people try to find 'the room' in the middle of 'the zone,' a region where nature has taken back control from human society, and within which one's deepest dreams can come true, including the wish to end all violence.

6. "Finally, consider the sacred places of the Ainu, the indigenous people who lived and still live on the islands now known as Japan. For the Ainu, an entire ecosystem was and is a sacred place, a "field" (*iworu*), ordered by a regional animal species, such as the Great Brown Bear or the Orca, important for [the Ainu's] way of life. These "fields" are by nature spiritual, infused with the spirit of the beings with which the Ainu are most in relationship. As such, the sacred place is not cut off from everyday life, as in a shrine or initiation site, but is *everywhere* in the circuit of everyday work and joy."[14]

These are all examples of sacred places; each one suggests some form of ecological identification at work in human culture. Of course, the presence of sacred places in a culture does not guarantee the culture is ecological. The presence may only point us to part of a culture. Shinto shrines, for example, coexist with a society that erases whole ecosystems for real estate development. And cultures can be thoughtless, too. Americans travel to the Grand Canyon because it is almost sacred. Yet to get there, they emit grand amounts of exhaust.

Nonetheless, sacred places demonstrate an important possibility. Ecological identification can be central to people's sense of humanity, and sacred places articulate it. The aboriginal initiation sites we saw are isolated from day to day activities, but they are meant to introduce people to the most important meaning of life. In fact, they seem to focus the meaning of life in these places, thereby revealing to initiates what life is about (they are like Diamond's limit experiences of life and death). Such focusing can also be seen in the Shinto shrines that contradict Japanese real estate development. The shrines remind people to respect nature and not simply follow the quickest profit. "Remember what matters," the shrines seem to say.

There is even a slim but significant tradition of sacred wild places in our culture. In the Romantic Age (roughly from the end of the eighteenth century until the middle third of the nineteenth, but with reverberations still with us today in many areas of cultural life), sacred places in wild nature began to become popular in Western culture. The Romantics included people like the poet William Wordsworth, and they prided themselves on revitalizing ideas they learned from reading about ancient Greek culture as well as ideas about Native Americans discovered through colonialism. One of the ideas they picked up from ancient Greece was of a natural place that was sacred because it communicated in some way with the divine. In ancient Greece, there were often shrines or locations that expressed in natural elements a divinity or the acts of divinities. One of these, for instance, is discussed in Plato's *Phaedrus*, the only Platonic dialogue that takes place outside the city.[15] Socrates and Phaedrus talk about love, madness, divinity, philosophy, and the afterlife of the soul under a tree surrounded by cicadas, across from a stream where a god of the wind swept down and carried off a maiden playing by the pure and clear water.[16] In other words, the sacred place they face symbolizes all the themes of the dialogue. So places would be marked as having been locations of divine history.

Millennia later, European Romanticism refashioned this Greek divinization of natural places. In countless poems that in turn illuminated movements like American transcendentalism and the culture that gave birth to Henry David Thoreau, lone poets such as Wordsworth walked out into the sacredness of nature and transcended human limitation in an experience of divine illumination.[17] This romanticism, in turn, helped Americans rediscover the Native American sacred places colonization had erased from public consciousness, as in the French novelist Chateaubriand's early romantic musing on America.[18] Both romanticism and Native American sacred places, then, helped develop ecological consciousness in the West today, and that ecological consciousness exists in the hiker's idea that a wild mountain is sacred, something people like the deep ecologist David Rothenberg appear to think.[19]

Yet ecological romanticism is not well integrated into our culture's common sense. By contrast, in cultures where sacred places are integral to the meaning of everyday life, respect for nonhuman life is more a part of people's everyday sense of the world. In such cultures—for instance, that of the Ainu—sacred places are integrated with the world of humans. This is an idea to which we will return in our closing lecture over a month from now: the idea of *integration*. The garden shrines of the homeless in New York appear to exemplify a similar integration for the homeless. For the Ainu and the homeless gardeners, ecological identification permeates the meaning of life, articulated with poetic power in sacred places. In this way, sacred places emphasize an everyday idea that nature is to be respected.

Lack of an absolute distinction between nature and humanity is fairly common to human cultures. We live on this Earth along with many other animals and all the elements. The original meaning of "environment" captures this fact. It means that which surrounds us, the world by our side. The world by our side is one we depend on, have interacted with throughout time, and is one that has been worked into the imaginations of cultures. Ecological integration can go very deep, even into a culture's sense of time. This is so in cultures—for instance, Greek and most preindustrial cultures—where time was cyclical, in step with the seasons and agrarian practice. It is also found in mythical time. For instance, aboriginal culture speaks of dreamtime, and Navajo culture involves a time when sacred places serve as an origin to both the human and the natural world. Some mountains are sacred to the Navajo because it is said Changing Woman worked her creative powers there in the mythical time before the world was fully formed. In such a time, both sacred places in nature and human life are intertwined.[20]

Thus, a brief glance at sacred places in various human cultures reveals something our deep ecologists might remember. Because sacred places are not found only away from society but commonly in the midst of society, it is clear they can join society and nature so that human life coexists with, and doesn't overpower, nature. *There is nothing intrinsically opposed to nature in our sense of humanity.* Perhaps what has gone wrong is something cultural—an excess of profit making and self-interest perhaps, or having powerful incentives to forget what is best in us, including respect for life. Perhaps we do not need misanthropy but cultural critique. Better politics, better economics, better laws.

Even middle-class culture suggests such cultural critique. This is my point about how ecological identification is more a part of common sense than we realize, yet should be brought out and exercised consistently. Think about sacred places in many people's homes:

> The recent history of private life and of architecture shows that people often create zones in the center of their very homes where they reconnect with the heart of life's meaning. Such places are sacred, but not by invoking a particular spirit or god. Rather, they invoke *the* sacred, which might be thought of as a dimension of experience in which many different values and emotions have their home, such as peacefulness, order, passion, and love. So people often have a small fountain with running water or a small area with a tree or trees in the center of their homes. Likewise, people can discover or make such places in nature. When they do, as when children build a treehouse back in the woods high up amidst the sunlit leaves, they may actually make a sacred place where no one god or spirit is invoked, but where the dimension of spirituality comes alive.[21]

The point here is not that middle-class consuming Americans are secretly deep ecologists. That's a funny thought. The point is rather that even in middle-class consuming American culture, one can see that parts of people's lives are at odds with other parts, for instance, the parts where they consume thoughtlessly: factory farmed meat, fossil fuel, non-biodegradable plastics and so on. People's lives are often in tension; while they may not be wholly laudable from the standpoint of an ecological critique, they are also not wholly bad. One might say: the better part of themselves shines through the part that is thoughtless from pressure or sheer inconsistency.

Sacred places thus have many forms and clue us into the widespread prevalence of relationships between humans and lands of an ideological kind. With sacred places, we see how analogical identifications form our sense of humanity as partially ecological already. This identification is close to the surface of our lives, too. It need not be buried deep in a culture that is exotic or archaic to the eyes of the global economy (that is, usually, a culture that was colonized in some form and which was quite normal on its own terms). New York's homeless gardeners, our heroes of identification, create sacred places in compressed durations of time, often across a few days. Because of territory battles between each other and with the city of New York, they move nomadically around the city. Yet the human ability and drive to make sacred meaning is strong enough that it can take root and then uproot overnight.

These gardeners do not have a media culture to cement their understanding. In fact, the media cements over them, neglecting to report on them as little more than a special interest story. They do not have an ancient mythological narrative. They have little more than the word on the street. They do not even have centralized resources and a genuinely collective set of rituals. They are anarchic, with groups forming and dissolving in transience. Yet their sacred places humanize them.

Given that we want to understand our humanity here, we should understand how humanization occurs. How do sacred places make us more human? Two of our examples formed initiation rituals around sacred places. Recall both the Aboriginal sacred place and that of the Boy Scouts of America. Even a fantasy sacred place such as the zone in Tarkovsky's film involves an elaborate ritual to reach it. Rituals are repeated. They steady us around an activity we have found meaningful. In Tarkovsky's film, for example, forlorn Soviet citizens in a nondescript future risk their lives to go into what seems to be a nuclear fallout zone where a meteor struck. The only person who can lead them safely is a kind of holy idiot: the searcher. He has to take them through contorted, invisible ordeals before they are ready inside themselves to reach the central room. This room is roofless, and its water-covered floor is populated by fish and algae. Rain pours in. The meaning here—as with all true art—is indefinite, but it is clear that the ritual of entering the zone, then the room, repeats the message of being worthy of baring (with an "a," not an "ea") one's heart. And that baring one's heart happens in a room open to the elements is not a coincidence. It is clear at the least that the movie sees nuclear holocaust as one of the profoundest antiecological and antihuman perversions of our humanity. In this example, the ritual of purifying oneself of anxiety so one can focus on what matters in life steadies the searchers to reveal what is best in their humanity, not what is worst. That best element of humanity, in turn, is a nonviolent respect for life, like the water that covers—and so nullifies—the weapons strewn along the floor of the room next to the movement of silver fish. Perhaps ritual is important for the development of sacred places.

At the same time, the gardeners do not have much time to develop rituals. So how do temporary sacred places nonetheless humanize them? The answer might be simple. Sacred places meet a drive inside human spirit to be connected with the places we inhabit. The homeless in New York are close to nature out of necessity. It is a harsh nature that kills many of them during the winter. By working their gardens, they not only tend life, they also integrate and identify with the elements. Out of this drive to establish a meaningful relationship with the place they spend their time, the homeless gardeners create sacred places, and this fact suggests, "one of the things crucial to the development of sacred geography is the need for a human home within the elements."[22] Finding that home, we feel more human.

*

I hope we see now that sacred places express relationships between humans and lands of the ideological kind, and I hope we see that such relationships are common in human life. Remember back to lecture one when I told you the root of the prefix "eco" comes from the Greek *oikos*, which means, roughly, the home? Today, that root makes more sense. Sacred places show us that we are ecological, because we are "*oiko*-logical." Our home is Earth. What are some environmentalists thinking when they assume that a sense of humanity is necessarily opposed to finding one's moral compass in nature? The philosopher Ludwig Wittgenstein—one of the most dialogical philosophical writers and Socratic teachers of the twentieth century—famously said to people who let theories cloud their visions: "*Look and see!*"[23] That is what we are trying to do here.

People and cultures make relationships with lands formed of analogical identifications central to their sense of humanity. This means they develop a limited or complete form of an ecological orientation involving respect for life, and it means that if we treat such cultures or people in ways oblivious to their relationships between humans and lands, we can wound their dignity and how they organize their universe's meaning.

It was easy for the Freeport Mining Company or the Zortman-Landusky Mine to run roughshod over two cultures' sacred places, because our courts did not look and see. You might think, at least, courts would see the analogy between the human right to practice one's religion and these cases involving spiritual mountains. We commonly think of mosques, temples, or churches as deserving some protections, because people worship there and have a right to do so in peace. Of course, people didn't gather under one roof and kneel on the floor at the mountains. Yet even if the mountains were not places where people went to worship, even if there were no rituals surrounding them (which there almost certainly were), they still shaped the cosmology of the indigenous cultures to such an extent that destroying them was destroying a focal point of the culture and, in the process, wounding the culture's ability to make sense of the universe. What kind of respect is that? For gold, you destroy someone's god? People living in the Christian Louisiana where Freeport is based should have known that *that* problem comes out of the Sermon on the Mount! "You cannot serve God and money!"[24]

Relationships between humans and lands help us understand practices whereby people think it is of utmost importance to respect some zone of nonhuman life. The moral reasoning in such cases assumes a link between nature and humanity in such a way that to act appropriately toward nature is to act out of a sense of humanity.

Moreover, sacred places bring out what is best in us. Sacred places emphasize human thoughtfulness and they reinforce the virtue of having a nondestructive soul. Thoughtful people are aware of the meaning in this world. They are careful. They do not lose sight of where we live, what matters most in the heart or the complexity of existence. Thoughtful people have nondestructive souls. Thought*less*ness wastes and is careless. It destroys without meaning to. Thought*ful*ness destroys only as a last resort—out of care, not an inner and destructive impatience. Thoughtfulness and a nondestructive soul are virtues of humanity, and we are most mature when we have them. Nor are they elitist virtues, but are available to people who take their time and who choose to live with the parts of themselves that are loving. Anyone who has been loved knows that love is available at some point in her being, and anyone who lives desperately needing love unconsciously knows it. Thoughtfulness and a nondestructive soul bring out human engagement and connection. And sacred places reinforce both. They make us remember that some regions of life are not to be violated, and that the ecological condition of the world deserves our respect.

Consider what is so special, or meaningful, about people who seem in touch with nature or respectful of other forms of life. Granted, it is not sufficient for being a moral person that you respect other forms of life or are in touch with nature, but it is certainly a good side of one's moral sensibility when one is. Also, if my argument in next week's lecture goes through, it's necessary for being fully moral that one respect life. Here, then, are two portraits:

Frog-on-the-Arm Man

My father is one of those people who is loved by almost every animal that meets him. He has a rare knack for befriending animals, and he loves them. In a card he once sent me when I was in graduate school, he showed his true colors. The card is called "Between Two Worlds," by someone named Schim Shimmel.[25] It is a painting of elephants and other animals from southern Africa with a sky that is underwater and filled with coral reef-dwelling tropical fish. The card is a fantasy, in short. I saved this card for many years and now have it in my office, because it feels like the unconscious true heart of my dad.

He never desists from showing his relation to other living beings. He loves to put insect stickers on envelopes and at sixty-five tattooed a tree frog on his left upper arm. That sort of thing. He reads natural history eagerly. His message is simple. We humans are part of this world of life, and we should respect the living beings with whom we share the planet. They are amazing. He has a global relationship between humans and lands, focusing on other animals. It is one of his moral excellences.

The Rock Lady

My mom is elemental. She loves rocks, and she is almost uncannily in tune with the world of the elements—a very Slovak trait, as I like to think of it. Rocks are not alive, but they bear the traces of the Earth—each one, a miniature icon of a whole terrain. Why does she love rocks, twisted dried wood, bougenvillias floating in water? Why does weather make her feel emotion so transparently it is like the world's energy is focused through her being? Why does that matter? Why is it moral?

It matters, because human life has evolved on Earth. We resonate with Earth's processes (I'm making a Thompsonian categorical!). The meaning of who we are is inextricable from our natural history, even if someday we move to the moon or other planets. Moreover, forming relationships with other lives and with the sources of life is a human excellence, because it shows we can appreciate life. What is moral about that is that when we appreciate life, we cannot be inclined to thoughtlessly do violence, waste, forget solidarity, or overlook order. Rather, appreciating life—zones of life, order that is different from our own—we must at least be given to thoughtfulness and a non-destructive soul.

Notes

1. This statement occurred in the May 1, 1987 issue of the journal *Earth First!* currently published out of Tucson, Arizona. This journal can be accessed online. There is also a subsequent history of debate around Earth First!'s misanthropy or lack thereof, much of it in the *Earth First!* journal itself, to their credit.

2. And perhaps also "trophic" in some way—an allusion to trophic levels in ecosystems?

3. Terry Gilliam, *Twelve Monkeys*, Los Angeles: Universal Pictures, 1995.

4. This view is commonly attributed to Arne Naess, although he is a more sophisticated philosopher than people make him out to be. Nonetheless, his *followers* often have this view. See Naess, "Identification as a Source of Deep Ecological Attitudes" in *Deep Ecology*, ed. Michael Tobias, San Marcos, CA: Avant Books, 256–270.

5. See Donald Worster, "The Ecology of Order and Chaos," in *Environmental Ethics: Concept, Policy, and Theory*, ed. Joseph Desjardins, Mountain View, CA: Mayfield Publishing, 1999.

6. Arne Naess, "Identification as a Source of Deep Ecological Attitudes."

7. I am assuming the class readily understands that being "green" is code in to-day's world for being *ecological*. Hence, the environmental party in Germany is the Green Party, and Greenpeace is an environmental activist group. Robin Wells sug-gested the expression "greener than you think" in a story I tell in the acknowledg-ments.

8. Andrey Tarkovsky, *The Offering*, Paris-Stockholm: Exile Production, 1986.

9. This is a view expressed in a compelling manner by the most powerful English-language environmental writer of the twentieth century, Rachel Carson. See Carson's *Silent Spring*, New York: Mariner Books, 2002.

10. See Fyodor Dostoevsky, "The Grand Inquisitor" in *Brothers Karamazov*, trans. Pevear, New York: Vintage Books, 1991.

11. Places one, four, and six come from Gary Snyder, *The Practice of the Wild*, San Francisco: North Point Press, 1991.

12. See my article, "Sacred Places," *The Routledge Encyclopedia of World Environ-mental History*, New York: Routledge, 2003, 1081–1082.

13. Andrey Tarkovsky, *Searcher*, Moscow: Mosfilms, 1978.

14. "Sacred Places," 1081–1082.

15. Plato, *Phaedrus*, in *Collected Dialogues*, ed. Hamilton and Cairns, Princeton: Princeton University Press, 1987, 475–525.

16. Plato, *Phaedrus*, 229 b-c.

17. See "Lines composed a few miles above Tintern Abbey."

18. See his *Atala*, Paris: 1801.

19. See David Rothenberg, *Always the Mountains*, Athens: University of Georgia Press, 2003.

20. Thanks go to Dave Aftandilian for teaching me these points about Native American culture.

21. "Sacred Places," 1084. The tree house is a memory of mine from Paris Rd./Hartford Terrace, New Hartford, N.Y., USA in the late 1970s.

22. "Sacred Places," 1082.

23. In his *Philosophical Investigations*, trans. G.E.M. Anscombe, New York: Prentice Hall, 1999.

24. Matthew 6:24 (New Revised Standard Version).

25. Schim Shimmel, "*Between Two Worlds*," 1992, acrylic.

Being True to Ourselves

I am excited for today's lecture and hope you are too. It will be a long one, but it should be worth it. Whether we succeed with the argument we've been building or not, we will at least be grappling with the core of the philosophical justification for becoming an ecological citizen, for hearing "world" in an ecological way too when speaking of being world citizens. The world is not just some abstract national territory, but is also a globe of life.

Recall where we are. We are after a justification for becoming an ecological citizen. We want one more detailed than the reasoning set out for us in our first lecture. We want to understand better, too, what being an ecological citizen involves. In our second lecture, we began our search by seeing what reasons justice gives us for becoming an ecological citizen. We found some good ones. We also saw how justice might shape being an ecological citizen with modes of moral attention. These modes expanded our frame of mind toward the world's ecological complexity and made it clear respect for others often requires respect for the Earth that is their home.

Out of respect for others, then, we should become ecological citizens. What about out of respect for oneself? In the next lecture, we explored what reasons prudence might give us for becoming ecological. We found many. It turns out that if we want to respect ourselves and our future generations, we ought to develop an ecological orientation. It is a good idea to do so, because an ecological orientation helps us flourish. Here was a second kind of reason, then, for how respecting ourselves gives us reason to become more ecological.

These prudential reasons also led us to an ecological orientation. It turned out that such an orientation might be a surer way to do what is in our best interest anyway. The idea of an ecological orientation involves direct moral reasons to respect nonhuman life, not simply reasons of self-interested prudence. So we were left wondering about what moral reasons we have for respecting life. Should we respect life? If we could find sufficient moral reason to respect life, we could have a clear justification for becoming ecological, and we would have good reason for adopting an ecological orientation directly, not simply out of prudence, but out of what is right.

I then made it clear to you that finding moral reasons to respect life has been one of the difficult and contested areas of environmental ethics. That being so, I recommended we take a slow path to our goal. I suggested we begin by showing that it is possible to respect life out of our sense of humanity. Can we do it? Our sense of humanity is a settled dimension of morality today and can be shown to be a settled dimension of morality, period.[1] If we can respect life out of a sense of humanity, it's not inconceivable we could have good moral reasons to respect life. We thus searched for and found two modes of analogical identification. They conceptualized that possibility.

Still, many things are possible. For instance, we could all decide to throw erasers at each other and cover our clothes in chalk. We could then rampage through the administration building hugging random people and shouting, "The ghosts are in the belfry. Fly, fly away!" Would that be a good idea? After all, some of you have significant others. Is it good to develop the possibility? *That* was the question. So class last week explored obvious ways people have in fact developed the possibility. People do it, for instance, with sacred places.

We considered relationships between humans and lands of the sacred kind and the ways people create a home by identifying with regions of life. We saw examples of relationships people have formed with lands. I saw the looks on many of your faces in the light of the projector. Most people have nondestructive souls. Life wouldn't work without it. It's just that our institutions can catch us up in patterns surpassing our minds. Sometimes, too, the very concepts these institutions rely on cloak our minds from attention to what is moral. Subtly, incrementally, we are pressured, lose touch, or forget our priorities. Yet spaces of time and special relationships can bring us back to focus, and examining whether we really think something is, say, a *resource* as opposed to a *zone of life* causes us to reexamine our way of conceptualizing the world. This is what sacred places are for people who have made them a part of their lives. With land-integrated people, respecting zones of life appears to bring meaning into people's lives and demonstrates a morally ecological side to being human. Does that mean we *should* follow a more ecological path?

So we come to this week. Reverberating with each other is not enough. We should argue plainly that it really is moral to respect life out of humanity. I don't want any sympathy you happen to have or my *de facto* authority in being up here to lead you into believing some position is sound when it is not. Even if my argument is not as successful as I hope it will be today, my hope is that I will inspire you to make it better. What I am arguing here is hard to argue, and it comes out of five years moving slowly toward realizations about it. Remember our remarks about the spirit of philosophy at the beginning of the course? One still feels like a beginner, even in the midst of it, just as one does in the midst of life when faced with a deliberation. Philosophy takes time.

To echo the quote I put on the board two weeks ago but did not discuss directly, "My heart is a storm in me." Yet it is not Odysseus's downpour facing an ocean he must cross to reach home. It is a sand storm on a red sand plain, observed from a grey and brown mountain range circling the plain and its dunes.

*

The argument I will be giving may seem confusing, because I will be moving from two different areas. On the one hand, I will be arguing from our *idealism*. On the other hand, I will argue from our *identity*. Idealism moves in the realm of *ought*—what we should do. Identity moves in the realm of *is*—who we are. Quite frequently, the two don't meet.

I will claim there is a part of who we *are* when we become socialized that involves the best in us, and that we *should* bring that out. If you think about the structure of that approach, some things appear:

1. First, what is best in us will be doing a lot of work in the argument. We should bring out what is best, because it is best. So we will need to scrutinize carefully what I claim to be best. Why is it best? Am I just assuming it is best, or do I have an argument for why it is? Is my argument convincing? Does it speak even to people who don't care much at all about what is best? What makes it convincing?

2. Second, something tricky is going on with identity. Who we are contains norms. Norms tell us what we ought to do. What is added to the argument by beginning with identity instead of just going directly to an argument for the norms? Why should we care about our identity, also? Identity can be a problem for many people. People escape through identities, and some become self-absorbed with them. Why start with identity?

3. Third, the notion of socialization should be clarified. I know roughly what "society" is, because I know how to use the word. Well, we might not know what it is exactly, but at least it is part of ordinary language. So, too, with being social. We tell kids to "be more social" when they spend too much time alone. What is socialization, though? Why is it central to my argument from our identity? How does socialization re-late to identity? How does it relate to what is best in us?

Uniting all these remarks, what we can say generally is that the argument assumes idealism is part of our identity, a part we should keep. Moreover, the idealistic part of our identity joins with our socialization. We should bring it out. I will argue that if we don't bring it out, we can't be fully moral. In this way, that part in us which is best is something we have to follow, or else we lose touch with our moral potential.

*

I want to begin with one obvious way our identity and our idealism are one: in the moral dimension of personal character. Humans are moral animals; we couldn't be *im*moral if we weren't. Let me explain. There is a very common and cynical view of humans that says we are immoral. This may be because we are sinful, because we are pressured relentlessly by global capitalism, or because power, greed, or lust is so sweet to us it is hard to desist. According to this disillusioned view, humans are the *im*moral animal, said Rousseau, one of the most rhetorical people to express this view. The other animals don't slaughter each other in mass wars for the sake of an imaginary boundary (i.e., a national border).[2] What is mistaken about this view is that we could not be immoral if we were not first subject to moral norms. Rousseau understood this. He knew we could only be immoral because we are *expected* to be moral. No norms, no immorality. That means we are a moral kind first. Morality—according to philosophers—is conceptually prior.

Nor is it inconsistent to say we are a moral kind of creature and yet act im-morally so often. We are free. We can mess up. Yet, as creatures of freedom, we are responsible for our actions. There is thus no great mystery about why we are moral, subject to moral norms. Because we are responsible, we hold ourselves and others accountable. This is the first necessary condition on our moral nature. Without being accountable, we could not be moral.

Here's the second: as a species, we have to live together in societies. We are social animals. There may be individuals who live as hermits. Yet they are exceptions, and our species could not survive following their example. Here, then, is the consequence of our social nature: because we live together in societies, we have to be accountable to each other. Without having to be accountable to each other, there would be no morality. That's the second necessary condition on our moral nature.[3]

The third necessary condition is that we have to be accountable to our own selves. As children and young adults, we have to be raised. There can be no human life without care in child raising. A large part of this care's purpose must be to teach us to care for ourselves. If we do not learn to live through care, we have problems until we learn to care for ourselves. Because we need to learn to care for ourselves, we should be accountable to ourselves. Otherwise, how would we be able to live up to what is careful? Without having to be accountable to ourselves, there would be no morality.

The last necessary condition on morality is that we can appreciate life in ourselves. Life matters. This is a tough one, because many people forget that life matters. Yet when people forget that life matters, they become immoral. They become open to wasting life, their own or that of others. This proves the point indirectly.

Here's a more direct route, though. Part of our being human is being loved into significance. When care is given to a typical member of our species, that person opens up. As she does, she becomes interested in life. What we do when we raise children is love them enough that they develop an ongoing love for life and a broadly loving intelligence that is alive to the significances of life and of their interests. Moreover, we expect that a morally developed person realizes that others should have their love for life respected. In short, moral development makes it an obligation to realize life matters, if not for oneself, than for others. Moreover, if one stops finding that life matters, one has a moral obligation to take steps to overcome the depression out of care for oneself. Life matters, because it is astonishing and because in it, we can do and experience so much that is meaningful. That is precisely why it is depressing when life becomes uninteresting or blocked: we know at bottom it is not supposed to be that way. And when people, governments, or systems act oblivious to the life that matters for many, they are unjust. Life is not just something worthless, or we lose touch with at least what is moral. If our lives did not matter, we could not be moral, and we could also not be depressed, cynical, apathetic, or bored.

Now, when you join these necessary conditions together, they are "jointly sufficient." Together, they explain sufficiently why our nature is moral. Because we are accountable to each other and to ourselves, and because our lives matter, we are by nature moral. People who lose touch with one of these necessary conditions become *dehumanized*. They lose the nature of human life. When in proper form, we are moral animals (that is a Thompsonian categorical!).

Someone who is not accountable to others is a sociopath. Someone who is not accountable to himself is severely incapacitated. And someone who does not think life matters *at all* is depressed or nihilistic. These are not value judgments or moral condemnations (unless the nihilism is chosen outside severe depression). To the contrary, when people are sociopathic, incapacitated, or so depressed as to lose all sense in life, they are not subject to moral judgment. Rather, they require urgent care. The point is: we humans are moral animals when in our normative form.

That means, though, that we are subject to norms. Morality is an idealistic dimension of identity, a place where how we are includes how we ought to be. That we are by identity *idealistic* explains why we need to *think* about morality and why what you are doing through these lectures is so important for your development. Whether you prove me wrong, remain unconvinced, or agree with some things in this series, the most important thing for you developmentally is that you are thinking about what you ought to do. Humans have to do that. It's part of our identity, and when you don't get to exercise it, as when political correctness stifles real debate or moral tyranny stifles genuine questioning, you become stunted. The real harm of both political correctness and morally stifling communities is that they stunt people's development as humans. We need to think about what we should do to be human, and we need to talk about it a whole hell of a lot.[4]

Idealism, strictly speaking, is thus basic to our identity, and not whatever people say when, disillusioned, they think humans aren't moral at all. If we truly weren't moral animals, if we weren't truly idealistic (subject to norms), we could not be subject to such critique. It would be pointless to criticize us, then, a category error, like shouting at a rock for falling on your foot. "*Bad* rock! Bad, bad rock!"

*

So we have to be moral to be ably human. Being moral means being legitimately subject to moral norms. What do socialization and respect for life have to do with being moral? We saw that being moral necessarily involves accountability to others (part of being social) and some appreciation of life (not being nihilistic). But "socialization" and "respect for life" are new expressions, and they are important for this lecture's overall argument. The way to move from our idealistic, moral nature to why we should respect life straight up—as New York hip-hoppers used to say—is to go through our socialization. And we need to see especially why respect for *life itself*, not just our lives, actually belongs to socialization.

Think about this claim, which I'll write on the board:

1. *Life is something that does not deserve any respect.*

This is the negation of the following claim:

1.* *Life is not something that does not deserve any respect.*

This second, starred claim means that should someone say to me, "Life doesn't deserve any respect." I'd say, "No, it does. Life is not something that does not deserve any respect!" What I want to know is: do we learn this starred claim growing up in order to be members of society? *Must* we, from the standpoint of society?

The answer is clear if by "life," we refer to human life, and I've already gestured to the obvious place of such respect in our moral nature. There can be no society in which the lesson people learn while growing up is that human life, as a rule, does not deserve any respect. Not only would life in such a society be "nasty, brutish, and short," to cite Thomas Hobbes, but it wouldn't be life in *society*.[5] Society is at the least people living together. How can people live together if human life does not deserve any respect? People would then live alongside each other and go about their days and nights in a situation where no one could legitimately stop another person who was, say, randomly doing violence to you, humiliating you for fun, or being just plain pushy and say: "You shouldn't do that. I'm a person, too, you know." In other words, people deserve some respect. A situation where people in physical proximity and interweaving paths of action cannot legitimately demand some respect of each other lacks security or a sense of looking out for each other's well-being. It's not a society where we can count on others not just trampling over us and where there is *some* notion of looking out for each other, even if that simply means respecting each other's freedom.

Of course, the real question might be why human life deserves respect. Someone might point out that in many societies, some humans receive some respect, and some humans don't receive any respect, for example, if they are slaves, a minority group, or women. This is not a point about it being right to treat some people as lacking a ground for respect. It's a point about what is *possible* in a society. The idea in this objection is that we don't necessarily have to be taught that all human lives deserve some respect for us to have a society. Some societies seem to have existed where some people didn't get, and were not supposed to get, any respect. There were bad societies, this objection says, but still they were societies. Societies can exist while excluding segments of society, I am sorry to say.

This much is true. I will reply that in such societies, those who exclude others from respect are in bad faith. By this, I mean that they are in denial of something basic to human development: our compassion. It is human to put ourselves in the place of other humans, and we can identify with basic human suffering and joy, even though we may misunderstand many aspects of other cultures.[6] This is a reason why, I believe, it has been possible for there to have been significant advances in the inclusiveness of the human community over history, and why we identify the moral notion of humanity with such inclusiveness.[7]

Moreover, in exclusive societies, the rule is still that human life deserves some respect, and the *exception* is that some humans don't need to get that respect because of some quality that is seen as a rationalization for the exception. Even according to racists, for example, the idea is: were human X not a possessor of characteristic P, human X would of course deserve some respect. The rule is to respect humans and the exception is based on a loathed quality of the society—for example, being of a particular religious culture, having certain kinds of features or coloring, practicing romance in certain ways, being of a certain class or vocation, and so on. Also, please note that this is not about the number of people included or excluded. Some civilizations have excluded most people as undeserving of respect. Yet the way they did so was to come up with a story about the proper human being, and then they denied their own compassionate potential.

I want to explain this point about compassion further. When we are brought up into the world, we are brought up to interpret such things as *human suffering and loss, human joy, and expectation*. This holds true for racists and egalitarians alike. We could not even raise our own children if we ourselves had not developed an understanding of the human good. The human good is not a mere name. It is a category of thought referring to, at least, the objective circumstances of our ecological and biological condition. It involves such things as the *kind* of emotional responses, developmental junctures, and capabilities of human *kind*. To become an adult member of any society involves developing a grasp of the human condition and some grasp of the human good. Otherwise, no common good can make sense at all, let alone a pursuit of the good individually.

Here, then, comes the rub. To understand the human good requires being able to understand such things as *a human face twisted in agony* or *a human face beaming with excitement and joy*. To go back to our Raimond Gaita quote from a past lecture, these are things we are expected to know *in our guts and in our bones.*[8] Indeed, we feel them before we even think them when we meet them. They think us. They make us react, because we know them so viscerally. When a human being is not able to recognize a face twisted in agony, we are dealing with a serious incapacitation, for even very young infants come to recognize that and the impression of agony.[9]

All humans—it is a matter of humankind—at times have a face alight with joy, at times a face twisted in agony. It does not matter if you are sky-blue or practice the strangest religion or are romantic in the oddest of ways or carry an extra eyebrow or, or, or. *That* is a face. *That* is pain. We know that. The idea here is that human life is not the kind of thing that does not deserve any respect, because no matter how racist our society, we still have to learn to recognize the human condition and have some grasp of the human good. And the *human* good does not discriminate among races. In fact, the entire task of racist ideology is to try to make us forget that fact. Human *kind*ness is basic to human development.

Let me summarize the point here. To become a member of any sustained society, we need to acquire some grasp of the human good. The human good is not confined to merely *some* humans. When we acquire some grasp of the human good and develop compassion properly, we learn that it is not just open to us to do bad to people for no good reason. As a rule, we are not to act in ways that are bad to other humans. That is, we learn that people deserve some respect. But if we think that only some people deserve respect, we lose touch with the fact that respect involves respect for the human good— and everyone has one of those. And if we think that no people deserve respect at all, we can't be part of any society. To be a proper part of society, then, is to believe that human life deserves some respect, period.

If we were engaging in philosophical history, I would argue that this normative condition explains not only why moral inclusiveness is possible but why moral egalitarianism has made progress over human history and why it is right that it has. At bottom, the potential for moral egalitarianism is basic to our socialization. To become a part of society, we need to learn that human life deserves some respect, even if our society tries to trim the corners on how much respect that is for some people or for all of us. A sense of humanity is conceptually basic to socialization. Human kindness is basic to human development.[10]

*

Now, we need to ask why *life as such* deserves some respect as a matter of socialization. Let's first get clear about what we mean by "socialization." "Socialization" is a term I associate with American progressive education in primarily John Dewey's era, that is, the early to mid-twentieth century. Dewey was a Columbia University professor, founder of the Lab School in Chicago, co-creator of the original New School for Social Research in New York City and widely recognized as the greatest American pragmatist as well as philosopher of education.[11] Dewey revolutionized the philosophy of education, especially public education, by insisting that schools be places for socializing us as much as teaching us disciplinary knowledge such as physics or English. Dewey's idea about the goal of public schooling explains in large part why American high schools have sports teams, drama clubs, and all other manner of activities as part of them. In Europe, these activities are usually part of private clubs separate from the schools.

Dewey's idea was that education ought to be holistic. We have many sides of ourselves that need development, and most of them have to take place in our society. Therefore, education should render us able to coexist with our fellows in society in a powerful and good way for all involved. Society is one of the greatest wholes in which our development matures. The process through which schools, families, and communities bring children up into mature adult members of society is called "socialization." This is also what I mean by the term. Socialization is upbringing into mature societal membership. It is education for a working union between humans.

Socialization

Upbringing into mature societal membership

Why, then, should socialization involve respect for all life, rather than only respect for human life? The first point is that respect for humans is impossible without respect for life. How can we discriminate between hugging someone to death and hugging someone to *death* unless we have a grasp on life and respect it? Or is hugging someone to death respecting him? Not unless this is a very extraordinary situation. When we respect each other—as a rule, not an exception—we respect in part that we are alive. Respect for each other's lives is a part of respect for each other.

Of course, respect for each other's lives is not respect for some mysterious and abstracted thing. It's respect for the organization of our species form with reference to the health of that form.[12] It's respect for the functioning of humans, you might say. It's not that there is some property—life—that is somehow attached to humans, and then we respect that along with humans. To respect life in each other is to respect human life. As Michael Thompson (our philosopher from lecture two) noted, judging something as a life form is categorizing it in a special way that is used only for living beings.[13] Life is not some property of beings, but is part of conceptualizing a kind of living being. That rock is neither dead nor alive. That ant is either dead or alive. We can say this of the ant, because it is a kind of living being. The rock is not a kind of living being. Likewise, to respect life in each other is to respect a kind of living being—the human being.

Even so, when we respect life in each other, we respect the proper, functioning arrangement of our species form. We respect, for instance, an arrangement between a pumping heart and lungs, not a heart systematically out of sync with lungs. Or we respect clear functioning of our minds, not the irrational breakdowns of them. We seek people who are capable, not the incapacitation of people. In this way, respect for each other's lives involves respect for the capable form of human beings,[14] that humans should not be rendered incapable for no good reason. And we can see a like capability in other forms of life. Because it matters to us, we can see it matters for them. At least it enables them to have whatever life they can have.

Why, though, should we learn that life in any species deserves some respect, just as human life does? We *can* extend our respect. We went through that over the last two weeks. So why should we? Let me approach the point another way by writing something on the board:

2. *Life is not something you waste.*

Imagine a child who grew up thinking that life *is* something you waste. Let us further suppose that he makes one distinction and thinks that human life is an exception to this rule. For some special reason according to him, human life is not something you waste. Other forms of life, however, are some things you waste. Would this child be able to become a mature adult?

To begin with, this child would be extremely imprudent. Wasting life is dangerous. A limited grasp of ecology shows this. Living beings exist in complicated interdependence with each other, even if the relationship is often antagonistic. To think that life is something you waste is to run over this fact, because at the very least, wasting nonhuman life opens us up to ecological problems. We saw this reasoning a little bit in lecture three, under the prudential justification of an ecological orientation. It's not in the interest of society across generations to have people who think life is something you waste.

Yet we are searching for a more direct moral reason to respect nonhuman life, right? So consider this. A child who grew up learning life is something you waste would be thoughtless and destructive. Why is that? The child would be destructive, because the primary sense of being destructive is destroying life, and this the child would do as a matter of course, at least insofar as he acted on the belief that life is something you waste. "What a fine day!" the child could say. "Today I will go down to the stream and squash some toads. That is fun: to watch them die." Or he could say, "What a day this was! I walked home from school, tore out several bushes just for the hell of it, stepped on a lot of bugs, pushed the neighbor's dog into the road when a truck came by, and thought about how I might use the elm tree in the back yard for a hatchet-testing zone." Or this young man could grow up and think, "Well, today is a day to make a profit. I will sacrifice several species for the sake of cattle grazing land. I will then pump the cattle full of antibiotics and keep them in pens that make them break out in sores and distress them. I will make them eat the remains of their fellow cattle to save some money I would have spent on food for them. Then I will hack them to pieces and eat them." All that is destructive.

Why is it thoughtless? Life is something rare. Without life, nothing in *our* world of meaning would be, because *we* wouldn't be. We wouldn't be without other living beings. Take a look at the planet Pluto. There's no life there, just like in most other—or maybe all other—places in the universe. Who knows? All we know of meaning is possible because of life, specifically, other living beings besides ourselves. These are facts. Other living beings make our meaningful life possible, and the fact of life itself is rare and a source of wonder if only because it makes our meaning possible.

Moreover, when we attend to other living beings, we can't help but be open to analogical identifications. We may not choose to acknowledge these identifications, but we are open to them as humans. They are in the realm of our possibility. And such identifications are meaningful. They help us understand, at the least, our relationships with the wide universe of life. These identifications are so deep in human cultures that we literally could not understand *world literature, religion, history, architecture, painting, sculpture, design, jewelry, symbols, languages, tattoos, postcards, names of cars, children's stories, homeless people's gardens, poems, adolescent kids who love to go camping, old people who hike, gardeners, proud farmers who care for the land, Russian films, the connotations of colors, why oceans are mysterious, why birds are amazing when they fly, pets, songs, zoos, photos, and mornings,* if we neglected to understand and use these analogical identifications *at all.* To think analogically in the ways specified two weeks ago, to acknowledge how life is part of human meaning and one of its conditions, and to grasp how life is rare, is to understand that life is not something you waste. Wasting it is thoughtless. You don't get what human life is about.

What I'm saying is that it is thoughtless and destructive to think life is something you waste, and that a kid who grows up with that belief becomes an adult who is not fit for society. Why? Because he is clueless about what makes human life pulse and mindless about what destruction is. I contend that we can't think of such as person as someone who is maturely socialized. Something has gone wrong.

*

Do you want to take a break? I see hands up. No? Alex:
I don't get the point about how analogical identifications help us see life is not something you waste. You gave this long list of things we couldn't understand without that identification.

Good. Basically, I was saying that when you think life is something you waste, you are thoughtless, first, because life is a condition of all meaning and, second, because so much of human experience assumes that life is not something you waste. You take yourself out of human meaning by holding such a view. The idea here is that even if you could go around with such a view, why would you want to? Meaning—that subtle and often fragile thing—depends on life not being something you waste. At least, this is a precondition of meaning and holds true in countless areas of human experience. It is thoughtless to fly in the face of such a condition, although it may be nihilistically possible in some sense. Ecological identifications underline the thoughtlessness. For instance, when your child races out into the clear and sunny day after a week of rain, do you want to fail to identify with her joy?

There's another way to put this point, too. The meaning of human time is inextricably bound up with analogical identifications. That long list involved varying forms and degrees of respect for life. If you think life is something you waste, you lose touch with how to orient oneself toward the human good, because that good is made up of ecological identifications in the form of embedded analogies that constitute large stretches of the meaning of human time. The good of all the things on that list supposed ecological identification. If you have no respect for life, no goods from that list are open to you.

Finally, if we raise children who think life is something you waste, we raise children unable to hold ecological identifications consistently. That means the identifications lose their point and a great part of human culture becomes foreign. That's thoughtless of us to do that to the children, because it makes them thoughtless about shared experience. That won't do for socialization either.

*

Are you sure you don't want a break? No? Fine.

To bring the argument home, let me spell out why being destructive is bad. We just assumed it is, earlier. It is bad for society to have destructive people for a number of reasons. First of all, life's ecological interdependencies are often indirectly for our good, and so a destructive person increases the risk to our good. Second, nonhuman life forms are the subject of people's attachments so that one hurts people by hurting their attachments. That was somebody's dog, after all. And there are many who have a history in this forest. Moreover, many enjoy that river today. A destructive person is a greater risk to property. Even more, he risks doing away with what matters to others even if he owns it. Third, people who think they have license to destroy nonhuman life when they want are a risk to meaning we may someday want or need. Preservationists of biodiversity often make this point about the possibility of destroying a future cure for disease in making plants extinct. But there are reasons beyond medicinal uses why we might want or need that life form to be preserved. Given how meaningful nonhuman life is for so many areas of human society, it is not in society's interest to breed people who are willing to destroy what may some day be meaningful. Finally, destructiveness overlooks something we began with. When we learn to respect each other, we learn to respect each other's lives. And although life is not some mysterious, abstract property, it is a predicate we make of living kinds. In learning to respect each other's lives, we learn that life itself is something special. This is a large reason why analogical identification can work. Destructive people don't understand this. Life is something that ought to be seen as special, even if only human life is initially seen as so special as to deserve our respect while other life forms are just things. Nonetheless, destructiveness overlooks how *all* living beings are not just things.

For these four reasons and probably more (Can you come up with more?), destroying life for no good reason is bad, and mature members of society should understand this. The simplest way to do so, of course, is to understand that all life deserves some respect. That way, you don't destroy it without a good reason. Because you have to respect it, you have to have a special reason to destroy it. Taking life demands justification. Life deserves some respect.

Look, this old man needs a fifteen-minute break.

* * *

I want to begin again with an objection. Before break, I rephrased our point about respect in terms of the idea that life is not something you waste. That idea still needs explaining. After all, life could be something you don't waste because you *use* it. One can use something thoroughly and not give it any respect. In that case, one would not waste the thing but would not respect it either. Or what we mean by respect would be little more than how one works with a machine so that it doesn't break. Yet respect for life should not be the same thing as respect for one's BMW.

Here's how not wasting life and respect for life go hand in hand. In general, life is not wasted only when living beings are let be or integrated with our form of life. To just use nonhuman life would be to waste it and lose most of its meaning. When you look at what human culture has made of identifications with nonhuman life, what you often see is admiration for the freeness of that life or appreciation of the integration that life can have with our own. Such integration includes pets, gardens, and even meals where the feast on an animal involves gratitude for its sacrifice to us. Such integration is not mere use of the nonhuman life form, but is also treating it as a being with dignity. The freeness of a life form is its autonomy from us. It is not, of course, freedom or autonomy proper: free dominion and self-rule. Animals do not rule or have dominion, in the precise sense of those words. They do not use rules, give them, or establish realms of legitimate authority. Still, we say animals—and plants too—are free in some sense when they are let be. The freeness of a non-human is a large part of its flourishing. It does its own thing. This is what the early modern rationalist Spinoza meant when he said all living beings have a "conatus," something they push to be out of a drive to remain in the proper existence of their form.[15] Think of a caged animal wanting to get out or a tree turning toward the light once it is released from some sculpted gardening that bent it in a direction it would not naturally go.[16]

I want to say here that the meaning of nonhuman life for humans, both on its own and integrated with us, is bound up with this relative autonomy of life, the way it does its own thing. That is why it is amazing we have pets or make gardens, and why it is amazing to human cultures, across time and around the world, that birds fly or that oceans thrive with creatures like the vampire squid. Who would have thought it possible? Who could make the creature do that? It does its own thing. To not let life be, without justification, is to waste life and drain it of the core of its meaning. Letting life be, unless justified otherwise, is a necessary condition on not wasting it or thoughtlessly exhausting its meaning. When we live knowing that life is not something you waste but is something meaningful, we must let it be unless we have a justification. That is, we must respect it.

*

Without respect for life, there can be no full socialization. That is what I have just argued. Humans are social animals, and part of our identity is made of our socialization. In this way, part of our sense of humanity depends on respect for life. Without respect for life, we do not have a working sense of humanity. This means that respect for life is socially necessary to our identity as humans and that when we lose having at least some respect for all life, we become dehumanized. We lose part of our humanity and lose our *full* humanity as well. This means that in addition to being disrespectful, we lose touch with ourselves. This self-obfuscation is a further bad thing about not respecting all life at all. We can't know ourselves fully as humans without giving all life some respect. That is tragic, because it is in our power to change our ways, and yet we can persist obfuscating how we are fully the humans that we are.

One of my early points on the board was that we need to understand why identity is being invoked in this argument. I believe we can now see why. What's at stake in this argument is whether we can ever be fully clear with ourselves. It is not only the other animals and the wide reaches of the plant world that suffer or wither when humans are categorically disrespectful of them. *We* suffer too, an invisible suffering whose form is a loss of meaning and self-clarity. It is a subtle and meaning-eroding thing to lose one's humanity, part by part. It is like walking around with a wound in your back while you are high on drugs and can't feel any pain. As you laugh and run through the streets, you bleed to death.[17] Of course, the blood here symbolizes a meaningful life, and the wound is something we've done to ourselves. We can't know ourselves fully as humans without giving all life some respect.

This much helps us see why respect for life must be part of human identity for us to be true to ourselves as socialized humans. Why should we bring out respect for life, though? Why think respect for life belongs to what is *best* in us? These questions bear on our identity as humans in a further way than we've seen up to now. The answer to the first question is that we should bring out respect for life, because it belongs to what is best in us and because humans should strive for excellence. The answer to the second question is that respect for life belongs to what is best in us, because it leads us to being generous. I will explain these answers in the remainder of today's time.

First, assume until we answer the second question that respect for life is part of what is best in us. Why should we strive for excellence? The answer is that striving for excellence is part of human identity: our idealistic side realized. We are a kind of living being that develops through our ideas about where we should grow and what we should become. The motivator of that development is what is *good* and especially what is best. After all, only by reaching out of ourselves toward what makes us dynamically evolve do we truly grow. In that way, what is best is like the carrot that hangs in front of the donkey's mouth to make it move forward. Realizing ourselves as humans requires being dynamically engaged with the pursuit of what makes us develop, and the way we develop is idealistically, through what we should become.

Nietzsche put this point another way. He said we are "self-overcoming" when we are true to ourselves.[18] The idea is ingenious. To be authentic is to be true to who you are. Who are we if we are truly alive only when we grow? Answer: We are *developmental* beings. To be true to yourself as a developmental being is to be true to development. And the moment of development is the moment when your old self is overcome by a new one. Hence, *the authentic moment for a human is the moment of developmental transformation.* That is the moment where we seek what is best, the moment of pursuing excellence.

One of Kierkegaard's most intimate pseudonyms said this another way: *humans are a despair that ideals will not be realized, and to become more human must be and is to develop faith in those ideals.*[19] This is a subtle and emotionally powerful way of saying we are dynamic beings who, being idealistic at heart, must pursue excellence in order to be authentic.

Nietzsche and Kierkegaard help us understand why idealism is not after an elitist excellence, but is the kind of thing that could structure such commonly human endeavors as the American Civil Rights Movement and Martin Luther King Jr.'s speeches. "We shall overcome" is both idealistic and humane, humane *because* it is idealistic. "I have a dream" is, thus, what is fully human, not living without a dream.[20] As King well expects his audience to understand and as countless people have since then understood, to fail to have a dream is to go soul-dead. It's to fail to develop. That is a final way to state my answer to why we should pursue what is best in us as a constitutive feature of being truly human.[21]

*

That leaves us with our last question. If we should strive for the best, why think respect for life is part of it? We are true to ourselves when we are idealistic. The carrot at the end of idealism's stick is the notion of what is best. Why is respect for life in an extensive and pervasive way among what is best in us? There are a number of reasons with which I'll start. Yet at bottom I want to claim respecting life belongs to what is best in us, because it leads toward giving. And giving is best, because it is the self-overcoming *par excellence*.

What are some of those reasons? First, respect for life brings out what is meaningful. Second, it is thoughtful. Third, it is nondestructive. We have already visited these reasons by looking at why we should not waste life.

Respecting life, though, we are guided by them. It's as if respect for life is a part of a whole set of character traits that includes fostering what is meaningful, being thoughtful and not destroying things, and where every part of that set supports the others, with respect for life being the foundation.

Also, respect for life is a necessary condition on love for life. Without respect, there is no true love. Moreover, when we respect life thoroughly, bringing out the respect and deepening it, we develop what in practice (if not in sentiment) is love for life. True love wants the loved one to be free and healthy, and this is exactly what respect fosters.

There's more. Loving in practice is giving. Since bringing out respect leads us toward love for life, it should lead us toward giving ourselves. What we give is nothing less, but also nothing more, than our space and care.

People often forget that giving ourselves out of love for what is respect-worthy is what is most authentically human. Self-giving to what is respect-worthy is a way we devote ourselves to what is worthy of our time, care and attention. When something is respect-worthy, it deserves respect. That means it matters, and not in a fungible way. It matters, period. Basic respect is categorical. When we give ourselves to someone or something respect-worthy, we structure our lives in terms of what matters, period. Moreover, we let go of serving what is unworthy of respect to give our time to what is. When we stop to think about it, there is so much in our world that is unworthy of respect. There is so much that does not matter, period, but matters only because of how we can use it to make us feel satisfied for a short period of time. Later, we hardly remember it—what's the point? It's not something we die remembering as what made life worth living, and it's not something we tell our grandchildren with pride. But things that matter, period, are things worth remembering when we die, things worth telling our grandkids, and are things that mark life with significance. They have memorial power, perhaps because they are not fungible, but mark out the structure of our world. They are categorical features of our identity. When we give ourselves to what is respect-worthy, we clarify our lives toward what is fully good and worth remembering. Such clarity is no small thing.

Also, as I said above, even this clarity is secondary to the developmental importance of giving oneself away for the sake of what matters, here, for what is respect-worthy. Self-giving for what is respect-worthy is the essence of human idealism and so the essence of human development. The simple word for it is *devotion*. Devotion is part of the best of us, because only through it do we give ourselves to what is worth fostering and thereby grow. So bringing out respect for life brings out our devotion and in turn makes us grow. Without bringing it out, we fail what matures us, which is to fail ourselves. Striving to respect life is authentically human, and failing to respect life is both immature and inauthentic.

There are other benefits to devoting oneself to respected life. When we respect life around us more and more—appreciating it for doing its own thing, trying to integrate with it and not just destroy it, showing gratitude for its loss at our feasts—its meaning for us opens up more and more. The sense that it gives us life grows. What is amazing about it becomes more apparent. Our sense of relationship grows, as does our ability to care. This is the way it is with what one practically loves. More love, more openness to meaning. More devotion, more provision from what one loves. More attention to the respect-worthy, more wonder. More respect, more relationship. More love, more ability to love.

We can use the sea, and even show some respect for its life, having zones where no fish may be caught. But it is another thing entirely when we try to respect it as much as we can. *All that life* is there, unknown to us, the source of our very evolution, varied, and bizarre. Its incandescent creatures make a mirror, far beneath the surface, of the stars in the sky, high above the ocean, every night when we sleep. By letting that life be, we can appreciate it more. By trying to integrate with it, not just waste it (as our fishing industries and toxic practices increasingly do), we can form relationships with a wider world than our own. By giving ourselves to the life in it, sacrificing our pleasures for its good, we structure our own lives around what matters, period, and not something simply fungible or ephemeral. We grow up.

Of course, people can reply: Food on my table matters, *period!* I have kids. They need to be fed. Tuna is cheap. They need to eat. Don't *tell* me about sacrificing myself for the big blue tuna. My kids need to *eat* the big blue tuna.

I hear you. But this reply is desperate. We know (if we attend to our socialization and refuse to be pushed off the fact that life is something special *and we know it*), we know that in the ideal world, the blue tuna could be caught in ways that do not render it extinct, destroy the ocean floor, or involve tons of by-catch. We could be grateful for the blue tuna filling our bellies from time to time. And we know that we might even have a world where our children would not be so hungry, given all the potential for food production in this technological world, and that we might have time to think about what is best to do. Certainly, ours is not the ideal world. The point is, it is not the *only* world either. Listen to most children, by the way: they find it confusing that we read them stories filled with Tommy the Tuna and then eat him.[22]

All my argument commits us to is effort. And not on the back of single working mothers who have three jobs, alcoholic husbands who are regularly abusive, and lack of family support. It commits *us* to effort, those of us who can take this course or read books on citizenship. This is what we came for, isn't it? To grow up just a little? Or to recharge ourselves? Or to associate ideas for creative decisions? These are matters of our society, and they are matters of common humanity. All I am saying is that to live up to our identities as humans, we need to work for what is ideal. And—please!—don't tell me that with all the ingenuity in the world, all the luxury, and all the potential for passionate self-giving, we can't come up with a way to catch fish, respect species threatened with extinction, and feed each other that is *more* respectful of life. Because what we have now is not *even* respectful of life.

Notes

1. On both of these claims, see Jonathan Glover, *Humanity: A Moral History of the Twentieth Century*, New Haven: Yale University Press, 1999; Theodore Zeldin, *An Intimate History of Humanity*, New York: Harper Perennial, 1994; and Diamond's "The Importance of Being Human," in *Human Beings*, ed. David Cockburn, New York: Cambridge University Press, 1991.

2. See Jean-Jacques Rousseau, *Discourse on the Origins of Inequality among Humans*, Indianapolis: Hackett Publishing, 1993.

3. This condition is found in both sides of the Atlantic in different philosophical traditions. See T.M. Scanlon, *What We Owe to Each Other*, Cambridge, MA: Harvard University Press, 1998; and Emmanuel Levinas, *Totality and Infinity*, Pittsburgh: Duquesne University Press, 1969.

4. Although I do not think swearing is always or all that bad—it can at times be good—I am not swearing in this sentence, but referring to the problem of evil. Part of human moral life is dealing with the problem of evil. See Susan Neiman, *Evil in Modern Thought: An Alternative History of Philosophy*, Princeton: Princeton University Press, 2002. A "lot" is a luck of the draw. And some of our lots are unlucky: we end up in a hellish situation. Then we have a hell of a lot to consider: as Jews, Romanies, the mentally disabled, gays, prostitutes, and communists did in the 1930s in Germany; as Bosnian children did in Sarajevo in the early 1990s; as Palestinians in the occupied territories and everyday people in Iraq do; as people in domestic situations where there is violence against them do; or as people whose way of life attracts phobic violence against them do. The problem of evil, ironically, reminds us how deeply moral we are and how much we have to talk about.

5. Thomas Hobbes, *Leviathan*, New York: Penguin Classics, 1982.

6. On this point, see Vivian Paley, *The Kindness of Children*, Cambridge, MA: Harvard University Press, 1999; Rousseau, *Emile*, trans. Alan Bloom, New York: Basic Books, 1978; and Jonathan Glover, *Humanity*.

7. On this point, again see Zeldin, *An Intimate History of Humanity*.

8. Gaita, *The Philosopher's Dog*, London: Routledge, 2003.

9. This point about what we learn to recognize in becoming a member of the human community is a point one can arguably find in Wittgenstein's *Philosophical Investigations*, part II. The psychological (including early childhood neurodevelopmental) basis for it can be found in Stephen Mitchell, *Relational Concepts in Psychoanalysis: An Integration*, Cambridge, MA: Harvard University Press, 1988, chap. 1.

10. For more on this point, see Paley, *The Kindness of Children* and Mitchell, *Relational Concepts in Psychoanalysis: An Integration*.

11. See for instance, John Dewey, *Democracy and Education*, New York: Free Press, 1944.

12. This point is well made by Thompson, "The Representation of Life," in *Virtues and Reasons: Essays in Honor of Philippa Foot*, ed. R. Hursthouse, W. Quinn, et al., New York: Oxford University Press, 1995.

13. Thompson, "The Representation of Life," in *Virtues and Reasons*.

14. On this point, see Martha Nussbaum, *Women and Human Development: The Capabilities Approach*, New York: Cambridge University Press, 2000.

15. See Benedict de Spinoza's *Ethics*, Indianapolis: Hackett Publishing, 1991.

16. The image of the tree comes from Rousseau's *Emile*, book I, where it is a metaphor for *children* once they receive a humane education!

17. I read a story about a case similar to this one when I was in college. It haunted me, and I use such an image because I want to underline to listeners that the erosion of our humanity through thoughtless destruction of life is a troubling matter.

18. Friedrich Nietzsche, *Thus Spoke Zarathustra*, New York: Penguin Classics, 1978.

19. Søren Kierkegaard (a.k.a. Ante-Climacus), *The Sickness unto Death*, Princeton: Princeton University Press, 1983.

20. Thoreau, whom King read, prefigured this point in the conclusion of *Walden*.

21. See Martin Luther King Jr., *A Testament of Hope: The Essential Writings and Speeches of Martin Luther King Jr.*, San Francisco: Harper, 1990.

22. Cora Diamond makes this point about children in "Eating Meat and Eating People," in *The Realistic Spirit*, Cambridge, MA: MIT Press, 1995. Susan Neiman recently brought it up in an argument for vegetarianism, without knowing of Diamond's essay (personal discussion, Berlin, August 2005).

Maturity's Idealism

For Jim Davidson, a great teacher

Thanks for coming outside. We rescheduled to the afternoon, so we could enjoy the fall before it gets too cold, and we got lucky. The weather is warm enough. Remember, in two weeks, we will meet at the Forestry School's preserve out in the country. Your discussion leaders have the buses' departure time. Today, we're in this small amphitheater. Soon, the forest. Does anyone know: does the Drama Department perform Greek tragedies here? In two weeks, we'll be inside the preserve barn, which is an interesting place itself, historical, preserving early nineteenth century New England. Today, enjoy the trees over us with their rusts and reds.[1]

For the remaining lectures, we'll depart from the previous. Last week, we passed a threshold in our argument. We can now see what the world should be like if the argument holds. We will be looking at personal development and social change. What do we have to do to bring out what is best in us? We are already greener than we think, but that's not good enough. How do we intensify our connection with life on Earth? How should social change proceed so that the Earth is brought out in the politics and economy of the world?

If we have good reason to become citizens of Earth, and if doing so is a matter of common humanity, then we should change our characters and habits. Our institutions should increasingly show respect for all life. We should keep growing, because the upshot of our argument so far is that to be authentically human is to respect life increasingly. That devotion ought to be part of our effort to live well. Being true to ourselves entails greening our culture.

Today's lecture is about maturing. Next week and following, I will focus on social change. Remember, when we were introduced to ecological justice, I argued that institutional measures are often more fitting for ecological problems than are personal deeds. The scale of ecological problems and the difficulty of being personally responsible for them are large. Thus I already suggested that citizenship, not private morality, would be a theme in these lectures. Ultimately, these lectures are part of what you might call "citizenship studies." *I don't want us to think only of morality, and I don't want us to think only of politics, but I want us to think of both together.* The main place where morality and politics join is in citizenship. By maturing, we can become better citizens. The main point of becoming a better citizen is to make our institutions better, to produce positive social change. So today we explore forming citizenship. Then, over the next two weeks, we will explore how a citizen might induce social change, what she might aim for and how she might get there.

The title of today's lecture is "maturity's idealism," because that is what I think citizens should have to be true to earthly humanity. Maturity is an idea that resonates with the language of socialization used last time, the idea of becoming mature in a society. Today, we will explore some of the features we ought to acquire to become maturely socialized, given that our sense of humanity ought to be ecological. How should ecological respect for life pervade our characters? How should we behave so as to develop an ethos of respect for all life?

I want to begin our exploration of these questions by returning to the notion of socialization from last lecture. Socialization makes us a member of society, able to live well with others. What we have now argued is that it should also include becoming a member of a society meeting the universe of life. We should be able to live well with other forms of life.

Ecological Social Maturity

Ecological social maturity is being able to live well not only with each other, but also with other forms of life.

The key idea in socialization is the idea of *living with* others. What we have clarified is that the others with whom we live include what the ecofeminist philosopher Val Plumwood calls "Earth others"—the other forms of life living on, above or in this planet among humans.[2] How do we improve on respecting life so that we live maturely with other life forms?

Remember, idealistic self-overcoming is authentically human. Some philosophers call such a view "perfectionist." The perfectionist school of thought holds that we are *not* perfect, and so have room to grow.[3] The point is made less moralistically, however. As psychoanalysts and philosophers of education have long explained, one condition of a healthy mind is that it keeps growing. "You should never stop growing" is therefore an old wise saying, because it is developmentally accurate.[4] Accordingly, we seek a form of socialization that grows, that does not learn one lesson and quit. Socialization should not remain stagnant. What keeps us growing in our efforts to live with other forms of life? What makes a person keep greening over a lifetime? (By the way, "green" works here because it suggests growth, rejuvenation, and being ecological.)

As philosophers of education know, the heart of development is lifelong learning. Lifelong learning consists in habits and attitudes that hold us as learners throughout life and not just while we complete a degree. When we learn *how* to learn, we position ourselves to learn throughout life.[5] Analogously, when we learn how to develop ecologically, we learn how to live up to the ideal in socialization across changes in cultural, economic, political, and personal circumstance. That is authentic. Also, since our circumstances often change (especially in light of ecological problems), it is worth developing a habit of lifelong learning and setting it as the goal of our investigation. Such a habit would also be a characteristically American attitude, at least according to American pragmatism.[6]

Lifelong learning fits the idea of maturity well. After all, the key to maturity is to learn how to mature. Mature people know how to grow. The idea, then, is to find elements of our character allowing us to grow within the ecological dimensions of society. Within those dimensions, we seek habits, because habits keep patterns of action consistent. The habits we want, in turn, are habits that improve our understanding and practice of how to live with other forms of life.

How do we know what these habits are? Our contemporary economy certainly does not cultivate them. In fact, our contemporary economy erodes the very language of respect, pressuring everything toward a resource or a value. That is how powerfully the economy reworks our habits, even our speech. So we need to think. What concepts do we use to understand living with others?

One would appear to be the concept of *integration*. When we live with others, we are integrated. The first indication of a good, ecological habit might be that, through it, we can integrate with other life forms, or that the habit directly promotes integration. Does a society of people with these habits, whatever they turn out to be, coexist with the other species on this planet? Does a society of such people allow the biosphere to support human life well, rather than causing problems? Can we find habits that allow or create a balance between human needs and the needs of other living kinds? Call this demand of maturity "the integration criterion."

The Integration Criterion

A developmental habit is ecologically mature if and only if it helps us balance, or opens us up to balance, human needs with the needs of the other life forms on Earth.

I will discuss the logic of this criterion in a moment. First, let me find others. What else would solidify our ability to live with Earth others?

We know that when we develop socially, we become more human. Of course, it is not entirely clear what it means to "become more human." How do we judge that? Is it like a tingling in our human thalamus or the pineal gland?[7] Yet we commonly do speak of becoming more human, especially when we become more attuned to our collective life, true to ourselves, open minded about the shape life can take, and when we solidify our nondestructiveness. When we say someone is deeply human or some other like compliment, we mean she understands human life and what makes it meaningful across a range of life situations: death, birth, love, hatred, family, procreation, work, food, sleep, shelter, sickness, health … Also, becoming more human, we become more faithful to who we are.

Perhaps, then, there are ways ecological maturity makes us more human? We already saw an intimation of this during our discussion of the homeless gardener, Jimmy. If ecological identification could establish his self-respect and root his being at home, we might come to ourselves and attune our respect as we shade our world in green. In this way, the second principle of good developmental habits would be that they humanize us. Call this criterion "the humanization criterion."

The Humanization Criterion

A developmental habit is ecologically mature if and only if it makes us more fully human or maintains our humanity without undermining it.

The humanization criterion may involve restraint. Given the way our economy provides powerful incentives for states, corporations, organizations, and people to cater to economic interests, developing maturity should involve knowing when to say "enough"—or as Arabic speakers say, "cghelas"![8] The exploitative tendencies of capitalism pressure the Earth's life to give up resources for profit and pressure us, too, to work more for less. Maturity in such an environment involves drawing the line against what is dehumanizing, much as our culture drew the line against slavery, child labor, and the more-than-eight-hour workday. The humanization criterion selects habits that maintain the categorical nature of respect for life. It selects habits that do not let our identity erode through capitalist pressure, including ideological pressure to change the very language of our lives toward a resource- and value-centered life.

Are there other criteria of ecological maturity? As we saw in our second week's lecture on justice, moral attention in many environmental matters calls for an expanded sense of human agency in context. We saw this with reference to expanded temporal, spatial, and biological frames of reference. To take one example, global warming is likely to affect many future generations and to build over more than a lifetime. Moreover, it seems to be affected by actions patterned across the globe. Finally, it makes us realize that our health is dependent on our ecosystems and the overall stability of the biosphere. This point about interdependencies is one we haven't emphasized enough. But the great environmentalist Aldo Leopold did. He even made the point into something he called "the land ethic."

In his classic book from 1949, Leopold urged his readers to "think like a mountain."[9] What this meant is that we should think of our existence in a natural order where there are many checks and balances—that is, antagonisms and symbioses. Drawing on an example from American history, Leopold noted that you can shoot all the wolves in Yosemite Valley, and this might seem a good thing not only for tourists and campers, but also for ranchers. Yet when the wolves go, the elk and deer proliferate without any major predator against them. The check has been lifted, and the imbalance starts. Soon the trees are grazed at an alarming rate and the saplings torn to shreds. If things go badly, other ground-grazing animals start to have a hard time, especially when they depend on the first six feet of trees. If things go very badly, fewer trees can mean fewer seeds and bugs to eat, a problem for birds, and much erosion due to decreased root mass in the area. Then topsoil drains away, and this decreases the fertility of the mountainside. By contrast, to think like a mountain is to contextualize human flourishing within its ecology and to be aware of interdependencies ahead of time. That requires a broad frame of mind and ecological knowledge.

Urged, then, by our discussion of ecological justice and also by Leopold's famous imperative, it seems to me that a good habit in green development will be one that sustains our "thinking like a mountain" (or "like the atmos-phere" for that matter). We seek a habit cultivating our sensitivity to eco-logical interdependences and our ecology, so that we conceive of ourselves as part of what Leopold called a "land community." We want a habit of open-ing our minds so that we comprehend how our good is bound up with the good of other living beings. For brevity's sake, I will call this criterion "the Leopoldian criterion," in honor of the environmentalist from the twentieth century who first developed a new, moral picture for our ecological future.

The Leopoldian Criterion

A developmental habit is ecologically mature if and only if it cultivates, maintains, or allows our sensitivity to ecological interdependence and to our ecology.

There is one last criterion that seems obvious. So far we have looked to how developmental habits might balance our lives with Earth life, how these habits should deepen our sense of humanity, and how they should relocate agency within a broad, ecological order. What, though, about the other lives themselves? Should respect for them call us to think of their good all on its own? It might seem we have a self-defensive view of ecological development at the moment, not the kind of expansive maturity for which our rhetoric seems to call, and as does our location today under the rusts and reds. How directed toward others should our habits be?

The answer, it would seem, is *very*. The entire sense of the respect for life in our socialization is to respect *that life*—whatever it may be. Society is not made solely of a self-regarding respect, a self-vigilance clearing space for oth-ers. Rather, society is also composed of our looking out for each other's good.[10] Just so, we have duties, born of respect we owe each other.[11] Where is our equivalent in ecological matters? Genuine society shows people at-tending thoughtfully to each other's good. We need something analogous for environmental matters. I propose it will be found in habits thoughtful of the good of other living beings. Thus we search for developmental habits thoughtful of other forms of life. Call this "the thoughtfulness criterion."

The Thoughtfulness Criterion

A developmental habit is ecologically mature if and only if it keeps us attentive to the good of other life forms, or does not interfere with our background commitment to respect life as a socialized human.

The way I've framed this last criterion deserves comment. Remember that we established respect for life as a background commitment of proper socialization. This commitment was part of the background idealism of being human. Given these conclusions, we should remember that the picture I've presented is one in which idealism and morality are authentically human. Out of the drive to be true to what is worthy of our time, human life exists within a background pressure to evolve in respect for life. I count on this pressure as one counts on human spirit. Human kindness is authentic, unless we are trained to be unkind, as children often are by the institutions into which we grow.[12]

Let's summarize and reflect on these criteria now.

Four Criteria for Habits That Help Us Mature Ecologically

1. The integration criterion
2. The humanization criterion
3. The Leopoldian criterion
4. The thoughtfulness criterion

First, about the logic. We should note that each of the criteria poses necessary and sufficient conditions on green developmental habits. Each one states a habit is green "if and only if" some condition. The "only if" signifies a necessary condition, and the "if" signifies a sufficient condition. Since each criterion is a necessary condition, each must be satisfied to make a developmental habit green. Since, too, each criterion is sufficient, *any* of the four satisfied makes a developmental habit green. Does this pose a contradiction? On the one hand, we are saying each of the four criteria must be in place, and on the other hand we are saying that any one of them will do. What is taking shape?

The answer is simple. Any one of the criteria implies the others. For instance, being thoughtful of other life forms makes us more human, balances our needs with those of other living beings and leads us to knowing our ecology. Or consider the Leopoldian criterion. Coming to know that our good is bound up with the good of other living beings makes us conceptualize integration, and so in turn thoughtfulness, and it makes us more human because it highlights our human condition. As a thought experiment, you might try seeing how the other two criteria imply the rest, practically speaking (go ahead; try it).

* * *

Also, the above criteria do not exclude the human good from being an ecological matter. That's what's cool about them. After all, according to the view presented here, what humanizes us should help us balance our needs with those of other beings; maintain, cultivate or at least allow a sense of our interdependence with those others; and keep us, or at least not hinder us from being, attentive to the good of those others. All this might seem strange, because I'm claiming when we are humanized—even if not in a directly ecological way—that humanization is nonetheless ecological. In other words, I'm conceptualizing our development as essentially ecological. Can I do that? I mean, it would seem some things that humanize us don't have ecological implications.

Let me give some examples. Take love for each other, which humanizes us. It helps us know our needs, a condition on balancing needs. It should produce more of a capacity for care in us, and it should support a grasp of the human condition of the loved one, which is ecological. Finally, because we learn to attend to each other's good, we are better able to identify analogously with the good of other kinds. So love for each other is indirectly ecological.

Or take humor, which humanizes us. When does humor humanize us? Or rather, when does it not? It certainly does not when it excludes members of the human community, or when it detaches us from the human good. Rather, what is humanizing about humor—as Bergson saw— is that it maintains our connection with our mortal and imperfect condition.[13] In that sense, it enables us, even if indirectly, to be thoughtful of the good of other kinds, of our interdependence with them, and of our mutual and often competing needs on Earth. This really isn't hyperbole. A sense of humor helps one relate to nature. Eric, Maclean's story that you love so much, *A River Runs Through It*, demonstrates that point. Because the brothers in the story can laugh at their own and others' clumsy attempts to live, they are freed up to see how much nature involves pragmatic innovation and a determination to survive. Having a good sense of humor does not hinder us from being ecological, but frees us up to see ourselves and our relation to the Earth, even if that is not its intent. In this sense, a habit of laughing could be ecological. I'm not saying that all good jokes are about nature, but that all humanizing jokes leave us be and at the least do not interfere with our understanding of the human condition. In that way, they support our being part of the natural world. We need to learn to hear how the dimensions of our humanity are saturated with ecological implications.

If we weren't so used to thinking humans are antiecological, what I'm saying would be common sense. We are part of nature, and we are ecological. Our human good is a part of ecological considerations, just as we are a part of the world's systems of life. Thus, humanizing ourselves is not antiecological.

On the contrary, it is necessary for being ecological, and to humanize ourselves is itself an ecological act. We are a species among many, after all, a specific kind of life. What the criteria underline yet again is that it is antiecological to respect life without including humans in that respect for life, and alternately it is antiecological to conceptualize human life as if it existed in a vacuum.

We seek habits, then, that keep us developing in ways that improve, or at least enable, our thoughtfulness with other forms of life, our open-mindedness about interdependency, our sense of meaningful and resistant humanity, and our integration with Earth life. What are some of those habits?

*

One way to look at determining these habits is to think about the obstacles we face against becoming ecologically mature. Then we can think about how the above developmental qualities gel with the problems with which we're faced. There are a number of major obstacles to ecological maturity. Here are four:

Four Obstacles to Ecological Maturity

1. Moral invisibility
2. Ecological illiteracy
3. Lifestyle rigidity
4. The political block

Let me explain them:

1. *Moral invisibility.* How can people be respectful if they are ignorant of what deserves respect? When you are ignorant of something, you have no idea how it exists. Much thoughtlessness is the by-catch of ignorance. The moral invisibility of life forms and of ecological destruction is a serious problem. As we've already indicated, this invisibility is perpetuated at the level of our language, much as the expression "collateral damage" masks the reality of civilians killed by bombs. Fish are living beings, not "resources."

Have we remembered the concerns of Dr. Earle when we have eaten aquatic life (for instance, at the recent dinner to honor philosophy majors)? We do not stop to consider what cost bringing those filets to us had. The workings of the industrial fishing industry are invisible to us unless we make a special effort to discover them. The question of by-catch and habitat destruction from industrial fishing nets is not even a passing thought in our minds. Abuse of life goes on for our suppers, and we don't blink.[14] A person who is ecologically mature should be in the habit of knowing the general conditions of industries like the fishing industry, so as to remove the moral invisibility of nonhuman forms of life. One of the ways she might start is by making sure she thinks of fish as living beings, not just resources. What kind of habit will help her do that?

2. *Ecological illiteracy.* Remember Leopold's example of culling wolves in Yosemite? One of the ways to understand what went wrong in that example is that people who culled wolves in Yosemite were ecologically illiterate. They didn't know how to read ecosystems and understand the indirect effects of their actions. Much the same could be said of the example concerning global warming from our lecture on justice. There we met up with an every-day American woman, well meaning and industrious, who like most other Americans unwittingly contributes to an ecological process that could have massive and severe consequences for future generations. A large reason such a pattern of action can seem tolerable to everyday people is that most people are ecologically illiterate about the risks associated with the plausibility of global warming. In these cases and so many others, not understanding how our actions affect ourselves and other forms of life makes for an obstacle to ecological citizenship.

3. *Lifestyle rigidity.* A further problem with developing ecological maturity is having a rigid style of life. There are many people aware of how their lifestyle contributes to ecological destruction, but who are fixed in their habits. Too much about our lives seems either comfortable or necessary as is. For example, a good many Americans do not see how they could manage to ride public transportation instead of driving, let alone work politically to en-sure swift, clean, and reliable public transportation is available. Or how might we begin to ensure that the packaging for food we eat (especially at restaurants and take-out joints) is biodegradable? How about greening the standard detergents we use so that they biodegrade nontoxically? Or wean-ing ourselves of large quantities of meat? In a world that is quickly becoming ecologically aware, there are a myriad of ways in which our lifestyles come under pressure to change. But change is often overwhelming to people. Lifestyles can harden against it. This is especially so in a highly competitive economy globally restructuring at an alarming rate since the 1970s.[15] Who has the time, energy, financial means, or job freedom to change one's ways within an economy such as ours?

4. *The political block.* How do you become greener when you are more op-pressed than you think? Saints will rise to ideals even by dying. But societies cannot be made of saints, because, to say the least, saints die or sacrifice their family life, thereby making generation impossible. Saints are exceptions in a

society, a dead-end street that gloriously reminds the society what it holds ideal (unless they are violent martyrs, who should remind a society of where its criticism should be focused). For an idealism of everyday life, we need situations that can be handled by people with families to raise and rough trade to keep. That is, we need political situations that are not so oppressive that changing ecologically is possible only for the saints. Let me give three examples:

i. *Stalinism*. Remember our example of the Tarkovsky film about "the zone"? We discussed it when discussing sacred places, and I showed you some slides of that shelled-out room with rain pouring through the roof where people come to bare their hearts. Tarkovsky's films are retrospective analyses of the psychology of living under totalitarianism, and Stalinism in particular. Tarkovsky's early life was lived under Stalin, and he never forgot how oppressive that was.[16] Imagine, then, that you live in Russia under Stalin, and like Tarkovsky did in *Searcher*, awaken to the fact that the Soviet production process and nuclear science program are ecologically destructive on an unimaginable scale. This was true, by the way. Soviet ecological damage was even more massive than that which occurs routinely under capitalism in the democratic West. And *that* is massive. Imagine you envision a disaster like that which happened at Chernobyl[17] in the near future and want to do something about it. Well, that would have been no easy thing to do under Stalin. He regularly killed people merely because a rumor had been circulated about them with no evidence the person was critical of the government at all.[18] Would you want to be critical of Stalin's productivity program?

ii. *Neo-colonial Corporate Cronyism*. Imagine you live in a country—such as Nigeria—that has been violently colonized in the not too distant past and exists in a vulnerable economic situation vis-à-vis the powerful transnational corporations that power the world's economy. Imagine your country is a source of resources, such as oil, for those corporations. Let's say the corporations smell billions to be made and start controlling the government through bribes, mercenary violence, and powerful economic incentives. As a result, where you live, oil is king. Perhaps even, as happened in Burma in the 1990s, your government forcibly enslaves citizens to work the oil industry (in the case of Burma, it was pipeline building). How much freedom do you have to protest the iron grip of the oil economy on your society? You have some, but you also have a high chance of being killed for speaking out.

iii. *The Multi-job Grind.* States also engage in less high-profile economic badness. They serve as regulatory conduits for the accumulation of capital within their borders and internationally, depending on the specific interests they serve. Within their borders, too, they strategically serve certain elements of society over others.[19] Sociologists call this situation "uneven development," and the idea is that state regulations—including tax breaks, investment opportunities, loopholes in labor law (or lack of labor laws), and so on—end up privileging specific regions and sectors of society and sometimes specific corporate interests, such as the corn-growing industry or the military-industrial complex. These sectors of society experience greater development than others, with ripple effects that extend into civil society, for instance, in the quality of schools available to some sectors of the citizenry. Meanwhile, other sectors of society experience little development or even economic depression.

If you happen to be caught in one of the more depressed areas of society, it is hard to make a living. For example, in America today, it is increasingly common to find people who have to work multiple jobs to make ends meet (by the way, graduate students are among these). Such jobs do not often come with benefits such as medical insurance. If you are in such an economic situation, life is hard to change in radical ways, although people (and often the most oppressed people) are inventive. It takes something of a superhuman effort for someone working more than one job, with kids (and sometimes as a single parent), to have the time and opportunity—including the financial flexibility—to change one's life. You may not be threatened by deportation to a gulag if you criticize the government, but in reality, it is hard to become active as an effective political voice and catalyst for social change. And the point is, political regulations make this inactivity a likelihood. The state *could* ensure, or seriously work to ensure, that every citizen has the minimum standards of humanity in their lives, as required by human rights, but the state instead (pressured to provide a fix for capitalist interests) makes whole areas of its citizens' lives practically desperate. Take an elementary sociology course on America today. Or, for a jolt of reality, go to Mexico City.

In all three cases, a political block makes it hard to exercise one's moral creativity in a way that is sufficient for the ecological development we should practice. A political block poses a problem for maturing. I want to reiterate: there are such blocks even in democratic countries. Put yourself in either a typical working class home in the Bronx, New York City; or a shanty suburb of Mexico City, Calcutta, or any of the major democratic population hubs of the world economy. You live under democracy and have liberties of life, some ability to critique your government, and your country pays at least lip-service to human rights. There is no Stalinist KGB, and your government doesn't send a death squad to kill you if you seriously protest the oil industry. Your country is probably even signed onto some international environmental accords such as the Rio Declaration we discussed in our third lecture on an ecological orientation. Yet how much real freedom do you have to change your lifestyle and become consistent with whatever ecological beliefs you have? When you have to look after your kids, put food on the table, and try to get an education, you do not have much freedom to buy expensive ecologically aware products, spend days lobbying governments to change, or buy expensive access to media. You work—or search for work—eat, and sleep. When you have time off—please, just a little fun! A cool walk on a hot night. Some time with your loved ones. Some loving some of the time.

These and situations like these are the real conditions with which ecological maturity has to deal. Real idealism will have to, as well.

How about a break? People brought food to share, and it's here along the stage. We'll regroup in about . . . twenty minutes?

＊ ＊ ＊

Listen up! Let's start again. A bunch of you were up here during break—Judy, Eliot, Malcolm, Omer, Elizabeth, Maureen, Kate, Joel, Saleem, Andy, Nashwa, Nisreen, Alex, Eric, Ahmad, (did I get everyone?) . . . Ayla and Abdullah. They were just telling me about their field-class experience with people opposing the destruction of the rainforests for cattle-grazing land. They explained how hard it is to protest when the companies doing the bulldozing of the forests have powerful allies in government. They left a discussion of the problem up here to the left of you on the stage, along with ways you can get involved in making the international community monitor human rights abuses. If you are interested, please come up and take a look in about half an hour when class is through.

Let's pick up from where we were. We have practical blocks to green maturity. We also know what has to go into a developmental habit to make it green. Can we articulate ecological habits that handle the problems we detailed before break?

Here are four habits I came up with. Each corresponds to a problem we posed. I mean these habits to stimulate your thoughts in case you encounter other problems calling for different habits. I'm reflecting pragmatically from problems.

Four Habits of Ecological Maturity

1. Moral perception
2. Ecological literacy
3. Moral creativity
4. Political-economic liberty

As we explain these, it's important to remember that each habit assumes our commitment to respect life as a background pressure within which the habit takes shape and acquires direction. Given that we are to develop in our respect for life, these habits interact with that assumption to produce green developmental habits that satisfy our criteria. Let's go through each proposed habit:

1. *Moral perception.* Moral perception is a developmental habit of learning to see the morally invisible. The morally invisible are those who deserve some respect but are not receiving any, enough, or the appropriate form; and those too whose use or abuse is unjustified. People who are in the practice of dissolving moral invisibility fulfill all of our criteria for a green developmental habit. First, seeing what is respect-worthy but has been occluded is the beginning of integration. Second, recognition of the unseen also shows a deeper attention to life and so makes us more human. Third, because moral invisibility is about what slips our mind because of our narrow frame of action, a habit of discovering the invisible must produce broad-mindedness (For example: Earle urges us to find out what is going on in ocean valleys; she wants us to "think like a sea-floor"). Finally, recognition of the unseen shows the essence of thoughtfulness. Perhaps, then, a habit of self-critically searching for moral invisibility is one developmental habit of ecological maturity? Perhaps the beginning of wisdom is to recognize the limits of our minds?

2. *Ecological literacy.* Ecological literacy is a habit of learning to read one's environment and consider its ecological nature. In response to being ignorant about the environment, we seek a practice of learning about how the ecosystems work where we live and when we affect them. This might start, to echo the words of a forest ranger turned environmental philosopher, with "a basic appreciation and interest in a wide variety of natural phenomena."[20] After all, how can we learn our ecological context if we don't look outward and consider the other forms of life and the biotic conditions in which we live? Of course, such appreciation should also be joined with scientific un-

derstanding so that we have further methods for knowing what our actions cause indirectly. Ecological literacy, then, combines a genuine receptivity to the wider universe of life with specific learning about how the environment works.

It also meets, in some form, our criteria for habits that would seem to be good developmental elements of green maturity. For one, a habit of keeping ecologically well-read handles our Leopoldian criterion. It allows us to stay informed of ecological interdependencies. It also appears to meet our integrationist criterion, as ecological literacy opens us up to know how to balance the diverse needs of other beings within a flourishing ecological order. As to thoughtfulness, it is clear that no respect for other forms of life can be effective without understanding that form of life, and so ecological literacy, because it helps us know another form of life, enables our thoughtfulness. The question that remains, then, is whether a practice of being ecologically well-read humanizes us. Yet if what we said about analogical implication several weeks ago is true, then we should learn about our humanity by becoming more ecologically literate. Ecological literacy opens us up to the human condition.

3. *Moral creativity.* To see lifestyle rigidity as a serious obstacle to ecological maturity is to advocate, by contrast, an aptitude for modifying one's life to fit moral demands. What is such an aptitude called? It is not simply conformity to moral law, but is rather an ability to be both deliberate and creative enough to change how one is living in order to catch up with new moral demands. This is no easy task, even to be deliberate. One has to feel in control of one's life, have time and space to think, have options (economic and political ones most of all!), and follow through on new courses of action often involving the creation of anything from new ways to go to work to new laws for one's city. No one says any of this is easy. It involves a new style of life, since our culture is lacking an ecological orientation.

When we change our style of life, we aren't simply switching one color of shoe for another. We alter patterns of action, advocacy, and economics, and these go along with many consequences. How will we make sure we don't disturb things we want to keep, such as relationships with people who are uncomfortable with our changes or the ability to have a job we want (or any job at all)? We will have to be creative at times, articulating compromises, shortcuts, and new forms of options. An aptitude for this sort of change might be called *moral creativity.* How would that fend as a habit?

Moral creativity is a habit of innovating our socialized respect in ways that allow us to meet new demands. It seems, on the surface, to be a good candidate for developing ecological maturity. After all, moral creativity would make sense in any situation where moral demands call us to change our lives in innovative ways, and many of those are ecological demands. Accordingly, ecological literacy and moral perception are pointless without moral creativity, because without moral creativity, all the ecological literacy and moral perception in the world won't add up to a better style of life. Moral creativity would also seem to help us integrate better with nonhuman life, since integration requires careful and often novel balancing of interests. In a similar vein, moral creativity would appear to help us handle the complicated causal chains of the Leopoldian criterion, which should often make us realize we have not conceptualized an institution in a sufficiently ecological manner. Moral creativity should also give more room for a thoughtful style of life by giving us the habit of positioning ourselves to be thoughtful. Finally, moral creativity would appear to make us more human. Becoming more in line with what we think is humanizing. We are deliberate animals, and self-control and moral integrity are not optional for our well-being. Moral creativity thus passes our test for being an ecologically mature habit.

4. *Political-economic liberty.* This is our last habit. Recall the problem: political blocks are hard to overcome. Yet it is possible to overcome them. Think of the homeless gardeners and how they manage to create ecologically advanced gardens of recycled goods even while being among the most oppressed members of American society. Many examples of ecological creativity come not from rich, modern Americans but from poor members of the world. Poverty does not prohibit becoming ecologically creative. In fact, as someone who grew up for a period on food stamps and many hand-created toys, I can tell you that poverty is often a scene of great inventiveness. This doesn't make it good, especially when it goes along with stunted educational and medical opportunities, but it helps explain why so many philosophers and religious figures from many world traditions have seen poverty as having moral advantages. There is room for being ecological in poverty. Still, economic conditions are a real block to ecological maturity for most people, and those economic conditions are possible only in the space of political regulations that enable—and even promote—them.

Thus, the political block to ecological maturity seems to me to remain one we must handle in our developmental habit. What kind of developmental habit could handle it? Some kind of habit of political-economic liberty? We should find out, because without the political-economic freedom needed for moral creativity, it will be hard to effectively balance our needs with the needs of other living beings in a way that is thoughtful. We also know that since humans are social animals, a habit that makes our political-economic order better suited to our moral core will humanize us—at the least, by keeping us free of oppression. Furthermore, making our governments reflect, or at least allow, what is ecologically mature will be one of the greatest enablers of the Leopoldian criterion we can discover. The single biggest block on recognizing the interdependence of our actions with complicated Earth biospheric processes currently in the world is a political one—for instance, the U.S. government's refusal to sign onto the Kyoto Accord, or the systematic avoidance of state and interstate regulations on economic transactions involving thoughtless use of the Earth's living beings.[21] Finally, political-economic liberty should also help us be thoughtful of other forms of life, because it will give us the freedom to identify with them as having a dignity analogous to our freedom.

Thus a habit of removing political-economic blocks is needed, and it is this I call "political-economic liberty." Think of "liberty" as freedom. We sometimes speak of a free way of living or even a habit of freedom. That is the sense in which to hear this last shade of green maturity. Political-economic liberty is a habit, even a fierce one, of dealing with political and economic blocks to our freedom to solve the problems that dehumanize us or keep us from doing what we should do. If the previous three habits are the moral genuis's, the ecologist's, and the moral artist's habits, this last is the political activist's habit. As I said, we are after the point where the moral and the political join: citizenship.

There is a moral genius we might all develop. It is a habit of moral perception, including being self-critical about moral invisibility. There is also an ecologist we might become, found when we develop a habit of ecological literacy. Nor is the moral artist, the artist of living idealistically, far behind. She is there in a habit of moral creativity. Finally, as Rachel Carson found out when it was her 1960s housewife readers who forced the American chemical industry to clean up its toxic act, there is a political activist in many a housewife even from a gender-conservative age: she is there in a habit of liberty, when she realizes the ecological injustice at hand.[22]

*

Let me take matters a step further now, so that we can organize our grasp of green maturity. I will be looking for a master habit, that is, an overarching developmental habit that organizes the more particular ones responding to the problems we imagined. After all, there are probably more problems out there, no? Even though we've explored how to think in support of growing ecologically, it would help to have a key for the unseen problems we will face when we depart from this idyllic spot and disperse into our lives.

The four particular habits mentioned so far are unified around a simple idea. To keep developing ecologically, we should keep learning about our ecological interdependence with other forms of life and about Earth biotic conditions, keeping aware of how our actions affect other forms of life that are morally invisible. In the process, we should be creative enough to modify our lives according to our moral and practical insights, and we should have the political-economic freedom to act on that creativity in a society free of oppression. Thus, the above habits center on a complex but relatively clear idea. We should keep aware of our interrelatedness with other forms of life and with biotic conditions (note that we assume by now a relationship with another life form involves respect!), and we should be able to practice what we envision. Let me write out the idea this way:

The Basic Constituents of Ecological Maturity?

1. Being aware of our interrelatedness with other forms of life and their biotic conditions

    (theory)

2. Being able to do what we think should be done

    (practice)

I am using "theory" in an archaic sense. The Greek root of "theory" originally meant "to see." Thus we might say that we are after a master habit that makes sure we join theory and practice. The point is, we seek a habit of conceptualizing our situation that involves moral self-vigilance and knowledge of the environment. And we seek a practice of living out our best, conceptually-attuned judgment in a creative and politically enabled way.

Finally, not only should we articulate better what such habits of developing citizenship are, but we should also reassure ourselves that they do meet our criteria for development. For instance, does each of them truly humanize us, or have I been bending reasons to fit the case? How do we argue with the astute critic who thinks that the notion of something making us more human is vague and that almost anything could make us more human? At some point, we should argue convincingly that becoming ecological does make us more human, where the use of that category is conceptually rigorous and well justified.

*

The way I'll take up these demands proceeds through a comparison with one of the original philosophers of character ethics, Aristotle. In his *Nicomachean*

Ethics, Aristotle describes the major habits of action and judgment that make an excellent person.[23] These include temperance, courage, generosity, and justice. He also articulates the kind of good judgment that guides our understanding of when courage, temperance, or justice are demanded. This judgment is a kind of master habit. Translators often call this judgment "prudence," but I choose to call it "moral wisdom," after the translation my father gave me while I taught a class long ago.[24] Moral wisdom involves an overall sense of the goals and meaning of human life. It also includes a good grasp of our life's conditions and the contexts wherein courage, temperance, or generosity are needed. No person can exercise her habits well without the moral wisdom of how a flourishing human life fits together. She must know when to act, when not to act, how to remain committed to one's ideals, and how to be creative in the right ways when creativity is most helpful. On this point, Aristotle is surely correct. There has to be a street-wise brain and a solidly good heart behind someone mature.

In this Aristotelian spirit, then, I propose that the master habit which will give us the ability to keep learning how to live with the universe of life is *ecological idealism*. Ecological idealism is not moral wisdom, because I do not assume—as does Aristotle—that an ecological idealist is perfectly wise. Remember, I'm after a developmental habit here. It assumes we have much to learn, not that we are done learning. However, since ecological idealism does include human flourishing under its purview, its domain is as overarching as moral wisdom. In fact, it inscribes a grasp of the human good within a grasp of our ecological good (much as, in two weeks, I'll argue human rights are a species of ecological law). And since our ecological good involves respect for life, ecological idealism is broader than anything Aristotle envisioned. For instance, it includes justice to other animals and temperance with the use of the Earth.

Ecological idealism is also like moral wisdom in that it frames the discussion and exercises of more specific ecological habits. It is the general spokesperson for developing our habits in matters ecological—the brains and heart of ecological maturity. Let me say how:

Our Overarching Developmental Habit

Ecological idealism is a habit of conceptualizing our ecological situation and acting on what we think is best in the service of respect for life.

Ecological idealism is a habit of conceptualizing our ecological situation in rigorous and critical moral terms and in well-informed and extensive scientific and experiential terms. It is likewise a habit of acting on what we think is best: true, good, and beautiful within a background pressure to respect life. Idealism is a two-faceted dimension of personality. It involves thought—ideas—and it involves living up to what one thinks. It is reason in action. An idealist doesn't just act thoughtlessly. She has ideas. She conceptualizes her situation and how to live well. An idealist also does not just speculate and think. She acts. She makes ideas happen.

Ecological idealism is the habit that handles both theory and practice, both the demand for ecological awareness and the demand for free creativity. When we looked at obvious obstacles to environmental maturity, we saw that we should be self-critical about moral invisibility and continue learning about our environment. The idealistic counterpart to these obstacles allows us to be ecological in both senses: respectful of life and informed about our ecosystems. That is the conceptual part of the *idea*lism. Thinking about the obstacles to ecological maturity also made us aware of how we should be creative with our lives in a society free of oppression. These obstacles called for us pushing the beat on our political systems and our calcified habits so that they enable us to live what we think is good, true, and beautiful. That is the practical part of the idea*lism*.

Putting theory and practice together, we should be in a lifelong habit of living an idealistic life. The way to be mature is to be idealistic, and not anything else that imperils that. How else can we remain conscientious about our situation on this planet and then live in accordance with that conscience, if we are not idealistic, if we do not put thoughtfulness and knowledge into the skeleton, blood, and guts of our lives?

Here, then, is what I want to conclude about ecological maturity. First, without being ecologically idealistic, we cannot be ecologically mature. Ecological idealism is a necessary condition on maturity. Second, being ecologically idealistic is sufficient to make us ecologically matur*ing*, if not mature. At the same time, are we ever done being mature? Or is maturity, like citizenship, a matter of becoming? The people who are adult are the ones who keep growing (people who don't grow begin to regress). In this way, then, idealism—in the activist, pragmatic sense I've advocated—is a necessary and sufficient condition on maturity. That's my conclusion.

*

One reason I point to ecological idealism as a unified answer to our call for habits is that it keeps the big picture of what we should have in view and gives room for complexity within that big picture. What the habit of ecological idealism gives us is *an ongoing practice of informing ourselves, being self-critical about our moral complacency and limits, and making our lives express the best judgment at which we arrive.* It has many dimensions, as we've seen while focusing on the four habits we sought to meet four obstacles. At heart, though, these four specific habits are all part of a seamless organic activity for creatures of reason and conscience such as we are.

The idealism is a healthy activity, too, because it is not desperate. It does not let our humanity remain stagnant. No matter how much one might cynically bemoan the conscienceless world of power, violence, and greed, the fact is we are creatures with an idealistic and moral being. The critique of the moral in a cynical awareness of human corruption is itself a conscientious act. The point is to remember that it, too, is motivated by idealism. Moreover, such a critique is good when used to establish a goal for making our lives more humane. Then even desperation becomes hopeful, because we see a way to grow up. And this is what the dynamic character of idealism drives us to do: to see how the negative can be made positive.

We can see better, too, why the habit of ecological idealism should humanize us, a doubt I left hanging ten minutes ago. To become thoughtful, to learn, to establish a more moral and informed relationship with the world, to be creative and bring one's life in line with one's judgment, to be free to do so: these *are* humanizing, and experience shows they are. They make us more alive and responsible. We also develop a better grasp of the human condition, a better sense and ability to live for what is good within our condition and a richer expression of what we find meaningful when we are thoughtful and creative, informed, and free to live our lives accordingly. I think you know all this better than I do, because young adults have this kind of energy in them that *wants* responsibility and creativity. The cynicism so many of you feel at times is the reflection of the wish you see let down by us, the older ones. It's there, because you sense what would help you grow and become free as humans, yet it seems forgotten by the preexisting society.

Of course, talking about transforming one's life and doing it are different matters. Speculating on moral invisibility and confronting one's *own* moral limits are different affairs. But this is why we are after a habit of idealism, and why the habit is itself a developmental one. We should learn how to discover our moral limits and innovative ways to make our lives reflect insight. Learning to face difficulty, solve problems, and reflect on the lesson is the goal.

Ecological idealism would appear to be experimental, therefore, informed by the insight it can gather. It would appear to be benefited by soaking up all the possibilities for enlightenment and know-how it can obtain. It would appear to be benefited by being politically active, especially in the face of our world's main economy whenever it exploits life. Throughout, the idealism would appear to work and play in the spirit of Dewey and progressive educa-tion. That is, it encourages us to learn as we go.

*

So that's the spirit these lectures advocate. We should next approach some of the details, how maturity appears in practice. Thus, next week, I want us to face the difficult issue of how we consider—or *fail* to consider—animals. We'll do theory work on moral invisibility. I hope that way we'll clear our minds some.

Then two weeks from now, we'll discuss how to green our culture. We'll try to be pragmatic about how to face a contemporary capitalism that is thoughtless with the Earth's life and so massively powerful as to exceed our imagination and personal powers. *That* should exercise our creativity.

In this way, after we have gone through the next weeks, we'll have had ex-amples of ecological idealism in theory and in practice. We will have exper-imented with reconceptualizing our moral universe and reconfiguring our culture. I wish I could offer you more than a glimpse, yet you are amazing people—go and pursue what your consciences point out to you. It's better than what some professor professes, anyway. It's yours. Then you can teach us, because you've followed your mind and worked out answers through cre-ative and hard commitment.[25]

Notes

1. Stage directions: The professor is smiling here.

2. Val Plumwood, *Environmental Culture: The Ecological Crisis of Reason*, New York: Routledge, 2002.

3. See Stanley Cavell, *Conditions Handsome and Unhandsome: The Constitution of Emersonian Perfectionism*, Chicago: University of Chicago Press, 1993.

4. See Jonathan Lear, *Therapeutic Action, an Earnest Plea for Irony*, New York: Other Press, 2003 and his *Happiness, Death, and the Remainder of Life*, Cambridge, MA: Harvard University Press, 2001, or Gandini et al., *The Hundred Languages of Children*, Englewood: Axel Publishing, 1999.

5. This notion is first articulated in modern philosophy of education by Rousseau in *Emile*. It is central to a justification of liberal arts education over exclusively pre-professional or exclusively technical education.

6. See Louis Menand, *The Metaphysical Club: A Story of Ideas in America*, New York: Farrar, Straus and Giroux, 2001.

7. Descartes famously claimed that there was a gland, the pineal gland, through which body and immaterial soul interacted. His view is often cited as a famous brain-fart by a great philosopher.

8. See Bill McKibben's book, *Enough: Staying Human in an Engineered Age*, New York: Times Books, 2003, although there are voices that question whether McKibben has a view of our nature that is too static and not developmental *enough*.

9. In this paragraph, I am discussing Leopold from his *A Sand County Almanac and Sketches from Here and There*.

10. Attention to others is a constitutive feature of genuine, human meaning and identity. This point is made by Martin Buber, *I and Thou*, Edinburgh: T & T Clark, 1999, who inaugurated one of the most significant developments of Western moral thinking in the twentieth century.

11. On rights within intersubjective relations of respect, see Diamond, "Injustice and Animals," lecture given at the University of Chicago, March, 2001, and also my "Common Humanity and Human Rights," *Religion and Human Rights* (*Social Philosophy Today*, v. 21), Philosophy Documentation Center, 2005.

12. This point is made very well by Diamond in "Eating Meat and Eating People," in *The Realistic Spirit*, Cambridge, MA: MIT Press, 1995; and by Vivian Paley in *The Kindness of Children*, Cambridge, MA: Harvard University Press, 1999. Children can be cruel to animals, but they have a strong tendency to respect life and to have empathy and wonder for it. Perhaps this is why some ecopsychologists speak of a "biophilic" tendency in people (a point on which I am unable to comment, since it is outside my field of study). On "biophilia," see Peter Hay, *Main Currents in Western Environmental Thought*, New South Wales: the University of New South Wales Press, 2001, chap. 1.

13. Henri Bergson, *Le rire* [*The Laugh*], Paris: Editions de Christine, 1991.

14. "Alas, the time is coming when man will no longer give birth to a star. Alas, the time of the most despicable man is coming, he that is no longer able to despise himself. Behold, I show you *the last man*. / 'What is love? What is creation? What is longing? What is a star?' Thus asks the last man, and he blinks. / The Earth has become small, and on it hops the last man, who makes everything small." Nietzsche, *Thus Spoke Zarathustra*, "Zarathustra's Prologue," section 5 (New York: Penguin Classics, 1978).

Consider also these lines: "Let your will say, "the [self-overcoming human] will be the meaning of the earth! I beseech you, my brothers, *remain faithful to the earth* . . . ! . . . To sin against the earth is now the most dreadful thing. . . ." Ibid., section 2, my modified translation.

I am providing ecological connotations that Nietzsche did not appear to intend. Still within *my* Nietzsche, they work. And what is Nietzsche if not *your own* Nietzsche? (Nietzsche is famous for advocating our subjectivity and articulating how perspective shapes truth.)

15. On this point, see Neil Brenner, *New State Spaces: Urban Governance and the Rescaling of Statehood*, New York: Oxford University Press, 2004.

16. This time and memory is a major part of Tarkovsky's most personal film, *Mirror*.

17. On April 26, 1986, the nuclear reactor at Chernobyl, Ukraine experienced a meltdown during a failed, routine test. There are disagreements about how much

damage was caused by the massive plume of radioactive steam released into the at-mosphere to spread over Europe. A conservative estimate is that some fifty people died with many more radiated to unknown consequence. For the conservative esti-mate, see the Uranium Information Center, *Nuclear Issues Briefing Paper*, n. 22, Mel-bourne Australia, August 2004, at *www.uic.com.au/index.htm* (accessed May 23, 2005). "Chernobyl" is often a catchword for a potentially massive ecological disaster, such as the Bhopal, India Union Carbide / Dow Chemical plant disaster which killed up to twenty-thousand people from toxic fallout in 1984. See Greenpeace's recent campaigns against "Toxic Hotspots," at *www.greenpeace.org/international/campaigns/toxics/toxic-hotspots* (accessed May 23, 2005).

18. On this point, see Glover's *Humanity: A Moral History of the Twentieth Cen-tury*, New Haven: Yale University Press, 1999, chapter 5.

19. See Brenner, *New State Spaces*, again.

20. Phil Cafaro, *Thoreau's Living Ethics: Walden and the Pursuit of Virtue*, Athens, GA: University of Georgia Press, 2004, 31.

21. In *One World: The Ethics of Globalization*, New Haven: Yale University Press, 2003, Singer has a good critique of the WTO's avoidance of regulating ecologically destructive practices. See "One Economy," *passim*.

22. This was the case with the reception of *Silent Spring*. Moreover, Carson wrote the book to activate such a potential in her middle-class housewife peers, at the time emerging out of the conservative 1950s. Though they were gendered to keep private, they went public.

23. Aristotle, *Nicomachean Ethics*, trans. Terrance Irwin, Indianapolis: Hackett Publishing, 1985.

24. Thanks to David Keymer for the translation. After teaching Aristotle's *Ethics* many times, I feel the translation captures best the relationship to the human good I seek to articulate. However, it could be confused with the use of "wisdom" in Aris-totle's sixth book. This is not a point into which I can go here.

25. In Arabic and in Islam, "Aql" is the Arabic and Qur'anic word for "heart-mind," or "intelligence with conscience." Thus, we might say ecological idealism is a form of *aql*. I thank Professor Kareem Douglas Crow for teaching me this word in his talk, "Belief: Heart or Mind?" (American University of Sharjah, March 2005).

~

A Circle of Life[1]

Good afternoon. This is Osool. She is a goat, as you can tell. She's used to being near humans and in new places. The school wasn't happy we brought in the straw and pen. But I promised to help clean up. I told them Osool is the muse of our lecture today. She has to be. Her eyes are so silent. Goats, especially, are known for silent eyes. They are mirrors of a world without thoughts, or anything like what we know thoughts to be. To accept that creatures like Osool are "truthful signs of our life," to quote a phrase by Alain de Lille, is already to make a step to maturity. How does our life affect them? Even though Osool cannot speak, cannot think in any way we know as thought, and does not articulate joy or agony (although she does express both), she is a fellow living creature and we share the world with her.

"Osool" is an Arabic word that does not have a simple translation, because its meaning varies with the context of use. It means *roots* when applied to vegetation, *origins, tradition, ethics, custom, right, principles*, and sometimes *law* when applied to human life, and it also has a religious connotation for scholars of Islam that denotes a branch of theological study. In addition, Al Jazeera has spoken of "usulis," an Arabic media expression for fundamentalists. However, "fundamentalism" is not a term scholars of Islam apply to themselves. It is a Western term, created in the early twentieth century to apply to a form of Protestantism, and is used by extension to categorize extremist Islamic sects. Moreover, if "usulis" applies to people who take the right to kill innocent humans, then it is anti-Islamic, for Islam strictly prohibits the killing of innocents.[2] I first saw "Osool" on a sign for a financial company in the United Arab Emirates, and loved simply the sound of the word. Later, I found fascinating the combined meaning of *roots, origins* or *tradition* and *custom, law, principles* or *right*. It reminded me of a similar word in ancient Greek that has many meanings and a rich philosophical tradition—*arche*—or *origin, principle*, and sometimes *ordering pattern*.[3]

I named Osool as I did because of one night when I was in Sharjah, a city in the United Arab Emirates near Dubai. It was during Ramadan and after the evening prayers. Everyone was out now, the neoclassical cornice built around a mirror of Lake Geneva filling with people and especially families. The traffic is heavy in Sharjah and locks up around old British roundabouts—those circular intersections used in former colonies in place of intersections with traffic lights. I was stuck behind a pickup truck with about ten goats in the back of it. They were eye level with me when I stopped my car close behind the truck. They were white and black, and they were curious and a little nervous from all the traffic. The ones at the back of the truck could see me—they recognize humans—and jostled into place to get a look. Their eyes were so silent. Amidst all those cars and Ramadan lights, I felt like they were looking out at us and showing us what we are. In the middle of all our order was this different order. And this is why I called Osool what I did much later, back in the States. It was a question of remembering the significances.[4]

*

Today, I want to give an example of the theoretical work ecological idealism is supposed to do. I want to explore how ecological idealism leads us to reconceptualize our moral universe, especially by self-critically unworking moral invisibility and broadening our ability to respect. The way I propose to do so is through a critique of factory farming, the industrial raising of animals for food. I want to show how respect for life, adrift in our socialization, can take root in a critique of what I will call a "region of inconsistency." This critique will also be different from that given by the popular movement of animal liberation[5], because the critique will be *humanistic*.

To begin, let's make sure we know what our words mean. What is factory farming? Judy[6], tell us what you think:

It's the name for how big food industries raise and prepare animals for slaughter or use them for stuff like milk or eggs. The idea is that the animal farm is run like a factory—a kind of Henry Ford automatic processing plant. The decisions are made by the bottom line and any shortcut to cost effectiveness. The scale of production is huge, and science, particularly animal medicine, is brought in to literally manipulate the animal's life form so that it produces more for less.

Yes, that's clear. Factory farming is industrial meat or animal food goods production. It is an unsavory business by even the accounts of those performing it. Also, it is one of those areas of our culture that is morally invisible to the mainstream.

The conditions of animal farming are infamous to those who have read about it. Today's reading from Peter Singer's *Animal Liberation* should have alerted you to the conditions, if you weren't already aware of them. Singer's book empowered a movement having a significant effect on legislation that improved the quality of animal life. In the reading, you saw how beef cattle are kept and how chickens are raised for meat and eggs. Books like Eric Schlosser's *Fast Food Nation*, also in our reading for today, bring out further how beef cattle live before they are slaughtered.[7] These books create wider familiarity with the backstage reality of what the mainstream eats at a McDonald's or a KFC (Kentucky Fried Chicken). Still the conceptual problem of why we shouldn't just use cows and chickens the way fast food does remains unclear, much as the moral problem of destroying the ocean in search of tuna or shrimp currently is. This problem challenges our moral perception.

What are some of the most infamous conditions of factory farms? First, factory farms don't let animals live a life healthy for their kind. As Singer underlines, the animals are kept in small or overcrowded places. They aren't able to move around or practice their normal hygienic habits. Often, they are so crowded together that they live in their own excrement. Frequently when they develop sores or infections, antibiotics are bought in to fix the problem, rather than the farmers creating different living conditions to prevent future problems. The farms, run by the bottom line of a profit margin, permit many life-deforming means that accomplish profit-maximizing ends.

Second, factory farms frequently involve the mutilation of animals, including a great deal of animal suffering and distress. The most infamous example, perhaps, is the debeaking that has often occurred in industrial chicken farms. Because the chickens are in such small places, can't move or even keep themselves free, they peck at themselves. The cheapest "solution" to this problem is to have their beaks cut off. There are other forms of mutilation too. Veal cows are not actually cut, but they are so deprived of movement and a normal diet that their muscles are not able to develop properly. The point here is that the farms take it as in *principle* permitted to mutilate the animals in any way that promotes profitability. Let me write this on the board:

The Moral Structure of the Factory Farm (Its "Osool")

It is in *principle* permitted to mutilate the animals in any way that promotes profitability.

Third, factory farms destroy the social patterns of the animals used. Chickens can't organize themselves in the usual way they would. Nor can cows live together or raise their young as they normally would. The group dimension of animal life is torn to pieces through the production process. This loss of a social dimension is unhealthy, of course, but I've separated it out as a third condition of factory farms, because it seems to me more significant than a simple health problem. In destroying the social dimension of an animal's life form, something specific is being destroyed that goes beyond unhealthy living conditions or the animal's physical integrity. The closest thing to an animal's order of meaning is destroyed, although it does not make sense to speak of meaning in the linguistic way we think of meaning (although with dolphins perhaps it would).

What all three of these conditions have in common is the destruction of the animal's *dignity*. The conditions destroy the dignity of the animals, because the farms do not let the animals live a life fitting their kind. The animals are treated, in fact, as if they aren't even lives. Rather, they are treated as stuff.

Look through the photos in the Singer book to visualize some of the conditions of which we speak. As you do, I want us to turn to the conceptual problem I think these conditions pose. Here we begin to address the idea of moral invisibility more closely and so begin to see ecological idealism do theoretical work. What I want us to focus on is what I will call a "region of inconsistency." This expression is my own, yet once again its idea came to me after reading an essay by Professor Diamond, one called "Experimenting on Animals."[8]

In this essay, Diamond takes up the problem of experimentation on animals, one of Singer's topics as well. Her question is about inconsistencies in our lives, a theme she addresses in "Eating Meat and Eating People." What is an inconsistency? There are several kinds. I'll write them out:

An Inconsistency

1. Holding a belief and its negation or opposition
2. Holding at least two beliefs that entail others that are contradictory
3. Acting on a belief in one context but not in another, and without a good reason

Diamond deals with several of these kinds in her work. For instance, in "Eating Meat and Eating People," she's concerned with the mixed messages we receive in our moral education. On the one hand, we read children's stories showing considerable sympathy with animals—for example, *Charlotte's Web*. Many of us grow up with pets, too. Yet at the same time, we find dead animals on our tables at night, and we eat them. What is one to learn as a child when faced with this simultaneous respect for and disregard of animals? That is the first kind of inconsistency listed on the board. We're supposed to respect them *and* destroy them?

Similarly, when we read about animals as sad and deserving of pity, yet relate to meat as mere stuff, we face the second kind of inconsistency. That animals have feelings implies they are sources of our concern. But that they become stuff for us implies we shouldn't care about them, except perhaps as property. Can they be both sources of concern *and* stuff about which we shouldn't care?

Then, there is the third kind of inconsistency. In "Experimenting on Animals," Diamond discusses the way both laws and customs prevent us from certain forms of cruelty to animals whereas the most torturous behavior is permitted on animals once they are in the space of, say, a medical or cosmetics-testing laboratory. What she is specifically concerned about is the way one's moral attitudes are permitted to switch off in these laboratories under the language of doing science. It's as if once you don a lab coat and start talking natural science, anything goes. (This is a theme Tarkovsky considered in *Searcher*, too, as did many Russian writers of his generation.) She is not arguing with the point that some scientific testing may be of great usefulness to pressing human medical problems. She is concerned with the cloaking of our moral responses. Those of you who have studied war may note a similarity here, for a similar cloaking happens once "enemies" are cloaked behind the rhetoric, uniforms, and technology of battle.[9]

Unless we are vigilant, it seems we compartmentalize our applications of moral concepts and thus expose ourselves to the third kind of inconsistency listed on the board. That is the point Diamond makes. Compartmentalizing our moral contexts, we open ourselves to what I will call a "region of inconsistency," an area of our lives that is morally inconsistent with how we act in other areas according to considerations we take to be morally authoritative. For instance (please excuse a jarring example), a child might one day decide to apply certain kinds of household chemicals to a neighborhood cat in order to see how they affect the cat's skin. Doing so would be considered a form of cruelty to animals in American culture. Even if the child were acting purely out of ignorance and curiosity, a good parent would be expected to school the child in the impermissibility of her act.

Yet a block away in a laboratory, scientists apply similar chemicals to animals such as cats and rest assured their actions are morally permitted. They don't have to be bothered, let alone compassionate, on account of the animal affected. Science is science. Similarly, psychological work has been done on how professional interrogators who torture can do their jobs at work and go home to their families without remorse or discomfort. Work is work. What you might call "doubling" has occurred: there is one life at work and another at home.[10] Yet such behavior appears inconsistent. And it actually is, unless we grasp the sufficient reason for the exception of moral principle in the context which uses violence.

What could a sufficient reason be? It would have to be good, because we are using it to exempt ourselves from moral principle (from *osool*). The reason would have to be one according to which considerations that are morally salient in one context are irrelevant in another. The weave of life is composed of moral context, and a good deal of maturity involves grasping the special justifications for treating like considerations differently according to context.[11] For example, in *principle*, we aren't permitted to walk up and knock someone to the ground, let alone crush him by ganging up on him with others who similarly attack his upright posture. Yet in an American football game, knocking people to the ground in gangland fashion is not only permitted, it is desirable within the parameters of play. It's demanded of the defense as a matter of principle. There are of course some arguments against the unhealthiness of football sacking as well as the potential for educating young people into a love for body-crushing violence, but the point is, the context of a game changes what we take to be morally considerable. For one thing, people do not have to play football, and so being open to being sacked is consensual. It may not be the smartest thing, but, hey, neither is slam dancing at a punk rock / rockabilly show. We don't think Josh is chargeable with assault just because he charges into you at a Throw Rag concert while you are both in the pit![12]

Perhaps, then, there is a special justification for the kind of phenomena to which Diamond objects. Here are some that might apply:

Common Special Justifications for Doing Violence to Animals

1. In a laboratory, *science* gives us leave to perform otherwise cruel or disrespectful things.
2. When an animal is a *pet*, it deserves respect that it otherwise does not have to receive.
3. When we need *food*, we are permitted to treat animals as stuff.

What do we think of these special justifications? Malcolm:

Yeah, well, even if science requires us to use animals, that doesn't mean the way we use them is totally irrelevant, morally speaking.

Okay. Good.—Yes, Omer?

I'm speaking about the second one. It seems to me that a pet is a special idea. We treat pets a lot differently than other kinds of animals. They have names, and people hug them for affection. People bury them, and people go into mourning over them. Like, Rachel, look how you feel about your border collie!

Exactly. I once had a colleague who felt similarly about her border collie. So you think there is a point to be made about giving pets different treatment than other animals, that it wouldn't be morally inconsistent, and Rachel, you definitely agree! Yes, Eliot:

Even if animals are food, like, you can do that differently than just making them live a . . . a really bad life. Like Native Americans, they traditionally thank the slain animal for its flesh.

Good! You all have a lot of good ideas! Yes, one more. Emily:

I think all these special justifications don't make sense about the basic issue. When we should respect life, we should respect life. Pets are a kind of super respect, but that doesn't mean you can do whatever you want elsewhere.

Okay, yes. The question seems really to be about whether respect for life admits of special justifications for disregarding it, and if so, what those are and what kind of leeway they give us.

Diamond has an interesting idea here. She wants us to reflect on what special grounds permit our being inconsistent. Failing to find those grounds, we should reexamine our lives to ease the tensions in them. Although she does not say so, I interpret her reflections as helping us deal with what I call "overlapping": the way pressures on our lives push us to over-determine areas of our lives. I'll write this, too, if I can find room on the board! Osool, please, don't eat my shirt!

Overlapping, a Common Cause of Inconsistency

- The same areas of our lives have *more than one human good at stake in them.*
- Often, one of those human goods is covered by the other, *producing the moral invisibility of the first.*
- The underlying issue of *respect for life is thereby cloaked.*

For instance, the pet-owning scientist who abuses animals for the sake of determining toxicity levels has allowed his vocational imperative to overlap with his everyday awareness of animal pain. It is part of the human good to respect life. But it is also part of the human good to handle toxic exposure. The result is an unsorted tangle of moral life. The tangle, in turn, produces moral invisibility. It is hard to see underlying commitments when they are obscured by surface ones. Regions of inconsistency very often involve overlapping normative imperatives that create a cloak for moral practice. In that case, the way to face the moral invisibility is to focus on the overlapping and remove the inconsistency as much as possible. This is an interesting kind of moral work.

To summarize, then, a region of inconsistency produces moral invisibility by overlapping imperatives that cloak moral considerations applying elsewhere. For example, the manner of treating animals in testing laboratories is inconsistent with how we think they ought to be treated on a city street. The animals become morally invisible in the laboratories, mere stuff, live litmus tests. The reason they become invisible is that the norm of testing has overtaken moral sensitivity to life. It has overlapped with such sensitivity and taken precedent, based on a tacit special justification for animal testing when done to reduce harm to humans. That imperative to test under the special justification of reducing harm has cloaked our normal sensitivity to animal pain and the result is that the animal's pain becomes a nonmoral consideration, if it is a consideration at all.

Or consider factory farming. The way animals are treated in factory farms is inconsistent with all our laws and customs regarding cruelty to animals, and is surely inconsistent with the ideal of nondestructiveness and respect for life in human socialization. Yet its inconsistency is rationalized by an overlapping. *The economic bottom line of producing profitable food has overlapped with respect for life.* The production of food, in turn, has received a special justification for exempting us from the prohibition against killing life. Needing food provides a special justification to kill in some circumstances. Under the double cloak of this special justification and the increasingly powerful norm of maximizing profits, factory farming is thrown into moral invisibility. So the infrastructure of major sectors of global food production subsists on what appears to be an immoral act of massive cruelty. What needs to be done, in turn, is to look carefully at both the special justification and the purported authority of the overlapping norm, and to figure out if an inconsistency such as this is mature for human life.

*

Diamond has an interesting way of handling such an inconsistency. I would like to begin with her idea as we head into the critique of factory farming, and also to applaud her as we do. This will be the last appearance of her ideas in this lecture series, and she has been a suggestive source of them over the years. Of course, he who champions accuses, especially with a subtle source. So I will say only that she has sparked some thoughts in me and that my interpretations of her work have helped me approach environmental ethics in a different way from the mainstream. This way may have been less theoretically ambitious than some other approaches to environmental ethics, but I have found it closer to what I think when I settle into a life that is meaningful in a worn, human way.[13] If I've misinterpreted her or misled you about her views, I hope she excuses me.

In "Experimenting on Animals," Diamond discusses "putting pressure on the circle" of what we are calling moral invisibility. Her discussion goes like this. Even if we grant the special justification for treating animals differently in the laboratory than we should treat them on the street, it still remains the case that we should minimize our exempting them from respectful treatment. (This is her point. Note, though, that our argument over the last two weeks strengthens this consequence considerably. We are supposed to keep developing what is best in us.). Second, a special justification gives limited permission, not open license. For example, a person who uses the special justification of self-defense to justify striking an attacker has that justification on her side only insofar as she strikes in ways consistent with self-defense. If she suddenly turns and tortures the attacker after he is down, she has crossed a moral line. She does not have license to torture him when she has a special justification to strike him in self-defense. The same applies to experimenting on animals. Just because we might have a sufficient reason to use them doesn't permit us to forget about their dignity entirely and put them through all manner of torture.

Minimizing the violent treatment of animals has far-reaching institutional and cultural consequences. This is where putting pressure on the circle comes in. If we are to minimize exempting animals from our ban on inflicting abusive conditions on them, we should put pressure on laboratories to shrink the circle of permitted, violent experimentation. Options should be tried that can circumvent the apparent need for violent testing on animals. When nonviolent options exist, these should be chosen. Additionally, steps should be taken to treat the animals with as much respect as possible. For example, animals should not be classified as mere "stuff" but should be discussed using a vocabulary that acknowledges (a) that they are fellow lives and (b) that our using them takes a special justification that is best to avoid having to use. When you put pressure on the circle, you reduce it.

Imagine, then, that you can test toxicity levels by using smaller doses or an artificial skin substitute, or by eliminating toxicity from cleansers. Imagine, too, that it is possible to produce such cleansers at a decent price and that one could regulate against the production of toxic alternatives. Given such options, the point would be that we are morally obliged to use them, as a matter of elemental consistency, a way of avoiding mixed messages in our culture. I would add, of course, that the obligation would also flow from our socialization and the ideal commitment to increase our respecting life. Imagine, then, that we turn to the issue of altered vocabularies for any animals that are still tested, perhaps now with a nontoxic substance we nonetheless need to check. In such altered vocabularies, they cannot be thought of merely as *subjects* or *test cases*. Rather, they are *living beings we unfortunately have a special justification for testing*. It would be better not to have to use that justification, too. In being consistent even with the special justification, we keep the loss in view.

What is interesting about this approach suggested by Diamond is that it accepts the putative justification of someone who thinks animals can be experimented on and then demands that real steps be taken to creatively minimize violence done to animals. There is a kind of institutionalized thoughtlessness in not creating procedures and a culture that apply a force vector to the circle of exempted treatment so as to minimize it. Ecological maturity, by contrast, involves instituting just such a creative procedure of finding and articulating nonviolent options. Moral invisibility is not, then, a matter of some constitutional blindness we have. Rather it is an effect of inattentiveness and lack of methodological rigor. In fact, I suggest it is often an effect of capitalist excesses that overdrive productive areas of the economy to lose their rigor in respecting life. But respecting life should be a feature of our socialized humanity.

Now Diamond's approach assumes some awareness of the abused animal as an animal being used in a special way—for example, as a test subject. Yet such awareness is not found with all areas of moral invisibility. Here, factory farming is especially troubling. There doesn't seem to be an awareness the animals are being treated in potentially immoral ways. Factory farms, first of all, draw on the fact we think of animals in their midst as *meat, egg-layers,* or *milk-makers.* Hidden in these expressions is a special justification for the killing or extraction of animal resources: to eat and drink. Secondly, factory farms intensify the way the animals are conceived as food resources. These living creatures become stuff to be squeezed to produce food. This stuff is quantified through tabulations of productivity specifying particular aspects of its life, for example:

- how the stuff responds to a certain kind of multivitamin grain mix
- how many eggs the stuff produces under specific dietary conditions

- how many of the stuff die when cages are made smaller to fit more stuff inside the storage barns
- how the stuff's muscles develop, or fail to develop, when given a diet designed to soften them
- whether there is less loss of stuff when the beaks are cut off

Such quantification is typical in capitalism. Since the value of a creature from the standpoint of capitalism is in its ability to accumulate capital, the systematic tendency is to abstract the animal's life into a set of disconnected parts that act as instruments for profit-making. The living creature becomes increasingly conceived as an abstract value—capital.[14] Capital, however, is completely fungible. Respect for what contributes to it is not an issue. In other words, the respect-worthy elements of the animal become transformed and streamlined into means that are maximized for their efficiency toward capital accumulation.[15] Their lives become numbers.

In such a situation, pressure cannot be exerted on any circle, because the animal has become cloaked behind a vocabulary that erases its moral considerability. What needs to be done is to dismantle—some say deconstruct—the vocabulary itself so as to reveal the overlapping that has occurred.[16] Such a dismantling involves not just words, but institutional arrangements and habits related to the words. Here, idealism and maturity have a difficult task: the disentanglement of the animal's being from behind the apparatus of capitalist production. Once we realize the stuff in the cage is a living being like ourselves, it is no longer appropriate to extract stuff from that stuff as if its living reality mattered not one bit. We need to change our practices, too, asking whether it is humane to deny a living being a healthy life in such a *cage*, or asking whether it is justifiable for human beings with a nondestructive soul to *mutilate* the animals for the next surplus edge of profit.

One of the main goals of ecological idealism today should be to dismantle the cloaking effects of our profit-maximizing, global economy. It is not just a matter of putting pressure on the circle of exceptions to our moral rules. It is a matter of revealing that such circles have been set up, permitted, and expanded to a very large degree. To give a concrete image of what I'm talking about, the very cellophane wrapping that packages the bloody ground round one buys in a supermarket should be revealed for what it is: part of a food processing chain that distances us from the actual conditions of food production, from what we are doing to other beings, and from the fact we are eating other living beings. The *flesh* we eat is not just stuff, and we should de-cloak it from institutional acts and overt vocabulary that make it come out as stuff and little more.[17]

Moreover, to reverse Diamond's image, we should be concerned not only with narrowing the circle of exceptions to respect for life but also with widening the circle of respect for life. We should work on widening a circle of those relations to animals in which we deal with fellow lives. Exposing people to the truth of food production, rather than hiding that truth, is part of this process of widening a circle of respectful practices. It is none other than widening the inclusiveness of the world through ecological idealism. I am saying we as citizens should be doing this.[18]

Okay. Let's take our customary break on this long day. When we come back, we'll head into respect for life as it emerges when we widen our world's respect.

* * *

I noticed a number of you were unsure whether Osool likes to be touched. She likes it, but you have to be both confident and slow enough not to startle. Also, there are places she can be touched and others she can't be, and you have to receive her bodily permission, just as with a human being. . . . We still have a fair ways to go today. We might go a bit over time, if that's acceptable to you.

Before we took a break, we had drawn some rough ideas developed from Diamond's work. We discussed narrowing the circle of moral exceptions, removing obstacles to respect in our vocabulary and associated institutions, and widening the circle of respectful relations to animals. We discussed moral invisibility in terms of lack of attentiveness and also in terms of cloaking vocabulary and concepts. In the background was my claim that the major form of cloaking in factory farming is that provided by the aims, concepts, and words of our currently misregulated economy. Next week, I will argue that capitalism, while it may be good for many forms of efficiency and innovation, should also be held in check to moral standards through appropriate political regulation and moral vigilance. The problem is that capitalism is not appropriately fitted to our humanity yet.

I said earlier that the critique today is humanistic. It is, because an idealistic commitment to respect all life increasingly is a defining feature of our humanity. Accordingly, I want to discuss how ecological idealism brings us to reconceptualize our moral universe, and I want to do this by continuing our critique of factory farming. One of the driving forces of such a critique is the notion and importance of respect for life. It is because respect for life is so central to socialization and because we can continually and infinitely perfect the ways in which we do respect life. This means that we can continually

subject our words and institutions to moral scrutiny. What do I mean by respect for life being "infinite" though?

Respect is *an intensifying concept.* Respect can be worked on, just as care
can be made to improve in quality. The means of intensification are not
quantitative. They are qualitative and express thoughtfulness for the good,
freedom, or dignity of the respected. Since the good, freedom, and dignity of
the respected are holistic concepts that touch on almost every dimension of
a life, there is, for all practical purposes, an infinity of aspects that can be respected in being thoughtful of another. For instance, the freedom of a child
should be balanced with the child's emotional development, since overper-
missiveness can be experienced as a form of neglect. Hence thoughtful parents work on achieving the right balance between license and direction and
further question whether direction and license are the ways they ought to
nurture cooperative guidance and autonomy. Moreover, respecting a child
while achieving the balance between guidance and letting the child be is
open to much creativity. A good parent can reflect on her emotional tone,
on jokes, trial and error, discussion, games, media, instruction, chores, field
trips, grandparents, other children, sisters, brothers, and so on. I am only
tickling the surface. Respect is an intensifying concept. As with love, when
you are thoughtful with it, you find ways to improve, to open the relationship. So you discover yourself in the midst of new dimensions you hadn't
foreseen, a more attuned and intricate complexity.[19]

Secondly, respect for life is global. Anything that is alive is not the kind of
thing that deserves no respect, unless a special reason applies. We already argued this point two weeks ago. This means that in principle there is a great
deal we can intensify! As I see it, our situation is this. We have inherited a
history that contains a dense crisscrossing of special justifications for taking
animal life, using other forms of life, defending ourselves against pests, preda-
tors, and so on. We have also inherited an economy that gives immense incentives to abstract life into a value for profit-making, and that has harsh dis-
incentives against not doing so. This economy involves a massive and often
chaotic architecture of concepts, practices, and institutions that have ob-
structed the respect-worthiness of life. It has done so through drawing on the
historically inherited special justifications for taking or using life. Meanwhile,
abstracting life into value, the economy has proliferated many new justifications for abusing life, species of the single genus: "For Self-interested Profit."
Joining our history and economy together and including cultural dimensions
I have not gone into (religious attitudes toward soulless creatures or metaphysical beliefs about human superiority), there are many ways exceptions are

taken to apply against the global commitment to respect life present in our socialization. Thus, because of the complicated overlapping that cloaks respect for life, there are many areas available for intensifying respect.

The humanistic critique is irreducibly idealist, an ongoing charge to improve the quality of our care and our thoughtfulness with other forms of life. We should repeatedly clear away and examine our justifications for using life, rethink words that cloak life's respect-worthiness, and investigate alternative means to taking or using life. To do so is a mark of our thoughtfulness.

A Mark of Human Thoughtfulness

To repeatedly clear away and examine our justifications for using life, rethink words that cloak life's respect-worthiness, and investigate alternative means to taking or using life.

The preceding remarks about respect also help you understand why I haven't gone into detail specifying what exactly respect demands, especially in cases where we have to balance respect for life with other important human goods. I agree that these are the cases that matter and that ecological policy has to be able to answer them. But my argument is committed to our continual improvement of respect. Hence, what is important for me is to conceptualize why we have to keep putting pressure on *any* violence done to life so that we try to find a way to avoid that violence even when it's justified. I am concerned with establishing a developmental, idealistic imperative and think that respect's intensifying and global qualities support my task, not weaken it. There is always work to do.

*

Nashwa:
All life?
Yes—unless justifications apply. According to our argument, the burden of proof should be *against* letting life be abused. After all, life is not something that does not deserve any respect. In this light, the primary image we should have in our minds is of a vast and infinite circle of life. Everything in that circle deserves some respect. We have to prove we have good reason to take away some of that circle, to patch it in with areas of use, killing, or the like. What ecological idealism seems to demand—and here I depart from Diamond—is not that we put pressure on the circle of exceptions, nor even that we widen the circle of respect for life, but that we *begin with a global commitment to respect all life.* *That* is being a citizen of a world that includes the Earth. Then,

and only then, can we begin the process of giving regions of that circle provisional and special exceptions. And the point is, the primacy of the circle remains unchanged. Any of those provisions or special exceptions from respectful behavior should be open to scrutiny as we revisit our past decisions to make sure they still apply and are reasonable.

Your handout shows three circles that represent the evolution of this lecture's critical work:

| Diamond's Circle | The Widening Circle | The Basic Circle with Exception |

Diamond's circle represents what goes on when we try to reduce an exception. The widening circle represents what goes on when we try to work *back against* a culture whose assumption is that life is primarily of value, for example, a capitalist economy as currently practiced. However, the basic circle with exceptions represents the wide-open circle of ecological idealism. It restores the rightful place of respect for life within our culture, given that respect for life and idealistic love for what is respect-worthy are essential to our socialization.

How, then, do exceptions to the wide-open circle work? This is a place where abortion should be discussed. Since abortion is a very sensitive subject on all sides of the issue, please be patient with me as I discuss why we have to consider it here. Note, too, that in what follows I won't advocate or prohibit the practice, because a conclusion would take a separate course, and it would be irresponsible for me to barge in and hastily resolve an issue so important to so many. Rather, I want us to learn why the contested issue of abortion makes the issue of exceptions to respect for life a question of understanding what fits each species of life involved. In what follows, I'll argue that *one* reason we have an argument around abortion in the US is because of the kind of species we are: a free one that lives more through meaning (i.e., idealistically) than through biology.

Abortion is often thought of as an exception to respect for life. Now, there is a genuine question about if, and if so when, a fetus is a life. For the present purposes, however, I will assume that a fetus is part of the life cycle and re-spect for life would seem to want to show care for the life cycle of living be-ings. I will also bracket out the matter of the mother's rights, even though that issue is a focal point of those advocating the right to choose (in other words, there is no way my discussion here can resolve the debate, since I am not entering into it). It would then seem that abortion should be intrinsically opposed by the morality we have advocated. It would seem, after all, that these lectures are right-to-life (although the mother's life also counts). Yet the matter is complicated, because what it is to respect a human life cycle is not a simple matter of preserving us biologically, paradoxical as that may sound.

Remember, in lecture four we noted that respect for life must fit the species in question. As a result, the language of exceptions is too blunt to specify what we want to capture. We must also add in the idea of respect shaped to life forms. This shaping may produce what looks like exceptions, yet on closer scrutiny actually produces species-shaped thought about moral-ity. In this way, we don't simply remove areas of life from moral invisibility when we make sure our exceptions are legitimate. We also bring our life into focus.

One reason why prohibiting abortion is not a simple matter from the per-spective of respect for life is that the *human* life form is a form of (1) freedom and (2) meaning. Because we are creatures of freedom, matters that limit our freedom in the most basic of ways are extremely serious.[20] Because we are creatures of meaning, being unwanted or thrown into situations with desper-ate meaning is extremely grave.[21] For human life, an unwanted, meaningless, or violent life is hardly a life at all, especially if your caretakers are unable to provide for you adequately. That is how central at least some small glimmer of hope is for human life.[22] To put this point another way, being wanted is es-sential to feeling human.

Arguments for freedom to choose abortion make respect for human life more subtle than one might think, because they work off these two anthro-pological facts about humankind. They suggest it is essential to our being that we be wanted, and especially not unwanted. They try to show respect for *our* life form. Human life is idealistic in an irreducible sense. It is not just bi-ological life that makes up a life for a human, but the good of our lives de-pends on what we make of our lives and on what meaning there is to them. Human life is meant. If we are to discuss abortion thoroughly, we have to take seriously this fact about our idealism. When we do, we should see there can be a serious reason for choosing not to go through and birth prenatal life. Whether this reason is decisive is a separate matter, and it would be irresponsible of me to make a judgment here (note that it couldn't be decisive, because I have excluded from discussion the other main concerns of the debate, e.g., the sanctity of life, the commands of G-d, the mother's rights, etc.). The point I want us to note now is that what it is to respect human life is to respect the way we are ensouled with meaning: deliberate and requiring a context of hope.

Because we are ensouled with meaning, being wanted as opposed to unwanted can be constitutive of being human, and we can see ourselves as created in the realm of meaning and not just in the realm of biology.[23] Decisions to have children then constitute the proper meaning of the newborn human life, and having children while wishing you hadn't had them becomes a violation of the child's very being, a violation that stretches across its entire life. Much the same can be said of those born into contexts that cannot adequately care for them. In this way, it can be humane to decide on beginning a life: whether now is the time and place for it, or not.

Thus there is cause to stop and think about how the right to choose might be a proper dimension of respect for human life. At the same time, no matter what one makes of the reason just given, respect for life commits us to limiting the need to have to face any dilemma surrounding abortion. Just as respect for life involves putting pressure of any legitimate exceptions of the rule, so it should involve pressuring out the situation giving rise to the dilemma in the first place. It should urge creative means to head off the kind of conditions that give rise to abortion debates. Such means include education—making people thoughtful about intercourse and criticizing promiscuity in the media.

One of the greatest concerns, too, should be the culture of convenience that thinks of abortion as an option much like getting one's knee bandaged if one happens to have tripped and fallen. It often seems abortion for some has become a matter of convenience. Whenever it has, it is immoral, because it has lost the gravity of respect for life. To me, the cultural forms that make factory farming preferred are similar to those that make abortion a matter of convenience. In both cases, we have the pursuit of immediate gratification overtaking thoughtfulness.

There's more to be said here, but I can't responsibly go into it now. What I want the case of abortion to show is that granting an exception of respect for life involves grasping the specific dimensions of a life form and its good.[24] Again, we already saw this in lecture four on analogical reasoning. Chickens have to dust themselves to accomplish their basic hygienic habits. Cramped cages and a lack of dusting particulates on the floor are indignities for their form of life. The lack of the dusty floor would not be an indignity for a cat.

So when we turn to dismantling our exceptions to respect for life, we should keep an eye on how specific improvements in the conditions of animals may significantly improve the quality of their lives. One needs ecological literacy, specifically zoological literacy, to do this.

Additionally, I want our discussion of abortion to show how exceptions should proceed within the emotional register of thoughtfulness. Taking life should involve a sense of gravity, regret, or blue gratitude. Eliot mentioned this earlier. For example, putting a new house into a field ought to be done with a certain amount of gravity. To live, we are displacing a small ecosystem. We do need a place to live, but displacing life shouldn't be a mindless act. How can we develop real estate in an ecologically respectful way? Or to take another example, the eating of animal flesh ought to be done with a special form of consciousness. One could imagine a shade of blue tinged with that gratefulness. It is not a mindless, irrelevant thing that we take life. Exceptions within the circle of respect for life should be under pressure from our moral universe. That is the point. We do not need to live with *guilt* for them. When reasoned well, they are legitimate exceptions. Still it is a mark of our humanity when we manage to reduce them and open up the circle to a more thoroughly pervasive respect for life in our actions and culture.

Here is where we can answer the question of harmful bacteria from a month back. Remember, it seemed insane to respect harmful bacteria. Now, I hope we can see it is not always so. Note that the classification of harmful bacteria already designates them in ordinary talk as opposed to us. This is a use of analogical extension whereby we have placed them in our moral universe as enemies with a blanket exception to kill them when need be. Amongst ourselves, we have a right of self-defense against enemies. Yet, too, when we are out harm's way, it is considered inhumane to hurt our enemies. So, too, with harmful bacteria. As long as they are not attacking us and we have defended ourselves against such an attack, it is immoral to eradicate them. They have a strange life, but a life, too.

I know this conclusion sounds off to many of you. The idea is simple, though. Imagine we come across harmful bacteria in some other living being. We could be affected by it. It could jump species. However, we've taken precautions, even developing an antibiotic in case it attacks us. Accordingly, what justification do we have to eradicate it in a preemptive strike? None, I think, just as with preemptive strikes among states. The *worry* of an attack is not the same as the beginning of an attack. Killing is not justified simply because we are worried about being hurt, unless that worry is over a truly imminent and lethal attack. And even then, we should simply defend.

What exceptions, then, are legitimate when it comes to the raising, food-extraction, and slaughtering of animals? I spoke earlier of investigating our vocabulary for dealing with animals. One of the most basic ways to revise what counts as a legitimate exception to respect for life in the raising of animals for food is to begin with how we conceive of animals in our moral relation to them. Earlier, I noted that one of the main sources of moral invisibility when it comes to animals is their conceptualization as *value* for a capitalist production process. We should reconceptualize the animal as something other than valuable. This is a most elementary way to revise our exception-ridden relation to them. For once an animal is not primarily a value, we have a conceptual origin from which to scrutinize our practices.

To begin with, note that we should think of animals as fellow living beings and as respect-worthy, even when a special justification can be found for using or killing them. We begin with the circle of life wide open. Note, second, that when we think of someone as deserving a minimum of common human respect, we do not do it *because* we value him or her. We do it, because it is part of our identity as humans to respect other humans.[25] Common human respect is categorical, a feature of the identity of our kind. It is neither optional nor fungible. When a fellow human is to be respected, she is to be respected, period. Moral respect is simply there or not there, and it can't be exchanged. These remarks indicate that the value of a person is not a good reason to respect her. Rather, her identity is, specifically, in how she forms a kind with our identity. Such is human *kind*ness.

Respect for life works the same way. When we respect life out of earthly humanity, we do so because that is what a human being does with fellow living beings. The shared identity of being a living being deserves categorical respect for a socialized member of humankind. Accordingly, the primary way we should conceive of and relate to animals when raising them for food is as *fellow living beings* who deserve respect categorically as a matter of humanity. We should not conceive of them as value. This point is simple but has far-reaching consequences.

To begin with, how and when you use a fellow living being is an issue of some consequence, whereas how you use something valuable is simply a matter of seeing how much else that is valuable depends on it. A fellow living being is a source of a moral call on our humanity, whereas something valuable is not.[26] Rather, something valuable is a source of interest for our value-balancing mind. Interests are optional. Calls are not. Calls lock into and draw on our categorical identity.

You should know what I mean by a moral call. Stop and think about living beings for a moment. That they are not *things*. Thus, when we take the life of a living being, it should not be like kicking a stone. The gap of mean-ing between kicking a stone and destroying life is the place where we can rec-ognize an—even faint—moral summons on us. This is what I mean by a moral call, and it grows to the extent we realize we have no special justifica-tion for taking or abusing a life. Unfortunately, however, the call tends to be deadened in proportion to the world's anxiety to acquire and use, including the way that anxiety takes the form of rationalizations.[27] Yet a call on us is a call on our identity—what categorizes us as human beings.

Here is another way to see this. When something is merely valuable, we are not in the first instance supposed to maintain a humane relationship to it. It could be, after all, something that we wish to exchange for something more valuable. Even if we think that something is intrinsically valuable, and so not fungible, we still thereby do not conceive of it as categorically related to our own humanity. But respect for life *is* categorical for our own human-ity, as our lecture two weeks ago showed. Furthermore, something that calls to our humanity is not something exchangeable. We are supposed to main-tain a humane relationship with it.

What would a humane relationship to animals raised for food look like? To begin with, it would involve expressing as nondestructive a soul as possi-ble with respect to them. If we have to use them, the way we use them should minimize pain, waste, and destruction and be thoughtful about the animal's form of life. This is important enough to write out:

What If We Have to Use Animals?

- Minimize pain, waste, and destruction
- Be thoughtful about the animal's form of life

Consider two possible kinds of exceptions. The first is when using the an-imal is good for the animal. Some animals have developed symbiotically with humans. Two examples include dairy cows and elephants in Southern Africa. Dairy cows depend on humans to milk them, and elephants in Southern Africa depend on humans to prey on them because humans are their only major predator. When humans do not prey on them, the ele-phants increase their population to such an extent that they cause their food sources to crash. They overgraze.[28] Doing so, they severely burden the land and countless other species dependent on its foliage and root mass. In cases like these, the animals should be used by humans, and what humans then need to show is care and restraint. Cows deserve to be treated with care, not just processed ruthlessly by machines and given a minimum of space to move. Our killing of elephants should be done with restraint, and in a manner that reduces pain and a torturous killing process (especially since whenever an elephant cries in distress, all its kind for miles hear it and are themselves distressed).

The second case is when we have to use the animal. This is the situation most open to critical scrutiny. In what sense do industrialized humans have to eat flesh? "In no sense" is the strictest answer. It is possible to have a vegetarian diet supplemented with vitamins and minerals if need be. There is a looser sense of having to eat animals, though, and it comes from the habitual tradition of flesh eating. What interests me here is what it looks like to *revise* meat eating so that it moves toward being increasingly humane (in the way respect, like love, is an intensifying concept). I am a vegetarian, but let us suppose we grant flesh-eaters some customary sense of having to eat flesh. What would humane flesh eating be?

Eliot earlier mentioned the precedent of many Native Americans in this regard. Among many American Indian nations, we find flesh eating practices such as showing gratitude to the animal, using the animal entirely, and conceiving of the animal as a kind of kin—not a human kin, but not entirely foreign to the human family either. These cultural ideas are rich with meaning, and I think they present us with both a challenge and ideas for revising our own cultural practices, including the practice of flesh eating. They also suggest that many practices should change inside factory farms. What could some of those be?

In closing today, I'd like you all to make a list together of ideas that could erode and revise the practice of flesh eating more in line with Eliot's comment. I want you to do this to imagine possibilities. You may not agree with the conclusions of this lecture, and I support your divergence from my authority in the interest of what *you* have reasoned out. (Please let me know sometime what makes more sense to you, and why.) I'll be the secretary and list what you find. We'll take both *the consumers end* and *the producers end*, keeping in mind the idea of relating to animals used for flesh in as humane a way as possible. Go ahead. Take a moment and then give me suggestions.

*

The Consumer's End

1. Consumers see, on the packaging, how flesh is produced. (Nisreen)
2. Consumers who do not go through a short course educating them about the realities and morals of food production are charged a tax when buying flesh. (Abdul-Rahim)

3. Consumers make flesh the exception and not the rule at meals. (Omer)
4. Courses in public school teach children not only ecology but also the moral consistency (with documents like the *Universal Declaration of Human Rights*) of showing restraint and gratitude when eating flesh. (Judy)
5. Consumers at restaurants finish their entire portions or are charged double the price of the meal.[29] (Malcolm)
6. And so on.

The Producer's End

1. Animals are given adequate room to move. (Nashwa)
2. They are given the material conditions for a normal member of their kind—for example, dusty floors for chickens. (David)
3. They are not allowed to develop sores as a result of the food production. (Frank)
4. They are allowed their normal social practices. (Maureen)
5. They are not biologically altered in ways that create distress for them. (Saleem)
6. They are not mutilated. (Kate)
7. When killed, the killing is done in a way that minimizes pain and distress. For example, they are not killed in lines where the cries of those up ahead panic those behind. (Joel)
8. When killed, the killing must be done by people trained in zoology and who have gone through training about the morality of killing animals. (Abdulla)
9. Idealistic youth teams oversee the food production, with the interests of the animals in mind up until the time of death. (Tina)
10. Workers in factory farms must go through training for humane handling of animals. (Cody)
11. And so on.

These are good. Many of your suggestions are idealistic, of course, and many might not be idealistic enough. The point is to think how inroads might be created that slowly erode and revise the practice of massive flesh production and frequent flesh eating. By extension, many of these suggestions apply to other forms of factory farming, such as egg production.

We're out of time. I want to note, as you pack up, that these suggestions do not apply to the consumption of plant life for the reason that plants do not feel pain and do not have social qualities. There are different considerations that apply to industrial agriculture, most importantly the loss of biodiversity resulting from current agribusiness. A critique of that sector of our economy would take a different study.

The suggestions we brainstormed are just policy prompts, not answers. The point of this lecture is to prompt us into social change and to focus our moral perception, the idea part of being idealistic. Once animals are viewed as fellow lives and not values, there is a categorical pressure to remove the overlapping that occurs between our use of them in food production and our respect for them as living beings. From the standpoint of ecological idealism, this categorical pressure exerts itself as an infinite charge to keep perfecting the quality of conditions in which animals live when we use them and to minimize our dependence on using them. This task extends, then, across many generations.

Can there be a humane place for eating flesh and using animal products that either benefits the animals or does not hurt them? Ideally, humans should mature into realizing that flesh eating is unneeded most of the time and that it should be handled with care. The prevalence of flesh eating should wither away, although under current cultural and economic conditions it will not. This is why the main goal of ecological idealists should be to tackle the current economy and hold it to standards of humanity. In doing so, you will join the ranks of human rights activists and many more. There are many just, nonviolent means to use too, whether taxation, other incentive structures, regulations, or consciousness raising. We are up against an immense economic pressure to maximize profit that continually abstracts animal life into a value that cloaks inhumane treatment. That treatment isn't worthy of the silence in Osool's eyes.

Notes

1. When I showed friends and colleagues this book, I found out that this title has been saturated by connotations of Walt Disney Studio's *The Lion King* and the hit song by Elton John: "*The* Circle of Life" (emphasis added). Long immersed in graduate school, I was unaware of this movie's song. However, before the expression's illustrious fate, "the circle of life" referred to a widespread Native American vision of cosmic order. It is unfortunate that Walt Disney Studio's production has obscured this tradition. With the title I've given this chapter, I am thinking of that tradition and of my own use of the idea of a wide-open commitment to respect life. Because, too, I don't take myself as having a right to appropriate the Native American idea, I will use an indefinite article: "*a* circle of life." The one in this chapter, a circle of wide-open respect for life, is one circle among many, and is an association developed from both a moment in Cora Diamond's work and the North American Indian vision. Earth, too,

happens to be a circle—a sphere, more precisely—of life. I want to thank Dave Aftandilian and Brian Yazzie Burkhart for clarifying the Native American cosmological idea for me.

In other uses of this figure, see Julia Butterfly Hill's Circle of Life organization (*www.circleoflife.org*, accessed May 24, 2005). I also discovered this organization after writing the chapter. Butterfly Hill is infamous among environmentalists for living a year in a redwood tree, "Luna," slated for lumbering. The action was planned by Earth First!, but dissension grew from it around Butterfly Hill due to her settling with the lumber company to preserve the tree. Also, being attractive and young, she is seen as a mainstreaming of radical environmentalism that some feel is a sell-out to the media and consumer world. Nonetheless, she is an active advocate for environmental causes, and I would argue that in the field of activism, it is worth spending time criticizing those who destroy life thoughtlessly rather than tearing down possible coalitions among roughly like-minded people.

2. A prohibition that, for instance, the late Sheikh Zayed, founding ruler of the UAE, openly and repeatedly promulgated.

3. I wish to thank Saiyad Admad for explaining the meaning of *usul* (the Library of Congress transliteration) to me. I wish to thank David Weddle for explaining the history of the use of the word "fundamentalism." In using this word for the name of an animal, I want to clearly state that I in no way intend disrespect for Islam, and I apologize if anything inappropriate is perceived. From conversations with students in my environmental ethics class at American University of Sharjah, it is clear to me that Islam has a respectful view of animals, more so than Christianity, for example. Prophet Mohammed (peace be upon him, as Muslims say) even has specific directives for the respect of animals.

In Islam, G-d's creatures are seen as deserving of respect because they are His creation. In turn, His creatures can be killed only with proper justification, and when killed for food should be slaughtered in as humane a manner as possible (this is the analogue to *kosher* killing in Judaism; in Islam it is called *halal* killing). These moral *principles* surrounding the treatment of animals supports the idea that part of the right, part of our roots, should be in respect for animals. Humans, then, should be rooted in the humane treatment of animals—and indeed of all life.

4. This last expression is an allusion to and almost direct quote of Cora Diamond from "How Many Legs?" in *Value and Understanding: Essays for Peter Winch*, ed. R. Gaita, New York: Routledge, 1990.

The Ramadan goats were in likelihood being prepared for sacrifice during Eid Al Fitr—the celebration that comes at the end of Ramadan. Many of my Muslim students question whether the extensive sacrifice of goats (in the millions) is consistent with the prophet Mohammed's respect for animals, even though sacrifice was called for by him. I think they urge a reduced practice that is more symbolic than widespread, although according to their religion they can only urge such a view if they are backed by proper religious sources and authorities. Note that sacrificial killing of animals still shows some respect for life, whereas factory farming shows none.

5. On this movement, see Peter Singer's book, *Animal Liberation*, New York: Ecco Books, 2002.

6. Judy has worked on animal protection. In that, she is like many students whom environmental ethics courses are fortunate to have participate in them.

7. Eric Schlosser, *Fast Food Nation: The Dark Side of the All-American Meal*, New York: Perennial, 2002.

8. Diamond, "Experimenting on Animals," in *The Realistic Spirit*, Cambridge, MA: MIT Press, 1995.

9. See Glover's *Humanity: A Moral History of the Twentieth Century*, New Haven: Yale University Press, 1999, chapter 2.

10. Some of these points are summarized in Craig Summers and Eric Markusen, "The Case for Collective Violence," in *Computers, Ethics and Society*, ed. M. David Erdmann and Michele Shauf, New York: Oxford University Press, 2003, 214–231.

11. Moral contexts are an interesting and new area of moral philosophy. I discuss them in a preliminary way in "Common Humanity and Human Rights," in *Religion and Human Rights (Social Philosophy Today*, vol.21), Philosophy Documentation Center, 2005, footnote 3. For a theory of moral contexts, see Mark Timmons, *Morality without Foundations: A Defense of Ethical Contextualism*, New York: Oxford University Press, 1998; and Margaret Urban Walker, *Moral Contexts*, Lanham, MD: Rowman & Littlefield, 2002.

12. Throw Rag, *Desert Shores*, Better Youth Organiz Records, 2003. For what it is worth, the real Josh is an environmental lawyer, as well as a skater, surfer and carpenter. You thought Julia Butterfly Hill was cool.

13. On philosophizing from what fits in a well-worn way, see Thoreau's *Walden*, the opening stretch of "Economy," in *Walden and Civil Disobedience*, New York: Houghton-Mifflin, 2000.

14. On abstract value in Marx and abstraction of elemental life vocabulary and measures, see Moishe Postone, *Time, Labor and Social Domination: A Reinterpretation of Marx's Critical Theory*, New York: Cambridge University Press, 1996.

15. This streamlining does not occur only with animals under contemporary, inappropriately regulated capitalism. It also happens with humans, for example, corporate managers. See Robert Jackall's brilliant study of this phenomenon, wherein humans streamline themselves into efficiency maximizers for the sake of gaining power in, and making profits for, the corporation (*Moral Mazes: The World of Corporate Managers*, New York: Oxford University Press, 1989). What the managers lose when streamlined is their moral being or, in ancient ethical vocabulary, the order of the human soul.

16. Those interested in a deconstructionist exploration of the above might start with some very hard but rewarding texts: Georgio Agamben's *The Open: Man and Animal*, Palo Alto: Stanford University Press, 2004; Michel Foucault's *The Order of Things: An Archeology of the Human Sciences*, New York: Vintage, 1994; and Jacques Derrida, *Of Grammatology*, Baltimore: Johns Hopkins University Press, 1994. My suggestion is closer to Foucault's work, however, than to Derrida's.

17. Singer alludes to such a need in *Animal Liberation*, New York: Ecco Books, 2002, 95–96.

18. At the very least, truthfulness demands it, because it isn't true living beings are things. On the structure of this virtue, see Bernard Williams, *Truth and Truthfulness: An Essay in Genealogy*, Princeton: Princeton University Press, 2004.

19. On the inherent, perfectionist dimension of love, a perfection that is not oppressive but contentment-deepening or exciting, see Jonathan Lear, *Therapeutic Action: An Earnest Plea for Irony*, New York: Other Press, 2003, 170–178, on love as the origin of "second nature."

20. Here, consider Carolyn Mcleod's *Self-Trust and Reproductive Autonomy*, Boston: MIT Press, 2002.

21. On this point, see the jarring study by Jean Amery, *On Suicide: A Discourse on Voluntary Death*, Bloomington: Indiana University Press, 1999.

22. On hope, see Megan Craig, "On Courage," dissertation in progress, Department of Philosophy, New School for Social Research, 2006.

23. The centrality of being wanted is recognized, with reference to Kierkegaard, also by Furtak, in *Wisdom in Love: Kierkegaard and the Ancient Quest for Emotional Integrity*, Notre Dame: University of Notre Dame Press, 2005.

24. A point made, with reference to humans, by Philippa Foot in her *Natural Goodness*, New York: Oxford University Press, 2003. However, Foot does not adequately address the species-tailored fact about humans: we are free and live more by meaning than by biology. On this, see Rousseau, *Discourse on the Origins of Inequality among Humans*, Indianapolis: Hackett Publishing, 1993. In effect, Foot establishes in part of the book a *necessary* condition on thought about the human good, but not a *sufficient* one.

25. This is a point explored in very different ways by Glover in *Humanity* and Levinas in *Totality and Infinity*, Pittsburgh: Duquesne University Press, 1969.

26. On being a source of a "call," see Jean-Louis Chrétien, *L'appel et la re-ponse*,[*Call and Response*], Paris: Presses Universitaires de France, 1992.

27. Rousseau wrote that conscience has a "quiet voice" the world drowns out (*Emile*, trans. Alan Bloom, New York: Basic Books, 1978, 291) or rationalizes away (*Discourse on the Origins of Inequality among Humans*, first part, *passim*). Kierkegaard deepened Rousseau's reflection by first conceptualizing—even before Freud—the centrality of anxiety to the way people relate to meaning. See his *The Concept of Anxiety*, written under a pseudonym, Vigilius Haufniensis (Princeton: Princeton University Press, 1980).

28. David Schmidtz, "Saving the Elephants," lecture delivered at the Scholarship and the Free Society seminar, Institute for Human Studies, University of Virginia, 2001.

29. This is an idea practiced at a vegetarian restaurant in Montreal. I have forgotten the name of it, but thank Prof. Greg Mikkelson of McGill's Department of Philosophy for showing me it.

Thoughts and Laws of Earth

Hey you all. Welcome back. This wood structure dates from the early nineteenth century, when Thomas Jefferson lived and Emerson and Thoreau were young. April 30, 1820 is the birth date, I think. I don't know if it is true for this barn, but I've heard that in early colonial America, a community turned out to raise a barn. It was a way of helping one's neighbors and involved a meal afterward. I imagine the basic structure was assembled beforehand, and then all day men helped put it up, with children running errands and women providing water. Now it would be women with hammers and men with aprons, too. Sometimes we lose good things as society changes, like a communal barn raising where owners build the structure they use, and sometimes we gain good things, like more gender equality. Thoughts and institutions change.

We shouldn't idealize life back then. This barn is on land that was once tribal, and we know what early American colonialists did to Native Americans. What we now call "ethnic cleansing" and "genocide" were part of the expansionist policies of the state and the people during the early years of the United States. There was a great deal of profit to be had from taking Indian land. We should remember that the search for new riches led Columbus to the shores of this country. Not much in that economic respect—or rather, *lack* of respect—has changed today.[1] Can we have some new economic thoughts and institutions?

Since you're working on your final papers, I want class to be on the short side. That way, you can walk around the preserve for an hour or so before heading back to campus. I wanted you to know this preserve exists for you and that it's not too far from campus. You can come here when you like and, if you are so minded, you can sign up for the field study course on the elements of biodiversity preservation. That course focuses on the preservationist strand in American environmentalism. Yet it does have a conservationist section of the course thinking about how resource use might, if done creatively, be consonant with preservation.[2] I highly recommend some field work experience. Even if you are a philosophy student who plans to preserve ideas, you have to discover life. You shouldn't lose the trees for the forest.

*

Last time, we looked at the theoretical dimension of green idealism, how we confront moral invisibility and conceive respect for life. This week, we will look at the practical dimension, how we become agents of social change. This week will include more attention to capitalism, too.

How do we shape capitalism in a humane way? People commonly begin with law. Laws prohibit inhumane practices such as slavery and child labor. They limit capitalism's exploitative drive and channel the economy toward outcomes consistent with our morality. Yet we saw during the second week's lecture on justice that law is not a simple matter.

First, the interpretation of the law depends on common sense. The judge who ruled on Beanal v. Freeport did not see a compelling harm to the Amungme in destroying their sacred mountain. If the judge had been Amungme, would he have seen a harm? The judge in the 1997 ruling was attempting to fathom international consensus as law required. That consensus can change when people's perceptions do.

Change happened recently in America around intimacy. In the mid-1980s, a famous case ruled that a homosexual couple found making love in their own home was guilty of a crime.[3] Just recently, however, the Supreme Court of the United States ruled that a couple arrested in a similar case has a right to make love freely.[4] Why the change of ruling? One answer could be that perceptions have changed. Perceptions could with respect to sacred lands as well.[5]

Second, law isn't sufficient to handle all important ecological problems. We need institutions, too. Some problems of large scale, such as global warming, cannot simply be regulated. Responses to them must also be intelligently coordinated. Institutions are good coordinators, creating a locus of responsibility for large-scale collective action. And they can function as large agents of knowledge, keeping us informed. To take a simple example, an agent like the United Nations is one institutional locus for the emerging global human rights architecture. It has legal elements, such as the International Criminal

Court with which it is affiliated. But it does more than just regulate. It links up with national governments, regional policy bodies, and development agencies. It includes monitoring, reparative work, and education. A similar kind of institution could be organized to address ecological problems of vast scale. After all, ecological solutions demand coordination between national governments, regional policy bodies, and ecological agencies, too. This is because national governments have control over their own nations' policies. Ecological problems are often regional. And a good part of ecological work is done by nongovernmental organizations (NGOs).

It looks, then, as if we should work on both *perceptions* and *organizations*. For instance, we would benefit from a cultural perception of how respect for life is categorically basic to our humanity in a way that capitalist valuation is not. We would also benefit from organizations that coordinate ecological justice and various forms of respect for life when they are matters of large scale, such as preserving the ocean's biodiversity or monitoring the conditions of food animals. Finally, we require regulations on capitalism's exploitative drive that restrain our economy from doing inhumane things—for example, with farm animals, the ocean's life, or the likely living conditions of future generations.

How should we go about these different and sizeable tasks? Whereas laws require cultural perceptions that support them, institutions shape cultural perceptions. There is a possible *feedback cycle* between perceptions and institutions. We can imagine a culture thirty years from now when ecological maturity has grown. In this culture, it is international common sense that destroying a people's sacred land is a violation of their culture. Laws then pick up the trace of common sense and support it. Perceptions support new institutions.

Inversely, we can imagine a law ratified with great difficulty concerning the way the fishing industry is supposed to catch and package fish. Not only is the industry required to use new kinds of low-impact nets with greater selectivity for the species they are after, and not only are they guided in the amount they can catch and must replenish with young stock, but they must also include a short discussion of the ecological cost of catching fish on every package they make. This discussion is similar to warnings on packs of cigarettes. We know, though, that once it becomes the law to say "smoking kills" on cigarette packets and to limit smoking to particular places, a question mark around smoking is placed in the culture. This is especially so for young people with no prior memory of the culture without those laws. Just so, a similar question mark begins to appear around the fishing industry. The law has begun to select and reinforce a perception. Perhaps, then, in this future world, tuna and shrimp producers are permitted to market their products only if they pass the approval of monitoring agencies that prove catch standards are met (some of this monitoring is done now, in fact, only with much less restriction on what can be sold).[6] The monitoring agencies are like human rights groups that monitor crisis conditions throughout the world on behalf of the world's nations. Knowing of these monitoring agencies, we learn to think of our culture as expressing a core commitment to respect oceanic life as a matter of institutional habit. Institutions articulate new cultural perceptions.

The feedback cycle between perceptions and institutions gives us an interesting challenge for creating the collective action funnels needed to form a world with appropriate moral structure. After all, the feedback cycle between perceptions and institutions can become negatively aligned, where immoral perceptions give rise to immoral institutions, as when anti-Semitism bolstered the rise of Nazi institutions. Or the cycle can become misaligned, our perceptions conflicting with our institutions and vice versa, as when a perception that people are equal coexists with laws that treat some people less well, or as when laws that require fair trials coexist with a perception of legal bias. We should align perceptions with institutions in an ecologically reinforcing way.

Let me give you a longer example of what I have in mind. There are a number of prominent examples of reinforcing institutions and perceptions that have marked our civilization during the epoch of capitalism. Laws prohibiting slavery were important revolutions in the moral structure of capitalism. Before their inception, it was permissible to treat human beings as stuff. What regulation there was in capitalism concerned contract. The freedom of humans was not inviolate. But the abolition movement popularized perceptions against slavery, often advocating these perceptions through organizations. Perceptions around abolition solidified into what we'd today call NGOs. These organizations, in turn, coordinated advocacy for abolition, thereby mobilizing collective action toward legislation. When the tragedy of the US Civil War was over, the idea of legislating against slavery was available to the public. Once laws prohibiting slavery were instituted, our culture was instructed by them across generations, thereby reinforcing abolitionist perceptions more deeply. Today, we take slavery to be an uncivilized economic relationship, and see the movement past slavery as an evolution.

The example of slavery is important for ecological maturity. Animal liberationists often compare our treatment of animals with slavery. There's a point here. One thing that is instructive about the frequent analogy between animal liberation and abolition is this potential for a similar process of social change surrounding the treatment of animals.[7] What began in cultural beliefs and animal rights NGOs can focus our culture toward legislation. Thereby, we can deepen cultural reform. Perhaps one day, as with slavery, we can bring about a culture where it is common sense to protect animals.

Or here is another example. Several centuries of international relations theory, new laws of war, egalitarian philosophy, revolutions, and increased competition among colonial powers created a culture in the early twentieth century that called for an international regulatory body. This call was answered by Woodrow Wilson's League of Nations. But this institution was powerless, and World War II swept its hopes away. Out of the rubble of World War II, after the Holocaust and faced with the Cold War, the need for an international regulatory body was more apparent, and we saw the creation of the United Nations. This institution, in turn, became a building block of our international human rights architecture and allowed many NGOs and grassroots human rights groups to have a prominent international body that can focus accountability for human rights standards. The UN is still evolving today, trying to rectify its horrific failures in Rwanda and Bosnia during the 1990s.

Through the UN and its educational branch UNESCO, beliefs about the importance of human rights have gained increasing prominence throughout the world. These beliefs have been urged on by NGO and grassroots organizing, not to mention the considerable adoption of human rights ideas in underground and academic media. By institutionalizing a culture of human rights in the United Nations, human rights became part of an emerging civil society movement internationally. This social movement, in turn, has reinforced the role human rights plays in our culture, even among those who seem to act inconsistently with human rights, such as the current president's administration. If you look at his foreign policy speeches, President Bush has to rationalize his policies as promoting human rights, even if his track record shows he cares little about them when economic or geopolitical interests make them unprofitable. Through a process of cultural modification and institutional adoption, then, human rights have become a vital concern in today's world, even if they are still under daily repression from forces threatened by them. There can be an ecological analogue to the human rights story: the creation of an international ecological humanity architecture that understands how our responsibility to each other in this world includes the Earth. After all, even the UN already has the beginning of such an architecture, the UNEP—the United Nations Environment Program.

*

How do we *enter* a reinforcing cycle between perceptions and institutions? How do we do so when the world is being conceptualized and treated increasingly as value?

Let's start with *perceptions* and what we mean by the "world." I am assuming you are familiar with the word "globalization" as it is used in the national media. Contemporary capitalism broadcasts the promise of globalization, a frictionless and borderless world of capital flow, a world where the free market flows inevitably toward a better world. But this image is a fantasy. Global production and consumption are full of friction and ecological burdens. Even the fast world of information technology whose enabling of finance capital and multinational production most suggests a seamless, economic world, even computing requires material conditions to function.[8] For instance, it requires gold chips (maybe even from Sacred Mother!), laborers who often destroy their eyesight assembling microchips, and a good electrical grid usually powered by coal, oil, or gas. There's much human pain and uneven development in our world today. There is much ecological destruction, at a pace the human mind cannot grasp on its own.[9]

Thus, there is a truer way of hearing the "world." The "world" isn't simply a given, unchanging and non-culturally specific idea. What it means is a matter of culture.[10] What *our* culture has made of the world is misguided in that the Earth is not heard as part of the world, and the world has increasingly become conceptualized through the language of values and resources. As we have argued throughout these lectures, though, we have good reason to understand the world as green (and blue). Thus, we should modify our perceptions to reflect our understanding. The world should include the Earth.

To include the Earth in our world, we must have thoughts of Earth. By a "thought of Earth," I mean an understanding of our life on Earth through respect for life. I'll write out the definition.

A Thought of Earth

An understanding of our life on Earth through respect for life

To be citizens of Earth, we have to understand life on Earth respectfully, for both action and culture flow from understanding.[11] How do we cultivate a respectful sense of the world?

*

We saw several weeks ago that respect for life emerges out of our care, the thoughtful, nondestructive region of our socialization whose purest form is an unconditional and idealistic love for life. What this proposition indicates is that progress in our truthfulness with respect to life should proceed by way of the path back toward our love for life. In this sense, *the Earth should appear from within the world out of our care for life*. At the heart of the meaning of being human, there is this care, and returning to it opens up the field of life (for those of you who have studied phenomenology, this is a phenomenological idea).[12] The care lets us see what is most thoughtful, namely, a consummately socialized and nondestructive side of ourselves. This in turn opens up life as respect-worthy.

How does one return to care? There are doubtless many forms, but one of the most remarkable I've seen is found in Quakerism. I am interested in Quakerism here not as an advertisement for the religion, but as an example of a moral practice that could be helpful for creating a more ecological culture. In what follows, I want to sketch a Quaker practice, and I mean it as an example that might suggest other, different practices we make for ourselves. I am thinking of Quakerism as having made a *philosophical* discovery.

In Quakerism, one becomes thoughtful by being silent with others. The silence is not a frozen, alienating silence. Rather, it trusts that with the presence of a community, when one lets oneself fall back into being with others, one's truth comes to light.

. . .

The idea is simple, and understands in a pure way the relationship between socialization and what is best in us. When we trust in each other, the love disclosed should become nondefensive and open up dimensions of ourselves we may have closed off, forgotten, or never known. Like water through sheet-rock that suddenly shakes down the side of a gorge, our defenses to what is best in us should disappear. This is just an anthropological fact about humans, a mark of our socialization and the integral role *kind*ness has in our psyches.[13]

. . .

In the communal silence of a Quaker meeting, people listen to what they need to say and to what they want to say, but which is most often closed out from being said in the rush of daily life. Here is where the brilliance of Quaker meetings lies. People naturally want to mend and to love. This point is very deep in child development and psychoanalytic literature, although the view can be traced back to Plato.[14] People adopt attitudes of hate, destruction, and self-fragmentation out of deep and habitual defenses to overwhelming dimensions of life. These defenses fundamentally involve distrust about the world and others. When the context of one's silence is a community that unconditionally supports your right to feel and speak and whose one structural condition is to create a space of trustworthy nonviolence, defenses can be stripped away or *freed*.

. . .

In that freeing, the human core in people has a chance to emerge. When it does, respect for life emerges with it. The fact is, we can almost always be more thoughtful with life. One way we can be so includes dismantling the defenses to the unconditional and vulnerable love inside us. Out of this love, we can come to a form of truthfulness that reminds us of what is most important in our lives, and out of this truthfulness, we can see idealism as the realization of our humanity.

. . .

You hear how silent this preserve is, don't you?

. . .

Wittgenstein said something like this once. We mentioned it over a month ago. He said, "the miracle is that the world exists."

This is not a sentimental comment, but it is a reflective one.

. . .

We are alive in a world out of which we have evolved, which sustains us, and with which the meaning of human time has been shaped. As we've seen over the past month, to destroy this world is to destroy ourselves, the meaning of ourselves.

What misregulated, anxious capitalism must forget to go its way is just this truth. Current, immature capitalism seeks to maximally exploit the world for the sake of profit, and it cannot exploit anything if it must also respect it. For this reason, any expression—in art, speech, journalism, gesture—that flows from the nonviolent source of thoughtfulness is an authentic and important part of ecological activism, an activism of passivity, and it brings the Earth into relief within the world.

*

Thoughts of Earth emerging from our love for life can break down conceiving the world as value. When we establish loving relations to our world, we begin to understand its beings and elements as free from us, not as things solely to be used, but if used at all, only thoughtfully. Freedom, not use, is our assumption.[15]

Out of our idealism, our world should be rooted in love for life. Thoughts of Earth, born of an origin in our love for life, should be our "osool." [16] Roots, however, have stems or trunks above them, and thoughts are the architecture of action and our entire instituted world. Good thoughts, words, and images are not enough to establish respect for life and ecological justice. *Institutions* are called for, too. When our institutions and our culture are not aligned, we experience society as oppositional to our best judgment or even alienating to our souls. Yet when our culture and institutions are aligned around what makes sense, society reinforces what is best in us and brings up our children into a world grown from sense.

So we should turn now to activism for institutions. That's the other part of the reinforcing cycle we seek to enter. Once we are guided by thoughts of Earth, what should we seek to cultivate?

I claim we should seek laws of Earth. Laws of Earth are somewhat broader than court-enforceable laws. I will use the category to include institutions that pattern collective action just as laws do. Here, I am inspired by, but not directly following, an ancient Greek word for law, *nomos*, which includes customs. What I want to categorize under "laws of Earth" are institutions surrounding the moral structure we give to our life on Earth. That moral structure, in turn, is cultivated from respect for life. Laws of Earth, then, are institutional arrangements that create the normative structure for a humanity thoughtful with life on Earth.

Laws of Earth

Institutional arrangements that create the normative structure for a humanity thoughtful with life on Earth

What would such a normative architecture be? How should institutions coordinate to institute thoughtfulness? We can see the broad functions institutions should pursue if we recall the case of global warming from our second lecture this quarter. There, we indicated that we need institutions that can (1) recognize global warming as it occurs, (2) pattern our behavior collectively in ways that deal with its likely effects, and (3) serve as the agent responsible for handling global warming. These three functions of institutions can guide us now. They are: (1) knowing the Earth's condition, (2) patterning respect for life on Earth, and (3) coordinating responsibility for the Earth.

1. *Knowing the Earth's condition.* In order to act ecologically, we must know what is happening ecologically in the world. First, we must gather knowledge. Such gathering consists of both scientific work and work of the sort done by humanitarian groups monitoring crisis situations. For instance, Dr. Sylvia Earle's work gathers knowledge. Her institutional position in the National Geographic Society and in US governmental oceanic institutes have allowed her to complete many studies of ocean life, and she has also presented her findings in reports on the Earth's oceans.[17] During her long life, Earle has also, inevitably, been involved with universities, another kind of institution that coordinates knowledge gathering.

Second, we must learn. Institutions knowing the Earth's condition include all those that provide ecological education. Formal schools and nonprofit groups have historically performed this function, as have some governmental agencies not primarily conceived as educational, such as national park services. Yet there are many ways to educate each other, and the range of kinds of educational institutions is as broad as our imaginations. For instance, some activists use touring buses as mobile classrooms. Others create Internet sites, and still others create theatrical productions.

2. *Patterning respect for life on Earth.* Once we know our ecological condition, we should find ways to organize our lives according to what we have learned and to what is morally wise. There are many ways to do so. Patterns of action can be made of laws, but need not be. They can also be formed by tax incentives, procedures, moral codes, and other non-legal normative forms such as everyday rituals. An ecological idealist will use action-patterning measures to create pathways of economic activity that remain humane.

The notion of patterning action comes from the theory of action and the notion of actions we are supposed to perform as a matter of propriety, whether we like to or not.[18] When a patterning principle of our action is in place, we must do a certain *kind* of act simply because it is what is appropriate for a human to do. Hence, if it is illegal to be cruel to animals, a socialized human will refrain from cruelty or find ways to confront cruelty against animals anytime it comes up. Similarly, if we have a ritual of refusing to take excessive packaging when we buy food so as to consume less, we refuse these materials even if we would like to take them or are too lazy to tell the employee to return them to their shelf. Being appropriate, our rituals are just what we have to do as socialized beings. They are the *kind* of things we do— acts without cruelty, or moderate acts. Patterns of these and other types are what we have to institute to shape the world thoughtfully. We already have with sacred places.

3. *Coordinating responsibility for the Earth.* Yet knowing our condition and patterning our lives accordingly still leaves open the question of how we will be responsible for large-scale ecological problems. Since any one of us cannot be held accountable for the entire problem, institutions are useful.[19] Hence, we should also seek institutions accountable for large-scale ecological processes affected by humans. The Environmental Protection Agency is one such body for accountability in the United States. A central administration of accords such as the Kyoto Accord is too, although it delegates responsibility to national governments for their share of the emissions cap and should evolve to penalize them if they exceed their limits. Finally, the World

Trade Organization (WTO) is supposed to function as such a body, ostracizing member states from trade benefits and partnerships if their products violate human rights or environmental standards. However, the WTO is faulty in practice.[20]

Institutional responsibility for large-scale ecological problems can involve everything from monitoring and lobbying groups to policing. It can also involve making information readily available so that people know where to go to have an ecological matter addressed. Think how often you *don't* act ecologically, because you don't know how to, where to, or with what institutional support. To take a common example, many people don't know where to go to recycle. Almost every major sector of society can become involved in providing information for ecological remedies: the media, the health sector, the police force, law courts, educational institutions, even religious orders. There is no need for us to feel overwhelmed by ecological responsibility. Rather, we can form organizations that institute collective responsibility in unified, corporate agents.

*

Through our three institutional functions, we can glimpse very broad areas of a global earthly humanity architecture. Just as there are laws of humanity (for instance, laws of human rights, humane treatment of prisoners, and the like), so our argument implies we should legislate laws of Earth out of respect for life. Since the category will probably strike you as immense, you might think of the laws of Earth as a genus containing many species—for example, the laws of animals, the laws of climate, the laws of sacred land, and the laws of human rights (after all, humans are one kind of living being deserving respect on Earth).

Some Species of Laws of Earth

- Laws of Animals
- Laws of Climate
- Laws of Sacred Land
- Laws of Human Rights
- and so on

We already have some laws in each of these species, such as human rights law, laws preventing cruelty to animals (that is, only *outside* farms and laboratories!), laws on permissible atmospheric emissions, and laws protecting some sacred, historic sites. But these laws are not enough, nor are they always the right ones. Remember Tom Beanal? New and well-developed species of the laws of Earth can hold the world to its proper ecological dimensions and institutionally pattern us as ecological citizens. Documents like the *Earth Charter* from our third lecture, idealistic though they are, point us toward the future of the laws of Earth. They include the Earth in the world, and so *include* human rights in the broader domain of norms governing respect for living beings. They make us one among many.

. . .

(I want you to note how radical that is: making human rights a species of ecological thought!)

. . .

In this lecture, we've talked about laws, an obvious way to reform our world, but only one method, often a blunt one, and one about which we should be wary. Law is a serious matter, because it implies the authority to coerce those who do not comply with it. Yet at the same time, it is important to dissolve hasty worries that come up when we talk of regulating people's lives and economies. One of the main worries is that no market will be free if we regulate it. But such a worry is misplaced. There is no such thing as a free market where "free" means "unregulated." All markets are constituted by regulation, for instance, contract law. There are other noncontractual forms of morality that have profoundly shaped the free market, too. As we discussed earlier, we prohibit selling people as slaves. It is therefore misguided to suggest that ecological regulation of markets will in principle make them unfree. On the contrary, ecological regulation should make them more worthy of a freedom we call "human."

We are free only because there are laws against violating each other for no good reason.[21] Regulating our use of other forms of life is consistent with liberalism's philosophy, once we extend it analogically. Liberalism's point is to allow us to flourish freely.[22] Once we include other life forms within the scope of our socialized respect, we must consider how they flourish as well. How free are they? What do the truthful signs of their lives tell us? They may not have free choice as humans do, but they do have a life all their own that can be blocked and dominated.[23] Are we liberal with those lives?

We have to use other forms of life to eat (at least plants), and we displace life when we build. Yet laws of Earth would try to open up, maintain, and enable as nondestructive a human world as is commended by our idealistic moral scrutiny. Such laws would set minimum standards of humanity for ourselves and future generations as well. They would shape our world in line with thoughts of Earth.

*

We are in this barn, created by a community and made for economic activity. It could provide some cold weather shelter for an animal like Osool if need be. Outside this barn are the redder trees, the trees under which we sat in the amphitheater two weeks ago. Many of the leaves have fallen, covering the ground with blankets of unexpected sound.

There is no reason why in principle morality, culture, and institutions cannot support each other. Yet bringing all three in line is a complicated, synthetic process. We may know that our world should express respect for life. That would be a world grounded in what is humane, not in the lifelessness of value. What we may not know exactly is how to articulate such a world, both verbally and institutionally. How do we figure out what works?

Social change is *complex*. Consider just some of the institutions that are part of our lives. There are schools and publishing houses; churches and sacred sites; courts and police forces; NGOs and communication grids; governmental administration and taxation systems; media centers and systems of production, distribution, and sales. We should write these out just to get a sense of our options.

Institutions We Can Work On

- schools
- publishing houses
- churches
- sacred sites
- courts
- police forces
- NGOs
- communication grids
- governmental administration
- taxation systems
- media centers
- systems of production, distribution, and sales
- (and there are more, too!)

How do we work on all these?

Social change also does not occur in a linear fashion. It often occurs through a *catalyst*. For example, modern international law emerged as a cultural answer to the seventeenth-century wars of early modern religion and of colonialist states. These wars forced a legal articulation that remade parts of society, especially so when in the twentieth century two World Wars and an imminent Cold War forced people to adopt human rights as the moral ideal of international regulation. There were historical events that catalyzed social change.

Underneath catalysts, though, there's usually *condensation*. Social change rarely has only one source. Confluences of cultures and institutions enable more pervasive change to arise. For instance, Enlightenment humanism worked together with the events of World War II to shape the *Universal Declaration of Human Rights*. In turn, Enlightenment humanism was the amalgam of early modern natural science, democracy, capitalism, anticlericalism, the age of exploration, the natural law tradition, Shakespearean self-culture, early modern forms of feminism, Cartesian ontology, and so on. Imagine how many other influences went into forming the *Universal Declaration* when we include the overlapping consensus that went into the multicultural authorship of the document—for instance, Confucianism as found in Article 1![24]

The point is, social change is not something we can simply create like G-d at the beginning of *Genesis*: "LET THERE BE ECOLOGY." Given how complicated social change is, given how multisided our sense of humanity is, and given how difficult, unknown, and complex many ecological problems are, I expect we will have to be *experimental*. As a teacher of mine once said, solutions that appear right from one angle often appear narrow or wrongheaded from another.[25] What is it to be experimental? I'm trying to think about how we can create condensation so we are ready for catalysts.

Let's see. *To be experimental with morals* is to discover whether a particular belief, patterned into actions it guides, creates tensions with other moral beliefs, attitudes, or habits. If it does (as when, say, the belief that killing is wrong creates a tension with the belief that we have a right to self-defense) then the experimental task is to come up with a mode of behavior that minimizes or resolves that tension. For instance, the police are taught to shoot to disarm, then to temporarily disable. A moral police officer will shoot in this way and only when, out of self-defense or the defense of another, he has to shoot. In this way, the tension between the wrongness of killing and the rightness of self-defense is resolved. Similarly, we might learn to eat in ways that use animals raised and killed humanely, and to do so rarely, only with ritual gratitude.

To be experimental with our collective imagination is to discover how well an expression accords with what is truly alive in a culture, and to then modify one's expression, in accord with what one learns from the interaction of one's expression with the culture. Does the expression connote things one did not intend and which are in tension with what one intended? What makes sense for people? How does it make sense? Are there beliefs which, if touched, will so shock the culture that people will become defensive and irrational? What is most imaginative for people? What emerges as important once a new belief is thrown into the cultural mix? Do I learn something from what has been brought to light in the exchange? Do I need to revise my beliefs in light of a discovery of cultural wisdom? Questions like these indicate that cultural modification involves trial and error attuned to the interconnections of the culture's beliefs, images, and styles. Only by genuinely listening to one's culture can a sustained response be generated.

Finally, *to be experimental with institutions* is to discover if they fulfill their functions well, and if not, to remake them. Just as moral beliefs may clash with others and cultural expressions may bring to light unseen tensions and lessons, so new institutions very often disclose problems, alliances, unseen advantages, weaknesses in the face of specific challenges, and many lessons concerning how people work best and worst together. People who know how to build organizations, modify schools, evolve churches, effect governmental change, or advocate successfully for new laws are among the unsung talents of the world. Such creativity is as prodigious as artistic creativity and involves a talent for dealing with other wills that few artists ever have to develop. As you will learn if you haven't yet, dealing with other wills is the greatest difficulty in life. To make institutions meet the various functions we sketched just a few minutes ago calls for much trial and error.

Take just one example (my favorite example this lecture). The League of Nations did not work well, but the United Nations has worked better. Yet it has failed miserably, too—for example, in Rwanda, Bosnia, and Darfur. Many today think, rightly, that the UN must be revised, including dismantling the current Security Council and developing a rapid response system that has international authority for genocidal wars such as those in Bosnia and Rwanda in the 1990s. The UN's secretary general, Kofi Annan, has even proposed such changes.[26] With the UN, we see an institutional response to humanitarian needs that has proven more effective than an earlier attempt at meeting similar needs, but which is far from being effective enough for the ideal of humanitarian respect.

As the UN suggests, being experimental with institutions may be the most challenging form of experimentalism of the three we've just discussed. Yet all three forms of experimentation have their difficulties, don't they? It's hard to get governments to strengthen the UN properly, but it's hard to deal with the outrage moral experimentation can create (not least in your families!). And good imagination often seems contingent on the gods. Yet morals that humanize us, expressions that catch into the air of our culture (hear this, you artists and musicians!), and institutions that handle ecological problems responsibly will bring the Earth out in the midst of the world in a way that helps our entire *culture* grow up. If the Earth should be conceptualized and institutionalized through respect for life, we have a *creative* goal.

So here is a challenge. For those of you who disagree with these lectures' reasoning, it can just be a thought experiment. There's at least an hour to walk around this preserve today. You can talk as you go. [27] How could you, as the next generation of idealists:

1. unwork the cloaking of Earth life;
2. popularize why respect for life is at the core of our humanity (why our identification with life has formed humankind across history and around the world); and
3. create the laws of Earth?

. . .

Enjoy the birds migrating in the sky!

Notes

1. The overt oppression of Native Americans has not stopped in recent history. See Ward Churchill and Jim Vander Wall's *Agents of Repression: The FBI's Secret Wars against the Black Panther Party and the American Indian Movement*, Chicago: South End Press, 2002. It is unfortunate that Churchill has been irresponsible in recent years comparing corporate capitalists with Eichmann, the primary administrator for the Final Solution in Hungary and other parts of Central-Eastern Europe. Eichmann was a direct and conscious agent of death, not an indirect agent of effects that can lead to exploitation and sometimes death.

2. I am assuming students understand that there are two strands in the American approach to dealing with uninhabited areas. One seeks to preserve that nature as wilderness (the National Parks approach founded by John Muir) and another seeks to conserve nature for wise use (the Forestry Service and Bureau of Land Management approach found in most schools of forestry). I wish to thank Phil Cafaro for first explaining this distinction to me.

3. *Bowers v. Hardwick*, 478 U.S. 186 (1986), Docket Number: 85-140.

4. *Lawrence and Garner v. Texas*, 539 U.S. 558 (2003), Docket number 02-102.

5. Stephen Rich (in an e-mail from May 12, 2005) tells me the comparison of the three cases is "apples and oranges"—, that is, of different kinds of cases. The Beanal case, as we saw, fell under an antiquated international law, whereas the Lawrence and

Bowers cases fell under civil rights law. My point is not a precise one in legal scholarship, but a presentation of a general possibility. Rulings in many kinds of cases depend on perceptions of what counts as common sense to the interpretation of terms in the law. When that common sense changes, so can the rulings.

6. See Peter Singer, "One Economy," in *One World: The Ethics of Globalization*, New Haven: Yale University Press, 2003.

7. See Peter Singer's *Animal Liberation*, New York: Ecco Books, 2002, again, especially chapters 5 and 6 on our culture of dominating animals.

8. This is a point made, albeit sometimes reluctantly, by Manuel Castells in *The Rise of the Network Society*, Oxford: Blackwell, 2000.

9. On ecological destruction, see Bender, *The Culture of Extinction: Toward a Philosophy of Deep Ecology*, Boulder: Humanity Press, 2003.

10. On this point, see Heidegger, *Being and Time*, New York, SUNY Press, 1996, and Henri Lefevre, *The Production of Space*, New York: Blackwell, 1991.

11. See Plumwood, *Environmental Culture: The Ecological Crisis of Reason*, New York, Routledge, 2002.

12. This point is suggested by Heidegger in *Being and Time*, New York: SUNY Press, 1996. See also Jean-Luc Nancy, *The Inoperative Community*, Minneapolis: University of Minnesota Press, 1991 and Jean-Luc Marion, *La phenomene erotique* [*The Erotic Phenomenon*], Paris: Grasset, 2003.

13. See again Paley's *The Kindness of Children*, Cambridge, MA: Harvard University Press, 1999.

14. See Jonathan Lear, *Love and its Place in Nature*, New Haven: Yale University Press, 1998, and Plato, *Symposium*, in *Collected Dialogues*, ed. Hamilton and Cairns, Princeton: Princeton University Press, 1987, 526–574. See also Paley, *The Kindness of Children*.

15. This is a freedom like that experienced by Meister Eckhart. See Bernard McGinn et al., eds., *Meister Eckhart*, vols. 1 and 2, New York: Paulist Press, 1981, 1986. See also Jean-Luc Marion, *Being Given: Toward a Phenomenology of Givenness*, Berkeley, CA: Stanford University Press, 2002. Also, consider the music of Windy & Carl, *Depths*, Chicago: Kranky Records, 1998; Sonic Youth, "The Sprawl" in *Daydream Nation*, New York: Geffen Records, 1988; or Steve Reich, *Music for 18 Musicians*, 1976, New York: Nonesuch, 1996. Finally, see Reiner Schurmann's *Heidegger on Being and Acting: From Principles to Anarchy*, Bloomington: Indiana University Press, 1988. Tarkovsky's *Mirror*, Moscow: Mosfilms, 1974, also contains a vision of freedom in the nature and early childhood scenes. The link to early childhood imagination is key: see Bachelard, *The Poetics of Reverie*, New York: Beacon Books, 1971.

16. "Usul," by Library of Congress transliteration.

17. See, for instance, "An Ocean Blueprint for the 21st Century: Final Report of the US Commission on Ocean Policy," Washington, DC, September 20, 2004, at *www.oceancommission.gov/documents/full_color_rpt/welcome.html* (accessed May 26, 2005).

18. On the idea of appropriate actions, see Vogler, *Reasonably Vicious*, Cambridge, MA: Harvard University Press, 2003. She is explaining Aquinas's reading of Aristotle, through the work of Elizabeth Anscombe.

19. This point first became clear to me in a seminar on moral responsibility held by Michael Green during the spring of 2001 at the University of Chicago.

20. See Singer, "One Economy," in *One World: The Ethics of Globalization* for an excellent, clear discussion of how the WTO has avoided its own commitment to respect life on Earth by manipulating a distinction between inhumane products and inhumane *processes*. Simply, the WTO does not count inhumane production processes as prohibited, but only inhumane products (such as child prostitution). Yet very little humanly or ecologically destructive production appears *as* the product. Most destruction is part of the *process*. Think of sweatshops for computer chips that make workers go blind under the working conditions. Think of toxic waste that is poorly treated and disposed of during the process of making paper.

21. See Philip Pettit, *Republicanism: A Theory of Freedom and Government*, New York: Oxford University Press, 1997. Could you ever violate me for a good reason consistent with freedom? Yes, if I were attacking you, and you had to defend yourself by bringing me to the ground.

22. See John Stuart Mill, *On Liberty*, Indianapolis: Hackett Publishing, 1978.

23. People who have studied the concept of freedom as it is classically understood in both religious and post-Kantian philosophy will have many problems with how I use the word in these lectures. My use is even inconsistent with Rousseau's. This is not the place to go into the debate here, but I want to state that I take the lessons of Wittgenstein on ordinary language seriously. I think it is a philosophical failing to be blind to the *many* uses words have in our ordinary language. Those uses may have inconsistencies among them, but most often they have sense to them, and what we have to do as interpreters is understand how different senses of a word link up. In the present case, I believe that freedom is *primarily* a word applying to humans, but that—because we are so essentially free, because freedom is so central to us—we extend the word analogically to understand other beings in a way that tries to appreciate their dignity as well. As with an analogy, in *some* but not *all* features, other animals can be free as we can be. For instance, they can be dominated or have their inner principle of motion (what Spinoza called their "conatus") blocked.

24. On the process of drafting the document, see Johannes Morsink, *The Universal Declaration of Human Rights: Origin, Drafting, Intent*, Philadelphia: University of Pennsylvania Press, 1999. Thanks to delegate Chang, Confucianism is found in Article 1 in the concepts of "brotherhood" and "conscience." They overlap *fraternite* (from the French revolution and the Semitic religions) and *ren* ("two-human-mindedness," from Confucianism).

25. Charles Larmore, "Why I Do What I Do," *University of Chicago Humanities Division Bulletin*, Chicago: University of Chicago Humanities Division, Spring 2003.

26. Kofi Annan, "In Larger Freedom: Towards Development, Security and Human Rights for All, New York: United Nations, A/59/2005, March 21, 2005. See *www.un.org/ largerfreedom/report-largerfreedom.pdf*, accessed May 27, 2005.

27. In ancient Stoic practice, wise people were trained to find the *kairos*, the right time. This is the time, similar to the moment of perfect virtue in Aristotle's *Ethics*, in which action is decisive and done well. Martin Luther, Kierkegaard and Heidegger developed this idea by speaking of the moment, the instant, or the "blink of an eye," when we decide on something meaningful or *are* decided by events. In Christianity, the word is sometimes used to refer to the fullness of time, as well, when love appears in the world.

~

The Sky inside the City

Hey, you're so talkative! Listen up. We've reached the last session of our course. Oh, don't clap—it wasn't that bad. There was no fundamentalist moralizing, and you even got to pet a goat.

I loved walking in here this afternoon and hearing so many people talking. We did at least one thing well this quarter. We had a class that found connections. The only thing that would have been nicer is if this entire lecture course had been a dialogue. But the organizers of this lecture series said it had to be a *lecture* series. Still it's nice to be back in this hall with you one last time. Don't be strangers next year. Contact me over e-mail when you want to talk.

Megan and Nick were up here talking to me about painting this time of year. I know what you mean, you two, about the end of the fall quarter and this time of year. After the lecture today, I am going down to New York to enjoy the late fall, early winter air. The holiday lights are out along Central Park, and there should be some dusting of snow still on the trees from yesterday, mixed with what's left of the fall. Those lights burn electricity. Yet if every office building turned off its floor lights after working hours, we'd have enough surplus energy to enjoy something beautiful. I guess I don't think it's bad to expend energy on something public and beautiful. In my own home, by contrast, I don't use much in the way of holiday lights.

In this weather, my Aunt Ruth Bendik loves to go for walks. So we'll probably go for a walk together before stopping in this neighborhood Hungarian place to eat, where everyone's a local and the waitresses look like they're either going to insult you or offer you timeless wisdom. Ruth and I talk about things like we discussed in this course. She's one of those conscientious citizens from what used to be a Democratic Ohio who cares about having a good world. She's one of the many everyday people who make the world go and who are relatively incognito from all that makes its way into the media. Yet without people like her, the world would go to hell. And with people like her, the world is basically a good place. In any event, I've always enjoyed talking with her. You know, I hope you communicate well with your families. Families do a lot to help us feel community when families are made of communication.

I've enjoyed spending time with you this quarter very much. You have no idea how invigorating it is to be around people your age. You feel the pulse of idealism and questions, and so you open up the world for the people around you. You're still working at your basic relationship to the world and to life. So thanks for having me. You are life for culture and hope for society. Believe in the best in yourselves.

*

Here, I've put this poem up on the overhead projector,[1] an odd poem about going out at night in New York City when the mood is like the Steichen photograph of the Flatiron Building taken in 1904 (fig. 10.1).[2] I will keep the transparency of the photograph on the overhead too. Together, the photograph and the poem make a diptych to remember our course by, and I will let them filter into your imaginations as we talk. Today, alongside these mementos, I want to add some framing thoughts for our quarter. I want to categorize the approach taken in this lecture series.

The approach we've taken this quarter is *integrationist*. You don't hear that term very often, but it fits what we did these past months. If you look in an English dictionary, that term denotes someone who advocated social integration—for instance, among races as was the case for integrationists in the 1960s. By now, my intended modification of this term should be clear. Out of our socialized nature, we should be integrationists with nature. That is, I advocate ecological integration, which, on the humanistic account we've given, is also social integration, a way of integrating our social nature most consistently with the universe in which we live.

This fall, we tried to integrate, not oppose, the flourishing of humans and the flourishing of the environment. Integrationism in this sense has roots within classic environmentalism—for instance, in Carson, Leopold, and Thoreau. I think, though, it has been under stress from the environmental philosophy community over the last quarter century. There has been a strong

Figure 10.1. Edward Steichen (American, born Luxembourg, 1879–1973), *The Flatiron*, 1904, printed 1909, Gum bichromate over platinum print; 47.8 x 38.4 cm (18-13/16 x 15-1/8 in.); The Metropolitan Museum of Art, Alfred Stieglitz Collection, 1933 (33.43.39) Copy Photograph © 1998 The Metropolitan Museum of Art.

tendency toward misanthropy and the romantic exclusion of the human world from the pristine, nonhuman one.

I think we have to uproot the romantic extremism that is part of much ecological culture to retrieve the roots of integrationism. We are part of nature. It is part of us. Human culture cannot but make connections with the wider world of life, and our flourishing is a vital and beautiful thing on this planet. The problem is not in us per se, but in the thoughtlessness and systematic disregard our political-economy shows as we follow its compulsions. To become more human is to integrate ourselves more respectfully with the universe of life. That is because respect for life is at the core of our humanity, without which we are untrue to ourselves. Here, I am simply reiterating what we arrived at over the past months.

Now an integrationist perspective may seem confusing at first, because it gives room to use the environment while respecting it at the same time. The position can seem muddy. Yet it makes sense once you think about it, just like mud does. In what follows, I will chart integrationism and give several reasons for its desirability. Then I will close our course with a general discussion of earthly humanity.

*

How should we share the world with other forms of life? Imagine three different ways of living with the wider world of life. Here is the first, picture A. Sit back while I read it to you. My description will be like a prose poem:

Nature is a beautiful place and also a dangerous one. If it weren't for nature, we wouldn't be alive. At the same time, nature kills, as when a tornado tears through a town, an ill bear attacks campers, or a drought causes thousands to starve. We try to form relations with nature that help us live. When nature obstructs us, we challenge it. When we want something nature has, we use nature to get what we want. In the meantime, we enjoy the wind in the trees after work and curse the lightning shattering our homes or the rain making the homeless shrink back beneath cardboard covers. Call this picture *the instrumental relation to nature*.

Here is picture B:
Nature is a beautiful place and also a dangerous one. A girl walked down by the river, was caught in a mudslide as the bank gave way, and was carried out into the brown water's torrent. She died. Later, her family placed a tire swing by the place she fell, hanging high from the trees over the river itself. They set up a plaque in the tree and called the place "Theresa's Sound

World," for their lost daughter Theresa loved the river, where she heard the sounds of birds, wind, water, and the far off hum of cars along the overpass. The plaque says, "If it's raining hard, and the river is brown, turn back. If the river is lazy and green, stay and swing out high into the water."

People in the town sometimes use the river to float timber down so they can build cabins lower and deeper in the woods where the water flows. The water thrusts out across a series of falls as it nears the sea, and people use those falls to turn turbines, but not so many that the countryside is disrupted. The people using the river have a way of speaking. They say, "Keep the shoulders strong." They mean the river throws its shoulders into human work, and we want to keep it vital to do so. The connotation is that the river is in solidarity with us, and we with it. Call this picture *the integrated relation to nature*.

Lastly, here is picture C:

Nature is a beautiful place and also a dangerous one. Faced with danger, we should defend ourselves against nature. When our vital interests are at stake, all things being equal, we have a right of self-defense against nature. Still, this right must not be taken very far. We do not have a right of self-aggrandizement against nature. Our vital interests do not include wanton use of nature or even relative luxury. If we are to use nature as a resource for our luxury, we must do so only if we also protect, and absolutely do not interfere with, whole regions of wilderness. In fact, nature has a right against us to be left utterly alone, away from human hands. Humans often sully nature, and nature's beauty is sacred. Nature is so sacred that it should be excluded from society, untouched within large regions of unused wilderness. At heart, nature should remain absolutely other to us. Call this picture *the oppositional relation to nature*.

*

What do you notice about these three pictures? In A, people use nature as an instrument, use instruments to move nature out of the way, and otherwise enjoy nature. There is no explicit talk of respecting nature, no sense nature is to be respected in its own right. True, the people in A enjoy nature and seem to show reverence for it. But their reverence does not decisively distinguish between liking nature only when nature is enjoyable and thinking nature deserves respect even when it is not very pleasant.

By contrast, the people in B relate to nature with solidarity. They do take advantage of nature, but the advantage seems to have limits and to aim for something symbiotic. Moreover, they relate to nature as a separate realm of life that deserves respect and with which they are in (at least in the way they see it) a partnership. The integrated relation to nature includes some instrumental aspects. Yet these aspects of use are understood as part of a larger back and forth relationship modeled more like a friendship than a sometimes pleasant yet strife-filled exploitation. In B, nature is never solely a means, but is also worthy of respect in itself.

More radically still, C presents a view wherein nature shouldn't, ideally, ever be a means to our ends. Humans do have a right to use nature sometimes, but that right emerges through a conflict of rights. If we have a right to use nature, it is because unfortunately we must in that instance, but ideally we would never have to do so. This is the oppositional relation to nature. There is always something of a tragedy when using nature.[3] Moreover, nature's significance is discerned in nature's separateness from human life.[4] Ideally, nature should be a shrine appreciated like the prayer to the gods that goes "the holy is not this, not that, not this..." Across the border from the sanctuary, we imagine the sacred lives, but in our cities, not this, not that, not this is sacred, because the sacred is beyond us.

Now, the instrumental relation to nature is common to our capitalist culture. The oppositional relation to nature is common to romantic and deep ecological counter-cultures, often reactive against capitalist anthropocentrism. As you might surmise given the criticisms I've raised in lectures four and five against both deep ecology and the prevailing view of anthropocentrism, I think both sides of the polarity—cutthroat capitalism and reactive deep ecology—are to be avoided. The reason is that they are mistaken about our sense of humanity.

To my mind, the integrated relation to nature, picture B, makes common sense out of who we are. There are many forms of connection humans form with the wider world of life, and respect for life is a crucial part of our socialization into common humanity. The poetry of human time is highly ecological, not always of course, but in recurring and clear patterns across cultures. We make a home in this world. That home requires we use life to get by. Doing so is part of being alive. The difficulty and art reside in balancing our use with our respect, our taking away of life with our connection to life. That is what integrationism is all about, and of the three pictures, it makes the best sense of the kind of beings we are who struggle to live well in our condition, evolving through our time on Earth.

*

Let me explain more why integrationism makes sense. First, the integrated relation to nature is practical and far-sighted. Integrationists can use nature, but they must be wise. By contrast, instrumentalists are shaped in such a way that they remain open to rash use or wantonness. True, a smart instrumentalist will look into the future. But when your way of life does not assume nature's intrinsic respectability, yet does assume your prerogative to use nature whenever you want, it is easy to overuse nature. After all, who you take yourself to be and what you take yourself to do give open season to using nature in principle (your *osool* is use). As we saw in lecture three on an ecological orientation, though, assuming nature's respectability is a good way to ensure wise use. Integrationists make the assumption and so must think about preserving nature even as they use it. In this way, integrationism is practical and far-sighted.

Second, the integrated relation to nature is respectful and harmonious. Integrationists respect nature and by doing so harmonize themselves as best as they can with the universe of life. Alienating ourselves from nature is unhealthy. We are natural beings ourselves, and human development depends both ecologically and psychologically on relationships with nature. As we've noted several times this quarter, the lives of young children respond pervasively and developmentally to nature. Integrationists respect nature in a way that allows relationships with nature to develop. Integrationist respect does not entail radical separation from the respected. Relating to nature respectfully, integrationists take the means needed to harmonize their own humanity as best as possible with nature.

Third, the integrated relation to nature is insightful in its understanding of our ecological selves. One criticism some environmentalists throws at instrumentalist capitalism is that the culture does not understand itself.[5] Instrumental people lack self-knowledge. They lack self-knowledge because human selves are ecological both in the natural history of our evolution and in the social history of our culture. Nature is woven into the meaning of human life so profoundly that to instrumentalize nature must involve a lack of self-respect. But instrumentalists claim to be prudent. Yet it is imprudent to disrespect yourself. So instrumentalists must lack self-knowledge. Against such a lack of self-knowledge, some environmentalists take the moral high ground by claiming ecological self-knowledge as their own. Yet the more romantic among these dubiously assume we need sanctify nature's separateness.[6] It is as if, ironically, they do not accept we are a part of nature, even though they say we are.

By contrast, the integrated relation to nature opens up our self-understanding in fuller ways than the romantic alternative. There are moments of beauty in the integrated relation to nature and fascination about living in the universe of life. Yet the people in picture B are practical, realistic, far-sighted for their loved ones, and even clever about their integration with nature. They are also moderate. When you respect someone with whom you work, you do not tax his abilities unless you are helping him grow. So, too, when you work with nature. The self-understanding of ourselves as moderate members of nature is highly ecological, for it fosters interdependence between ourselves and nature. Cooperating with nature, we are more ecological than if we separate ourselves from nature and fathom its radical otherness.

Thus integrationism is preferable to both unfettered capitalism and reactive deep ecology on their own grounds. It is more *prudent* than capitalist license, and it is more *ecological* than reactive alienation from nature. Not only is integrationism common sense. It's also better at what A and C sought, and on their own terms. What do you think?

*

Integrationism could be thought of as a new humanism, if we have to use all these "isms" (which is in bad form!).[7] At the same time, it's an old one—as old as that common sense part of ourselves that has evolved in connection with the ecology of Earth life. Human beings are one among the many species of life on Earth and have evolved in thick interdependence with the world's land, sea, and air ecologies. A child makes this assumption before she has ever taken a course in Earth Science. She looks at her hands, the veins, a tree, and the leaf's veins. She looks into a dog's eyes, perceiving a glimmer of intelligence. She sees a TV episode on amoebas and later realizes she feels just like one on a hot day. Her coagulated motion is so similar, and the spreading, hot currents of air fanning the clouds are, too. It is in our common sense to identify with nature. A person who did not identify at all with any part of nature would seem from another planet and species. In Wittgenstein's terms, family resemblances between humans and nature belong to the grammar of human identity.[8]

There's another reason, too, why integrationism is part of common sense. Human practicality demands our integration. Our practicality is how we are as beings acting for ends that satisfy our flourishing. Such is an old Aristotelian definition.[9] For what kinds of things does our flourishing call us to act? One set of human ends concerns the development of our psychological, intellectual, and spiritual life—our *Geist* as Germans economically say.[10] Part of our development here calls for healthy relationships with nature. Humans as a species do not mature psychologically if they are systematically alienated from nature. Nor is full intellectual development possible. Finally, human spiritual life suffers without identification with nature. Though there may be exceptions among specific humans and in parts of development, human culture would be significantly thwarted without identifications with nature.[11] Just so, to flourish psychologically, intellectually, and spiritually, we as a species need to develop relationships with nature. That's a practical point.

Meanwhile, another set of human ends concerns our physical well-being. Humans need healthy environmental conditions, adequate sustenance, and materials for construction to obtain physical well-being. All of these needs depend ultimately on wise use of the environment. Certainly, technology can help us meet our physical needs in ways that at times re-create whole Earth ecologies. Yet even technological satisfaction depends on positive environmental conditions supporting or serving technology. While we may instrumentalize nature to obtain good conditions for our technological construction, we have already seen that, ironically, it is not wise to use nature without respecting nature. Here, integrationism is common sense once again. By forming relationships with nature wherein we get to know nature and use nature only moderately, we put ourselves in the best way to securing long-range health, sustenance, and materials. So for our practical being, integrationism makes common, human sense.

*

My favorite integrationists are writers or artists. What one has to grasp from the beginning is the way our humanity is connected with nature, and the artists of experience are best at reminding us of our connections. Among these artists, some of the best are nature writers. Let me mention one kind here: the practicing outdoorsman or naturalist. Think of Norman Maclean, Aldo Leopold, Rachel Carson, and Thoreau. Eric, as you know, Maclean wrote as a lover of fly-fishing. His descriptions of nature are filled with respect and awe, yet there is no alienation from nature. We should use nature, wisely and for our maturity.

Thinking about Eric's allusion to Maclean earlier this term, I found a passage in Maclean that shows integrationism exceptionally well. The narrator—presumably Norman himself—is sitting on the shore of a Montana stream during an exceptionally hot day. He has been having a hard time with his brother Paul, a guy who's always in trouble unless he's on the river fishing. In addition, the afternoon has been a crazy one, with a lot of stupidity from his visiting brother-in-law, Neal. The author wants to forget that stupidity so that he can have a new sense of strength with which to help Paul. Maclean writes:

> I sat there and forgot and forgot, until what remained was the river that went by and I who watched. On the river the heat mirages danced with each other and then they danced through each other and then they joined hands and

danced around each other. Eventually the watcher joined the river, and there was only one of us. I believe it was the river.[12]

This passage seems like a brilliant portrait of what deep ecologists seek when they talk of becoming one with nature.[13] And it is. But when you put it in context, it is nothing like deep ecological antihumanism, let alone misanthropy. The author is a fly fisher. He kills as an art. He doesn't zone out as a way of life, but just this once, in a revelatory moment. He doesn't think being human is somehow alien from nature's purity. He's used to nature and comfortable in it. The relationship is not exaggerated. At the same time, the author understands local ecology like few people do, and when people show they don't care to understand the land, the author and his brother have disdain for such a self-*dis*respecting way of being.

A page later, the author continues after he has extensively described the ecology of the river and how much he knows of it from having grown up with it. He writes:

> As the heat mirages on the river in front of me danced with and through each other, *I could feel patterns of my own life joining with them.* It was here, while waiting for my brother, that I started this story, although, of course, at the time I did not know that stories of life are often more like rivers than books. But I knew a story had begun, perhaps long ago near the sound of water. And I sensed that ahead I would meet something that would never erode so there would be a sharp turn, deep circles, a deposit, and quietness.[14]

I don't want to give away the story to those of you who have not read it. So there is only so much I can say here. In the context of the story, this is a luminous passage, like a shaft of sunlight appearing through a hole in the clouds and rotating silently along a river's shore. First of all, the narrator is echoing what he's just said about the actual ecology of the river—its turns, eddies, deposits, and quiet pools. These in turn become not simply metaphors but *order* for his life's patterns. He is so in touch with the river he's related to that his skeleton of meaning, his bedrock, comes from the river's shape and ecology. This is analogical implication, because the shape his life takes on concerns one of the most central loves and sadnesses of his life. I won't give that away, because you have to read the book, but you can hear it in the passage.

Not only does the river take on the author's cares—it becomes the shape of his story. Here nature is not simply part of history. It *structures* history. It's the background condition within which sense gets spun. Again in Wittgenstein's terms, it's grammar. And that is so obvious too! The Earth *is* our background condition for the Earth-evolved creatures we are. What Maclean's

story shows is that we become more in touch with who we are by acknowledging that. Sitting by a river is not the only way to be truly human, of
course. But someone who cannot relate to the author's experience has missed
something that is truly human.

*

Over this course, we've been doing philosophical anthropology. We've been examining what it is to be human. My thesis throughout this fall has been that
humanity can be, has been, and should be integrated with the universe of life.
Some things, you see, you don't value—they *are* you. They are categorical. That
is why Maclean's narrator and Paul the brother have disdain for people who
show up in Montana and act like they couldn't give a flying fish for the land.
To the brothers, such people have sold out on being human. Over a month ago,
I set up analogical identifications to help us see this kind of self-respect. From
the waste lots of the Village to the gorges of Montana, from the homeless to the
outdoorsman, identifications make up human self-respect in so much of world
culture. Here is rooting for a critique of our exploitative systems.

When some things are you, you don't let them become abstract without becoming abstract yourself. That's the way it is with human things. Calling civil-
ian deaths "collateral damage" is a way of becoming abstract to yourself. So,
too, with calling living beings "resources." They aren't resources. They aren't
things. They are alive. The more we treat them like stuff, the more we become
stuff in parts of ourselves. The more we treat them respectfully, the more human we become. That is integrationism in a line. Here, let me write it out:

Integration

The more we treat other life forms respectfully, the more we become
human.

Human beings are made of relationships. The best part of ourselves is our relatedness: to each other; to the world; to religious sources inside ourselves that
speak with something like voices; to our pasts and futures. We are amazing because we can relate. And when we stop relating, we stop being amazing. I say
this as a socialized human, and it is something the great Hasidic mystic Martin Buber also said and which my one-time colleague Dan Scheinfeld taught
me more than any other teacher.[15]

There is no good reason to think humanity stops when we meet other
forms of life. In fact, it is blind to think so. A great part of what is so amazing about human potential occurs in the intersections between us and them,

between species. As with dolphins, dogs, and chimps, we are a creature that can be social beyond our *species* and, unlike them perhaps, we can also know ourselves by knowing other forms of life. Earthly humanity expresses our ability to relate and to know ourselves.

Here is where the poem on the projector makes sense.

The Sky inside the City

Life among humans is more than you mentioned.
In the city, alone, live lives
A thousand times too deep within the ground,
I know. Silently, I watched them fall
Inside the space of my memories of other lives,
I dreamed. Timelessness makes sense only
Across the elements where species rise and descend.
As loved-ones, too, we walk
Out into the twilight as lavender as kisses—
The air intractable, an ether in change.

The city as we know it is older and more multiform than we commonly assume: "Life among humans is more than you mentioned." It actually includes natural history, the rise and fall of species: "Timelessness makes sense only / across the elements where species rise and descend." Certainly, no actual city ever did witness the reach of evolution, though. So the city must be metaphorical for something. For what, though?

This Steichen photograph, too, shows a city where the color of the atmosphere and the silhouettes of branches merge seamlessly with the shape of buildings and the rush of a man's top hat along the park. In the context of the poem, the photograph suggests something about our lives in society and about our relatedness to the world around us. What does it show?

To my mind, both the poem and the photograph suggest, perhaps, that there is a great unconscious to our city life, our social life, and that such an unconscious is the movement of a world where "species rise and descend." We know it, but we do not know it yet. The Earth—our presence on it, evolved within it—the Earth always floats up into the world at the end of the day. That is the idea—an integrationist one. The Earth always floats up into the world at the end of the day.

Notes

1. See the poem on p. 202.
2. Edward, Steichen, *The Flatiron*, 1904, gum bichromate over platinum print, New York: Metropolitan Museum of Modern Art, Alfred Steiglitz Collection, 1933, 33.43.39.

3. This was the view of Albert Schweitzer, whose reverence for life is admirable.

4. This view pervades a number of essays in David Rothenberg's *Always the Mountain*, Athens: University of Georgia Press, 2003.

5. See Carson, *Silent Spring*, New York, Mariner Books, 2002; and Leopold, *A Sand County Almanac, and Sketches Here and There*, New York: Oxford University Press, 1989.

6. See Rothenberg, *Always the Mountain*.

7. I began this lecture series with an allusion to Heidegger, and I wish to hint at one as I close. Heidegger attempted to deconstruct (*abbauen*) humanism in his "Letter on Humanism," in *Basic Writings*, ed. Krell, New York: Harper, 1987. His view is sophisticated. The gist of it is that modern humanism has emerged out of the tradition of Platonic metaphysics and conceptualized our place in the universe as primarily active upon the universe, destined to use and reshape it. He attempts to unwork this humanism by wresting our experience of meaning back into an openness prior to any activity and which should make us receive the world rather than attempt to use and produce it. There is an obvious ecological consequence to his view—his subtle attempt to integrate transcendent, free humans with the Earth's systems of life and the meanings they give our cultures. People call such a consequence "*anti*-humanist."

But it's mistaken to see our humanity as destined to exploit the Earth. My argument concerning analogical identification and the centrality of an unconditioned love for life in humankind could possibly be aligned with Heidegger's critique. Yet at the same time, my point is that it doesn't make sense to give up the promise of *earthly* humanity. No anti-humanism.

8. The expression "family resemblances" comes from a passage in *Philosophical Investigations*, trans. G.E.M. Anscombe, New York: Prentice Hall, 1999, where Wittgenstein discusses the experience of looking at the faces of a family in a photograph and knowing that they are of the same family, though the precise identity is hard—though not impossible—to pin down to specific properties.

9. From the *Nicomachean Ethics*, trans. Terrance Irwin, Indianapolis: Hackett Publishing, 1985, book 1.

10. As in Hegel's *Phenomenology of Spirit* or *Phenomenology of Mind*, depending on the translation. (*Phenomenology of Spirit*, New York: Oxford University Press, 1977.)

11. For one: we wouldn't have Tarkovsky's *Mirror*! (Moscow: Mosfilms, 1974.)

12. Maclean, Norman, *A River Runs Through It, and Other Stories*, Chicago: University of Chicago Press, 2001, 61.

13. Again as is Arne Naess's "Identification as a Source of Deep Ecological Attitudes," In *Deep Ecology*, ed. Michael Tobias, San Marcos, CA: Avant Books, 256–270.

14. Maclean, *A River Runs Through It*, 63, my emphasis.

15. In *I and Thou*, Edinburgh: T & T Clark, 1999.

~

Acknowledgments

This book came out of what Dan and Sandra Scheinfeld of the Erikson Institute for Advanced Study in Child Development call "growing edges." It also came out of what my father, David Keymer, calls "chance meetings," from his reading of Rachel Cohen's recent book on American writers and artists.[1] Although we are taught in our careers to be deliberate and specialized, I am happy that my first philosophy book happened about as randomly as a book can. That to me shows that the philosophy around it is part of life, even when you catch life unexpectedly. I think one of the greatest and unacknowledged worries of "assistant professors" (as Kierkegaard called us) is that philosophy isn't part of life. But it is, and that is why we professors are often in need of assistance.

I did not do my dissertation work on environmental ethics. Rather, I wrote about conscience and the sense of common humanity. As an undergraduate, I spent my time on Kant and Levinas, before being drawn to the voice of Søren Kierkegaard. From the first, my interest was in social justice and the centrality of love to moral life. I've felt for a long time that people are originally beautiful and good, but that the power centers of our world are often not structured to bring out human goodness. This is confusing for people. I've also felt, personally, that it's hard to focus on ideals and that philosophy can help one take a break from a fast-paced life enough to find one's center again.

When I was a graduate student, Breena Holland asked me if I'd teach an environmental ethics course. Ted Steck agreed, and I taught with Rodger

Field. I wish to thank you three and my students over three years of environmental ethics courses at the University of Chicago. Here, I want to thank especially Eric, Joel, Saleem, Kate, and Maureen.

During my first solo environmental ethics course in the fall of 2000, Roger Lopez sent me an announcement for a guest issue of *Philosophy in the Contemporary World* on environmental virtue ethics. Phil Cafaro edited the issue. I submitted the main part of what is lecture four here, and it was published. This article came out of teaching the first course in winter 2000, when I noticed Cora Diamond's arguments had something interesting to them, especially when used to criticize deep ecology. I want to thank Roger Lopez and Phil Cafaro, Phil especially, for he became a colleague when I moved to Colorado for my first full-time job down the road from him in Colorado Springs. I especially remember the hike he took me on to see the Aspens in their golden time, and what it felt like to breach tree line and look south toward Rocky Mountain National Park.

The next surprise came when I answered a call on the ISEE (International Society for Environmental Ethics) Listserv to review some books for Roger Gottlieb and *Social Theory and Practice*. I was chosen and wrote an essay for Roger and the journal. This essay, "Environmental Maturity," must have caught something in Roger's eye, and he started asking me about whether I had any book projects in mind. These questions, in turn, led to a process whereby I proposed and then wrote this book. I want to thank Roger and Brian Romer from Rowman and Littlefield for their patience and for giving me this opportunity. I'd also like to thank Lynn Weber, Rowman and Littlefield's production editor; Ginger Peschke, who copyedited the manuscript; and Karolina Zarychta, the graphics editorial assistant.

Along the way of writing this book, a number of people helped out, especially Flannery Hysjulien. Flannery took me camping a couple times, talked with me about the transcendent and the immanent on the way down from Delicate Arch in Arches National Park, showed me Grand Gulch Primitive Area in Utah (a zone, in Tarkovsky's sense), and introduced me to her Society of Friends (Quaker) meeting. Her family was generous with helping on what is now lecture two. I want to thank them all very much.

Judy Twedt also deserves a special thank-you. She was my research colleague during the summer of 2004 when she was awarded a student-faculty research grant from Colorado College. Judy and I went to the Raven's Nest three times a week to talk nonstop philosophy for two hours. I developed the central argument of this book, that in lecture six, due to conversations with her. She was an amazing student, because her seriousness allowed reasoning to come out. Thus she taught her teacher, and we were both taught by what we discovered over those cups of coffee on the nondescript corner by the eld-erly woman who tended her flowers. Judy also compiled the index for this book, for which I thank her.

The final surprise of the process came in the last months of writing and is a little complicated. It concerns one of the poetic cores of a book, its title. I was stumped on a title. My editors wanted certain words or clear connota-tions in it, and my love for oblique titles was not faring well. Robin Wells, a fellow baritone in the Dubai Chamber Choir, asked me what my book was about after rehearsal one night. I was exhausted from work, practicing Stravinsky's *Mass*, and writing. I told him very simply and informally what the book was about and told him I couldn't find a title. He immediately blurted out, "Oh, you should call it *Greener than You Think!*" Aurore Dib, who was with us, said she liked that. Although I didn't end up using this ti-tle, somehow it led me outward to hear what people were thinking. And in the process, I asked Megan Craig if her painting *West Side Highway* (2003) would open the book. Megan once sent me a tape (back when cassette tapes were used for mixes) called "Green and Blue," and what was greener than thought was the blue of her painting of New York City's West Side Highway, which shows the Hudson River and the drive along it.

Megan's painting is reminiscent of the good-hearted American who drives along Seattle's roads in lecture two. It also brings to mind many of the rea-sons why New York City is a place that feels like home, despite its problems (many of them ecological). Due to limitations on reproduction, we couldn't use Megan's painting,[2] yet the painting opens up a mood and a perspective that is central to this book.

I was still missing a title, though. Megan's painting reminded me of a poem I wrote about Chicago during the summer of 1999. I believe I wrote it 9/9/1999. I wish I had it here, but I don't know where it is. The poem had three parts. In the third part, I talk about driving along the blue lake, like the blue of Megan's painting. That lake is Lake Michigan.

The poem is very still. I'd been working for Saskia Sassen at the Univer-sity of Chicago all summer, and I had been learning a lot from Breena. Dur-ing that time, Breena and I went occasionally to the North Side of Chicago, its beach, and the Cafe Ennui in Rogers Park ("ennui" means, roughly, "bore-dom"). The weather was beautiful, and the time was not boring, but open. I associate this time with the best time of grad school. And it is certainly the time when I started to put my mind around the ecological life, a life of cities *and* nature, of shores between humans and waters.

Months after talking with Robin, Aurore, and Megan, and then remem-bering the summer of 1999 with both Breena and a sociologist of global restructuring, I met Brian in Portland to have lunch at Mother's Bistro. We still didn't have a title, but I had found the book's zone. As in the painting and the poem, I returned to California driving. I drove down Route 5 and past Mount Shasta, perhaps the most beautiful single mountain I have ever seen (if only my car had been solar powered!). It was during the first, distant views of the mountain from the plains and low hills of Oregon (or just into California) that "The Ecological Life" came to me. Aldo Leopold said we should learn to think like a mountain.

Our whole lives are threaded ecologically and are greener than we think. This book is close to me. It has drawn on early experiences, because I have always loved nature. I do not understand how people can be thoughtless with it. It is exceptionally beautiful and true, so much so that I think it is beyond being a gift, as if reducing it to a gift has already done violence to its freedom. This awareness of nature was a central part of my poetry when I wrote poetry seriously in the Yale literary scene of the early '90s. I think it was to such a degree because of early experiences: my mother's reaction to birds and her way of floating bougainvilleas in water, my father's friendship with animals.

I wish to thank here Jim Davidson, my sixth-grade teacher, who gave me the opportunity to work at Crumhorn Mountain Boy Scout Camp, where I had the honor of being a waterfront instructor for two summers during early high school. Second, I want to thank my Aunt Eleanor and Uncle Bill who asked me out to work on their Ohio farm for a couple summers when I was young. My cousin, John, took me once to a spot in the woods, where, from a fallen tree, you climbed up and saw nothing but a field of leaves.

In college, Susan Neiman and Anne-Christine Habbard brought out my need for social justice and taught me a lot about what philosophy is. Stephen Rich, Christopher Boerboom, and Irene Liu taught me what friendship is, and their long talks shaped my mind.[3] In graduate school, Martha Nussbaum and Candace Vogler guided me. Candace first proposed the expression "ecological humanity" after reading and listening to an early talk version of lecture four during our Medici writing coffees of summer 2001. Martha presented an example of someone with a global conscience. I feel so lucky to have met all these people. Leonard Linsky's five-year-long Friday afternoon reading group on Wittgenstein's *Investigations* that met at least forty-five weeks of the year gave graduate school its grammar (I attended only a third of these meetings!). Jean-Luc Marion's phenomenology reminded me of how we can enliven our mental grasp of meaning. Finally, Charles Larmore and David Schmidtz helped me refine my analytic thoughts about many of the matters in this book during my last years of grad school.

In closing, I want to thank: Dave Aftandilian, Neil Brenner, all my colleagues at the environmental philosophy gatherings listed below, the Dudzinskis (especially for memories of childhood games around their home), everyone at AUS and Colorado College who taught me something related to this book's content or who supported me while writing it (especially my 2003 Citizens of the World class, John Fox for being up late when the book was first being written, Hans Krimm for regular environmental philosophy discussions over two years, and David Lea for reading the manuscript), Joshua Graae, the extended Keymer family (especially for time on Spicer Lake and Grandma for her knitting of sheep on a pasture), Johann Klaassen, Antoine Lacronique (especially for time at St. Dalmas), Carolyn Mcleod, Jasmine Moorhead, Ratheesh Nair, the Paliks (especially Aunt Evelyn for her ecological quilt), the Pikes Peak Justice and Peace Commission, the Scheinfelds, George Streeter, Alan Thompson, Lauren Tillinghast, and Elizabeth Willott.

Finally, my thanks and love go to my family. I am lucky to have been raised by Dave and Esther and to have had such a close aunt as Ruth Bendik. If you remember one thing from me, remember that you have enriched my life so much and that I love you all with all my heart.

The following are places where I gave talks on matters related to this book:
(2001) The University of Chicago Environmental Studies Workshop; the University of Chicago Political Theory Workshop; the University of Illinois (Champaign-Urbana) Graduate Student Philosophy Conference; the North American Society for Social Philosophy Annual Conference: *Truth and Objectivity in Formulating Socio-Ethical Judgments*, Eastern Michigan University

(2002) Villanova University Department of Philosophy; Luther College; Whitman College; the North American Society for Social Philosophy Annual Conference, *Society, Embodiment and the Environment*, the University of Oregon (Eugene)

(2003) The International Society for Environmental Ethics section of the American Philosophical Association Pacific Division meeting; the Four Corners Environmental Gathering, Arches National Park; the Macalaster College Department of Geography and its Workshop on Political Ecology

(2004) The University of Washington (Seattle) Department of Philosophy; the 14th North American Conference on Environment and Community, Empire State College; Zayed University; the International Society for Environmental Ethics section of the American Philosophical Association Pacific Division meeting

The following are media where material serving as a sketch for this book was published:

(Chapter 2) "Mining and Injustice: the Case of Irian Jaya," *South Pacific Journal of Philosophy*, vol. 8, 2005.

(Chapter 3) "The Idea of an Ecological Orientation," *Social Philosophy Today*, vol. 19, Philosophy Documentation Series, 2004

(Chapter 4) "A Sense of Humanity" in my *Conscience and Humanity*, dissertation submitted to the University of Chicago Department of Philosophy, 2002, chap. 3; "Analogical Extension and Analogical Implication in Environmental Moral Philosophy," *Philosophy in the Contemporary World*, vol. 8, n. 2 (Fall–Winter 2001), 149–158; "A Sense of Ecological Humanity," *Social Philosophy Today*, vol. 18, Philosophy Documentation Series, 2003

(Chapter 5) "Sacred Places," *Routledge Encyclopedia of World Environmental History*, New York: Routledge, 2004

(Chapter 7) "Environmental Maturity," *Social Theory and Practice*, vol. 29, n. 3, July 2003

(Chapter 8) "Openness and Meaning," *Nature, Story, and Legend Humanities Net*, University of Michigan Humanities Net, February 2004, at *www.h-net.org/~nilas/* (accessed June 3, 2005)

(Chapter 9) "Environmental Protection and Social Justice: Two Expressions of the Same Idea," *Nature, Story, and Legend Humanities Net*, University of Michigan Humanities Net, March 2005, at *www.h-net.org/~nilas/* (accessed June 3, 2005)

(Chapter 10) "Weathered Nature: Integrationism and Conceptual History in Environmental Ethics," *Nature, Story, and Legend Humanities Net*, University of Michigan Humanities Net, August 2003, at *www.h-net.org/~nilas/* (accessed June 3, 2005)

Notes

1. Rachel Cohen, *A Chance Meeting: Intertwined Lives of American Writers and Artists*, New York: Random House, 2005.

2. Megan's painting can be viewed at *www.megancraig.com* in her portfolio and under the section on New York paintings (accessed September 5, 2005).

3. Steve also gave me *Transitory Gardens, Uprooted Lives* in 1994.

Bibliography

Agamben, Georgio. *The Open: Man and Animal*. Palo Alto: Stanford University Press, 2004.

Amery, Jean. *On Suicide: A Discourse on Voluntary Death*. Bloomington: Indiana University Press, 1999.

Annan, Kofi, "In Larger Freedom: Towards Development, Security and Human Rights for All," New York: United Nations, A/59/2005, March 21, 2005, at *www.un.org/largerfreedom/report-largerfreedom.pdf* (accessed May 27, 2005).

Apollonius of Rhodes. *Jason and the Golden Fleece (The Argonautica)*. New York: Oxford University Press, 1998.

Arendt, Hanna. *Eichmann in Jerusalem: A Report on the Banality of Evil*. New York: Penguin, 1993.

Aristotle. *Nicomachean Ethics*. Translated by Terrance Irwin. Indianapolis: Hackett Publishing, 1985.

"The Australia West Papua Association," at *au.geocities.com/awpab/environment.htm* (accessed December 20, 2003).

Bachelard, Gaston. *The Poetics of Reverie*. New York: Beacon Books, 1971.

Balmori, Diana and Morton, Margaret. *Transitory Gardens, Uprooted Lives*. New Haven: Yale University Press, 1993.

Beanal v. Freeport-McMoRan, Inc., 969 F. Supp. 362 (E.D. La. 1997), 382.

Bender, Frederic. *The Culture of Extinction: Toward a Philosophy of Deep Ecology*. Boulder: Humanity Press, 2003.

Bendik-Keymer, Jeremy. "The Apathetic Citizen: When State Institutions Do Not Reflect Human Rights Consistently." In *Annuaire Francais de Relations Internationales*, Belgium: Bruylant/la Documentation Francaise, 2006.

————. "Common Humanity and Human Rights," in *Religion and Human Rights* (*Social Philosophy Today*, vol. 21). Philosophy Documentation Center, 2005.

————. "For a Time as Shifting as Sand: *Walden* in the UAE," *Thoreau Society Bulletin*, n. 253, Summer 2005.

————. "Human Rights," in *Global Perspectives on the United States*. Great Barrington, MA: Bershire Publishing, 2006.

————. "Sacred Places." In *The Routledge Encyclopedia of World Environmental History*. New York: Routledge, 2003, 1081–1082.

Bergson, Henri. *Le rire* [*The Laugh*]. Paris: Editions de Christine, 1991.

Berlin, Irving. *The Complete Lyrics*. Edited by Robert Kimball. New York: Knopf, 2001.

Bowers v. Hardwick, 478 U.S. 186 (1986), Docket Number: 85-140.

Brenner, Neil. *New State Spaces: Urban Governance and the Rescaling of Statehood*. New York: Oxford University Press, 2004.

Buber, Martin. *I and Thou*. Edinburgh: T & T Clark, 1999.

Burkhart, Brian Yazzie. "What Coyote and Thales Can Teach Us." In *American Indian Thought: Philosophical Essays*. Edited by Anne Waters. New York: Blackwell, 2003.

Burnside, R. L. *A Bothered Mind*. Oxford, MS: Fat Possum Records, 2004.

Butterfly Hill, Julia, "Circle of Life," *www.circleoflife.org* (accessed May 24, 2005).

Cafaro, Philip. *Thoreau's Living Ethics: Walden and the Pursuit of Virtue*. Athens, GA: University of Georgia Press, 2004.

Carson, Rachel. *Silent Spring*. New York: Mariner Books, 2002.

————. *Under the Sea Wind*. New York: Penguin Press, 1996.

Carter, Alan. *A Radical Green Political Theory*. London: Routledge, 1999.

Castells, Manuel. *The Rise of the Network Society*. Oxford: Blackwell, 2000.

Cat Power. "Evolution." On *You Are Free*. New York: Matador Records, 2003.

————. "Maybe Not." On *You Are Free*. New York: Matador Records, 2003.

Cavell, Stanley. *Conditions Handsome and Unhandsome: The Constitution of Emersonian Perfectionism*. Chicago: University of Chicago Press, 1993.

Cawley, A.C. *Everyman and Medieval Miracle Plays*. New York: J.M. Dent & Sons/ Everyman's Library, 1993.

Chateaubriand, Francois Rene. *Atala*. Paris: 1801.

Chrétien, Jean-Louis. *L'appel et la reponse* [*Call and Response*]. Paris: Presses Universitaires de France, 1992.

Churchill, Ward and Vander Wall, Jim. *Agents of Repression: The FBI's Secret Wars against the Black Panther Party and the American Indian Movement*. Chicago: South End Press, 2002.

Coetzee, J.M. *Elizabeth Costello*. New York: Penguin Books, 2004.

Cohen, Rachel. *A Chance Meeting: Intertwined Lives of American Writers and Artists*. New York: Random House, 2005.

Craig, Megan. "On Courage." Dissertation in progress, Department of Philosophy, New School for Social Research, 2006.

———. *West Side Highway*, 2003. Oil on canvas. Germany, private collection, and at *www.megancraig.com* (accessed August 31, 2005).

Crow, Kareem Douglas. "Belief: Heart or Mind?" Talk given at American University of Sharjah, March 2005.

De Kooning, Willem. *Excavation*, 1948. Oil on canvas. Chicago, Art Institute of Chicago General Collection.

Derrida, Jacques. *Of Grammatology*. Baltimore: Johns Hopkins University Press, 1994.

Descartes, Rene. "Discourse on Method." In *The Philosophical Writings of Rene Descartes*, vol. 1. New York: Cambridge University Press, 1996.

Desgagne, Richard. "Human Rights in *Lopez-Ostra vs. Spain*," *American Journal of International Law* 89 (1995): 772.

Dewey, John. *Democracy and Education*. New York: Free Press, 1944.

Diamond, Cora. "Eating Meat and Eating People." In *The Realistic Spirit*. Cambridge, MA: MIT Press, 1995.

———. "Experimenting on Animals." In *The Realistic Spirit*. Cambridge, MA: MIT Press, 1995.

———. "How Many Legs?" In *Value and Understanding: Essays for Peter Winch*. Edited by R. Gaita. New York: Routledge, 1990, 149–178.

——— "The Importance of Being Human." In *Human Beings*. Edited by David Cockburn. New York: Cambridge University Press, 1991.

———, "Injustice and Animals." Lecture given at the University of Chicago, March 2001.

Dobson, Andrew. *Citizenship and the Environment*. Oxford: Oxford University Press, 2003.

Dostoevsky, Fyodor. "The Grand Inquisitor." In *Brothers Karamazov*. Translated by Pevear. New York: Vintage Books, 1991.

"Draft Declaration of Human Rights and the Environment," 1994, at *www1.umn.edu/humanrts/instree/1994-dec.htm* (accessed June 3, 2005).

Driskell, David. *Creating Better Cities with Children and Youth: A Manual for Participation*. Paris / London: UNESCO Publishing / Earthscan, 2002.

Earth Charter, at *www.earthcharter.org/files/charter/charter.pdf*, 2002 (accessed June 3, 2005) or in Nigel Dower, *An Introduction to Global Citizenship*, Edinburgh: University of Edinburgh Press, 2003.

Ferry, Luc. *The New Ecological Order*. Chicago: University of Chicago Press, 1995.

Foot, Philippa. *Natural Goodness*. New York: Oxford University Press, 2003.

Foucault, Michel. *The Order of Things: An Archeology of the Human Sciences*. New York: Vintage, 1994.

Furtak, Rick Anthony. *Wisdom in Love: Kierkegaard and the Ancient Quest for Emotional Integrity*. Notre Dame: University of Notre Dame Press, 2005.

Gaita, Raimond. *The Philosopher's Dog*. London: Routledge, 2003.

Gandhi, Mohatma. *Selected Political Writings*. Indianapolis: Hackett Publishing, 1998.

Gandini, Leila et al., eds. *The Hundred Languages of Children*. Englewood: Axel Publishing, 1999.

Geach, Peter. *The Virtues*. New York: Cambridge University Press, 1977.

Genet, Jean. *Funeral Rites*. New York: Grove Press, 1972.

Gilliam, Terry. *Twelve Monkeys*. Los Angeles: Universal Pictures, 1995.

Glover, Jonathan. *Humanity: A Moral History of the Twentieth Century*. New Haven: Yale University Press, 1999.

Gottlieb, Roger. *A Spirituality of Resistance: Finding a Peaceful Heart and Protecting the Earth*. New York: Crossroad Publishing Company, 1999.

Green, Sam and Siegel, Bill. *The Weathermen Underground*. Sundance Film Festival, 2002.

Greenpeace, "Toxic Hotspots: Bhopal," at *www.greenpeace.org/international/ campaigns/toxics/toxic-hotspots* (accessed May 23, 2005).

Hay, Peter. *Main Currents in Western Environmental Thought*. New South Wales: University of New South Wales Press, 2001.

Hegel, G.W.F. *The Phenomenology of Spirit*. New York: Oxford University Press, 1977.

Heidegger, Martin. *Being and Time*. New York: SUNY Press, 1996.

———. "Letter on Humanism." In *Basic Writings*. Edited by David Krell. New York: Harper, 1987.

———, *Poetry, Language and Thought*, New York: Harper & Row, 1974.

Hesiod, *Theogony*. Translated by Richard Caldwell. Newburyport, MA: Focus Publishing, 1987.

Hobbes, Thomas. *Leviathan*. New York: Penguin Classics, 1982.

Holland, Breena. "Capability and Environmental Value." Dissertation submitted to the Department of Political Science, University of Chicago, 2005.

Homer. *The Odyssey*. Translated by Richard Lattimore. New York: Perennial Classics, 1999.

Husserl, Edmund. *The Idea of Phenomenology*. Dordrecht: Kluwer Academic Publishers, 1994.

Jackall, Robert. *Moral Mazes: The World of Corporate Managers*. New York: Oxford University Press, 1989.

Kant, Immanuel. *The Critique of Judgment*. Indianapolis: Hackett Publishing, 1987.

———. *The Critique of Pure Reason*. New York: St. Martin's Press, 1965.

———. "What is Enlightenment?" In *What Is Enlightenment? Eighteenth Century Answers and Twentieth Century Questions*. Edited by James Schmidt. Stanford: University of California Press, 1996, 58–64.

Kierkegaard, Søren (a.k.a. Ante-Climacus). *The Sickness unto Death*. Princeton: Princeton University Press, 1983.

——— (a.k.a. Vigilius Haufniensis). *The Concept of Anxiety*. Princeton: Princeton University Press, 1980.

King, Martin Luther, Jr. *A Testament of Hope: The Essential Writings and Speeches of Martin Luther King Jr*. San Francisco: Harper, 1990.

Klaassen, Johann and Bendik-Keymer, Jeremy. "Of Blood and Money: War, Financial Collusion and Economic Citizenship." Manuscript, 2005.

Kohler, Avery. "Valuing Land and Distributing Territory." In *Geographies and Moralities*. Edited by Roger Lee and David M. Smith. New York: Blackwell, 2004, 135–148.

Kozol, Jonathan. *Savage Inequalities: Children in America's Schools*. New York: Perennial, 1992.

Kuehn, Robert. "The Environmental Justice Implications of Quantitative Assessment." *University of Illinois Law Review* 103 (1996): 116–149.

Larmore, Charles. *Patterns of Moral Complexity*. New York: Cambridge University Press, 1987.

———. "Why I Do What I Do." *University of Chicago Humanities Division Bulletin*, Chicago: University of Chicago Humanities Division, Spring 2003.

Lawrence and Garner v. Texas, 539 U.S. 558 (2003), Docket number 02-102.

Lear, Jonathan. *Happiness, Death, and the Remainder of Life*. Cambridge, MA: Harvard University Press, 2001.

———. *Love and its Place in Nature*. New Haven: Yale University Press, 1998.

———. *Therapeutic Action: An Earnest Plea for Irony*. New York: Other Press, 2003.

Lefevre, Henri. *The Production of Space*. New York: Blackwell, 1991.

Leopold, Aldo. *A Sand County Almanac, and Sketches Here and There*. New York: Oxford University Press, 1989.

Levinas, Emmanuel. *Totality and Infinity*. Pittsburgh: Duquesne University Press, 1969.

Light, Andrew and Rolston, Holmes. *Environmental Ethics: An Anthology*. Oxford: Blackwell, 2003.

Maclean, Norman. *A River Runs Through It, and Other Stories*. Chicago: University of Chicago Press, 2001.

Marion, Jean-Luc. *Being Given: Toward a Phenomenology of Givenness*. Berkeley, CA: Stanford University Press, 2002.

———. *La phenomene erotique* [*The Erotic Phenomenon*]. Paris: Grasset, 2003.

Marx, Karl. *Grundrisse: Foundations of the Critique of Political Economy*. New York: Penguin Classics, 1993.

McGinn, Bernard, et al., eds. *Meister Eckhart*. Vols. 1 and 2. New York: Paulist Press, 1981, 1986.

McKibben, Bill. *Enough: Staying Human in an Engineered Age*. New York: Times Books, 2003.

Mcleod, Carolyn. *Self-Trust and Reproductive Autonomy*. Boston: MIT Press, 2002.

Menand, Louis. *The Metaphysical Club: A Story of Ideas in America*. New York: Farrar, Straus and Giroux, 2001.

Mill, John Stuart. *On Liberty*. Indianapolis: Hackett Publishing, 1978.

Miller, Brian, "Justice and the River," in *studentwebs.coloradocollege.edu/ ~B_Miller/ justice%20and%20the%20river.htm* (accessed May 3, 2005).

Mitchell, Stephen. *Relational Concepts in Psychoanalysis: An Integration*. Cambridge, MA: Harvard University Press, 1988.

Morsink, Johannes. *The Universal Declaration of Human Rights: Origin, Drafting, Intent*. Philadephia: University of Pennsylvania Press, 1999.

Munz, Kathryn. "Mineral Development: Protecting the Land and Communities." In *Justice and Natural Resources: Concepts, Strategies and Applications*. Edited by Kathryn Munz et al. Chicago: Island Press, 2002.

Naess, Arne. *Ecology, Community and Lifestyle: Outline of an Ecosophy*. Translated by David Rothenberg. New York: Cambridge University Press, 1990.

——. "Identification as a Source of Deep Ecological Attitudes." In *Deep Ecology*. Edited by Michael Tobias. San Marcos, CA: Avant Books, 256–270.

Nancy, Jean-Luc. *The Inoperative Community*. Minneapolis: University of Minnesota Press, 1991.

Neiman, Susan. *Evil in Modern Thought: An Alternative History of Philosophy*. Princeton: Princeton University Press, 2002.

——. *The Unity of Reason: Rereading Kant*. New York: Oxford University Press, 1994.

Nietzsche, Friedrich. *Thus Spoke Zarathustra*. New York: Penguin Classics, 1978.

"Norms on the Responsibilities of Transnational Corporations and Other Business Enterprises with Regard to Human Rights." U.N. Doc. E/CN.4/Sub.2/2003/12/ Rev. 2, 2003.

Nussbaum, Martha. *The Cosmopolitan Tradition*. New Haven: Yale University Press, forthcoming.

——. *For Love of Country: Debating the Limits of Patriotism*. Boston: Beacon Press, 1995.

——. *Women and Human Development: The Capabilities Approach*. New York: Cambridge University Press, 2000.

Oates, David. *Paradise Wild: Reimagining American Nature*. Portland: University of Oregon Press, 2003.

Paley, Vivian. *The Kindness of Children*. Cambridge, MA: Harvard University Press, 1999.

Pettit, Philip. *Republicanism: A Theory of Freedom and Government*. New York: Oxford University Press, 1997.

Pinkard, Elizabeth. "Human Rights and the Environment: Indonesian Tribe Loses in Its Latest Battle Against Freeport-McMoRan, Inc., Operator of the World's Largest Gold and Copper Mine," *1997 Colorado Journal of International Environmental Law Yearbook*, 141.

Plato. *Phaedrus*. In *Collected Dialogues*. Edited by E. Hamilton and H. Cairns. Princeton: Princeton University Press, 1987, 475–525.

——. *Symposium*. In *Collected Dialogues*. Edited by E. Hamilton and H. Cairns. Princeton: Princeton University Press, 1987, 526–574.

Plumwood, Val. *Environmental Culture: The Ecological Crisis of Reason*. New York: Routledge, 2002.

Postone, Moishe. *Time, Labor and Social Domination: A Reinterpretation of Marx's Critical Theory*. New York: Cambridge University Press, 1996.

Regan, Tom. *The Case for Animal Rights*. Berkeley: University of California Press, 2004.

Reich, Steve. *Music for 18 Musicians*. 1976, New York: Nonesuch, 1996.

Rimbaud, Arthur. "Par les soirs bleus d'été" ["With blue evening, all summer"] in *Une saison en enfer [A Season in Hell]*. Paris: Gallimard, 1987.

Rio Declaration on Environment and Development, 1992, at *www.unep.org/Documents .Multilingual/Default.asp?ArticleID=1163&DocumentID=78&l=en* (accessed June 3, 2005).

Rolston, Holmes. *Environmental Ethics: Values in and Duties to the Natural World.* Philadelphia: Temple University Press, 1988.

Rothenberg, David. *Always the Mountains.* Athens: University of Georgia Press, 2003.

Rousseau, Jean-Jacques. *Discourse on the Origins of Inequality among Humans.* Indianapolis: Hackett Publishing, 1993.

———. *Émile.* Translated by Alan Bloom. New York: Basic Books, 1978.

Sassen, Saskia. *The Global City: New York, London, Tokyo.* 2nd ed. Princeton: Princeton University Press, 2002.

Scanlon, T.M. *What We Owe to Each Other.* Cambridge, MA: Harvard University Press, 1998.

Schlosser, Eric. *Fast Food Nation: The Dark Side of the All-American Meal.* New York: Perennial, 2002.

Schmidtz, David. "Saving the Elephants." Lecture delivered at the Scholarship and the Free Society seminar, Institute for Human Studies, University of Virginia, 2001.

——— and Willott, Elizabeth, eds. *Environmental Ethics: What Really Matters, What Really Works.* New York: Oxford University Press, 2002.

Schrader-Frechette, Kristin. *Environmental Justice: Creating Equality, Reclaiming Democracy.* New York: Oxford University Press, 2002.

Schurmann, Reiner. *Heidegger on Being and Acting: From Principles to Anarchy.* Bloomington: Indiana University Press, 1988.

Schweitzer, Albert. *Reverence for Life: The Ethics of Albert Schweitzer for the Twenty-First Century.* Edited by Marvin Meyer and Kurt Burgel. Syracuse: Syracuse University Press, 2002.

Seifert, Jaroslav. "Wet Picture." In Raymond Carver, *A New Path to the Waterfall.* New York: Atlantic, 1990.

Sessions, George, ed. *Deep Ecology for the 21st Century.* Boston: Shambala Press, 1995.

Shakar, Alex. *City in Love: The New York Metamorphoses.* Chicago: F6 Press, 2001.

Sheffler, Samuel. *Human Morality.* New York: Oxford University Press, 1993.

Shimmel, Schim, *Between Two Worlds*, 1992. Acrylic.

Singer, Peter. *Animal Liberation.* New York: Ecco Books, 2002.

———. *One World: The Ethics of Globalization.* New Haven: Yale University Press, 2003.

Snyder, Gary. "The Place, the Region, and the Commons." In *The Practice of the Wild*, North Point Press, 1991.

Sonic Youth. "The Sprawl." On *Daydream Nation.* New York: Geffen Records, 1988.

———. "Tuff Gnarl." On *Sister.* Lawndale, CA: SST Records, 1987.

Spinoza, Benedict de. *Ethics.* Indianapolis: Hackett Publishing, 1991.

Steichen, Edward. *The Flatiron, 1904*. Gum bichromate over platinum print. New York: Metropolitan Museum of Modern Art, Alfred Steiglitz Collection, 1933, 33.43.39.

Summary for Policy Makers: Climate Change 2001; Impacts, Adaptation, and Vulnerability, sixth session of the Intergovernmental Panel on Climate Change (IPCC) working group II, Geneva, Switzerland, Feb. 13–16, 2001.

Summers, Craig and Markusen, Eric. "The Case for Collective Violence." In *Computers, Ethics and Society*. Edited by M. David Erdmann and Michele Shauf. New York: Oxford University Press, 2003, 214–231.

Tan, Kok-Chor. *Justice without Borders*. New York: Cambridge University Press, 2004.

Tarkovsky, Andrey. *Mirror*. Moscow: Mosfilms, 1974.

———. *The Offering*. Paris-Stockholm: Exile Production, 1986.

———. *Searcher*. Moscow: Mosfilms, 1978.

Taylor, Paul. *Respect for Nature*. Princeton: Princeton University Press, 1986.

Thompson, Michael. "The Representation of Life." In *Virtues and Reasons: Essays in Honor of Philippa Foot*. Edited by R. Hursthouse, W. Quinn, et al. New York: Oxford University Press, 1995.

Thoreau, Henry David. "Civil Disobedience." In *Walden and Civil Disobedience*. New York: Houghton-Mifflin, 2000.

———. "Walden." In *Walden and Civil Disobedience*. New York: Houghton-Mifflin, 2000.

Throw Rag. *Desert Shores*. Better Youth Organiz Records, 2003.

Timmons, Mark. *Morality without Foundations: A Defense of Ethical Contextualism*. New York: Oxford University Press, 1998.

Todorov, Tzvetan. *Frail Happiness: An Essay on Rousseau*. College Park: Pennsylvania State Press, 2005.

United States Commission on Ocean Policy, "An Ocean Blueprint for the 21st Century: Final Report of the U.S. Commission on Ocean Policy," Washington, DC, September 20, 2004, at *www.oceancommission.gov/documents/full_color_rpt/ welcome .html* (accessed May 26, 2005).

Universal Declaration of Human Rights. New York: United Nations General Assembly, 1948.

Uranium Information Center, "Chernobyl," *Nuclear Issues Briefing Paper*, n. 22, Melbourne Australia, August 2004, at *www.uic.com.au/ index.htm* (accessed May 23, 2005).

Usef, Malik. "My City." On Common, *One Day It'll All Make Sense*. Chicago: Better Element Records, 1997.

Van Wensveen, Louke. *Dirty Virtues: The Emergence of Ecological Virtue Ethics*. Boulder: Humanity Press, 1999.

Vogler, Candace. *Reasonably Vicious*. Cambridge, MA: Harvard University Press, 2003.

Walker, Margaret Urban. *Moral Contexts*. Lanham, MD: Rowman & Littlefield, 2002.

Warren, Karen. *Ecofeminist Philosophy: A Western Perspective on What It Is and Why It Matters.* Lanham, MD: Rowman & Littlefield, 2000.

We're for Ecology. Poster photograph of farm animals made in the early 1970s, source unknown.

White, E. B. *Charlotte's Web.* New York: Harper Trophy, 1974.

Williams, Bernard. *Morality.* New York: Cambridge University Press, 2000.

———. *Truth and Truthfulness: An Essay in Genealogy.* Princeton: Princeton University Press, 2004.

Windy & Carl. *Depths.* Chicago: Kranky Records, 1998.

Wittgenstein, Ludwig. *Culture and Value.* Chicago: University of Chicago Press, 1984.

———. *Lectures and Conversations on Aesthetics, Psychology, and Religious Belief.* Berkeley: University of California Press, 1967.

———. *Philosophical Investigations.* Translated by G.E.M. Anscombe. New York: Prentice Hall, 1999.

Wordsworth, William. "Lines composed a few miles above Tintern Abbey." Reprinted widely.

Worster, Donald. "The Ecology of Order and Chaos." In *Environmental Ethics: Concept, Policy, and Theory.* Edited by Joseph Desjardins. Mountain View, CA: Mayfield Publishing, 1999.

Wu, Jean. "Pursuing International Environmental Tort Claims Under the ATCA: Beanal vs. Freeport-McMoran." *Ecology Law Quarterly* 28 (2001): 487.

Zeldin, Theodore. *An Intimate History of Humanity.* New York: Harper Perennial, 1994.

Index

conscience, 49, 141; Rousseau on, 170n27; and Universal Declaration of Human Rights, 8, 19n3, 184

consumer, 8, 23, 39, 165–66, 93

consumption, 16, 50

coordinating responsibility for Earth, 180

cosmology, 24, 95

cosmopolitan: contemporary, 9; meaning of, 5–6; semantic arguments against, 11

cosmos, Greek definition of, 5

courage, enlightenment, 2

courts: American, 25–26, 32–33, 172; European High Court of Human Rights, 31, 53; International Criminal, 13, 43, 51; Supreme, 172. *See also* law

Craig, Megan, 207

creativity, 140

Crow, Kareem Douglas, 144n25

culture: American, 35, 93; capitalist, 196; of convenience, 163; human, 111; Latin meaning of, 59; mass, 8; media, 94; and relationship to land, 23; Western, 91; world, 15

cynicism, 21, 141

Daily Caffe, 21, 45n1

Davidson, Jim, 121, 208

DDT, 23

De Kooning, Willem, 62n8

de Lille, Alain, v, 145

debeaking chickens, 147. *See also* factory farming

deep ecology, 66, 85, 86–88, 196

democracy, 133

Derrida, Jacques, 169

Descartes, Rene, 142n7

Desgagne, Richard, 45n21

destruction, 109–12. *See also* violence against animals

development, 5, 103–4, 107–8, 157, 197–99; ecological/green, 123, 125–26, 129; idealistic, 115; uneven, 132, 176

developmental habit, 121, 124, 127, 136, 139–42; definition of, 139; green, 133–38; personal, 121

devotion, 116–17, 121

Dewey, John, 107–8, 142

Diamond, Cora, 67, 72, 10, 154, 206; on animal liberation, 114–17, 119; on circle of life, 156, 158–59, 167n1; on Dickens, Charles, 69; *Eating Meat and Eating People,* 119 118, 220; *Experimenting on Animals,* 73, 148–49, 153–54; *How Many Legs?,* 69, 168n4; *The Importance of Being Human,* 73–4; injustice against animals, 142, 151; on mortality, 68–70, 74, 76

Dib, Aurore, 207

dignity, 113, 157; animal's, 76, 95, 137, 148, 153; culture's, 95; human, 53, 81 the divine, 89

Dobson, Andrew, 20n8

Dosteovsky, Fyodor, 89, 98n10

Draft Declaration of Principles on Human Rights and the Environment, 25, 43

dreams, vii

Driskell, David, 20n16

Dubai, 10; Sheikhs of, 1

Earle, Dr. Sylvia, 15–16, 134, 179

Earth, 3–4, 9–10; charter, 51–55, 57, 88, 182; conditon of the, 179; as dimension of existence, 7; Heidegger on, 7–8, 203n7; as home; 95; others, 122, 124; processes, 137; as source of relationship, 8; thoughts of, 176, 182; in the world, 121, 176–78, 202. *See also* citizens of Earth

~

About the Author

Jeremy Bendik-Keymer is assistant professor of philosophy in the Department of International Studies at American University of Sharjah, United Arab Emirates. He grew up in upstate New York and France, studied philosophy at Yale University and University of Chicago, and, before moving to the Middle East, taught at University of Chicago and Colorado College. He received the 2001 Wayne C. Booth Prize for excellence in undergraduate teaching from the Humanities Division, University of Chicago for the course on which this book is based.